ORGANIZING THE
MULTINATIONAL ENTERPRISE

ORGANIZING THE MULTINATIONAL ENTERPRISE: AN INFORMATION-PROCESSING PERSPECTIVE

William G. Egelhoff

Ballinger Publishing Company
Cambridge, Massachusetts
A Subsidiary of Harper & Row, Publishers, Inc.

International Standard Book Number: 0-88730-170-3

Library of Congress Catalog Card Number: 88-16611

Printed in the United States of America

Library of Congress Cataloging-in-Publication Data

Egelhoff, William G., 1941–
  Organizing the multinational enterprise.

  Bibliography: p.
  Includes index.
  1. International business enterprises — Management.
2. Strategic planning. I. Title.
HD62.4.E38 1988   658'.049   88-16611
ISBN 0-88730-170-3

To William H. Newman,
Teacher and scholar

CONTENTS

LIST OF FIGURES

LIST OF TABLES

PREFACE

There is a twofold purpose to this book: (1) to review and extend conceptual theory about macro organizational design and strategic management and (2) to develop a more comprehensive model of strategy and organizational design for multinational corporations (MNCs). The first is important because without better conceptual theory there is a serious limit to our ability to model a wide variety of organizational phenomena, including the strategic management of MNCs. Because it is more abstract and general, conceptual theory serves to integrate the many operational theories and models that make up a field of study. Without it, operational theories cannot be compared or aggregated to build a more complete understanding of the field.

The second purpose, developing a more comprehensive model of strategy and organizational design for MNCs, is important because the various features of organizational design (structure, centralization, staffing) always exist together in organizations, and their impacts on organizational performance are usually not separable in practice. While these features are conceptually separate, theories and models are more useful if they can provide a common denominator for integrating the impacts of these features on organizational functioning and performance.

There are two distinctive characteristics of this book that make it different from previous books and studies that have addressed similar subjects. First, it uses an information-processing perspective to conceptually develop contingency relationships between five important features of organizational design (structure, centralization, control, staffing, planning) and twenty-two aspects of MNC strategy and environment. Second, it develops a two-level model of the parent-foreign subsidiary relationship. Eight of the twenty-two aspects of strategy are elements of company-level strategy while fourteen are elements of subsidiary-level strategy. Organizational design at the parent-subsidiary level of analysis is related to both levels of strategy.

The operational model and hypotheses are tested with data from a sample of fifty large, successful MNCs (24 U.S. and 26 European). Data was gathered through structured interviews in the international headquarters of the firms, and ninety-four specific parent-foreign subsidiary relationships were studied (generally two in each firm).

This book is primarily addressed to researchers and students interested in organization theory, strategy implementation, and MNCs. The conceptual ideas and literatures discussed come from all of these areas. In this book I have attempted to explicitly discuss some of the critical issues surrounding structural contingency theory research and to provide useful references for those interested in further exploring an issue. These issues include the impact of the population ecology and strategic choice perspectives, the measurement of organizational performance, the notion of fit in organizations, and the use of information-processing concepts in developing organizational models. Many of these issues are surrounded by controversy. While the study takes specific stands on these issues—as operational studies must do—the style of the book is intended to invite evaluation and criticism.

To facilitate this, I have tried (1) to make explicit the assumptions and weaknesses associated with the approach taken, and (2) to provide enough of the data and analysis that the reader can critically evaluate the conclusions drawn from the study. While the book is written with a conclusive tone, the intention is to sharpen debate more than to convince. The underlying idea is that many of these issues need to be more actively debated and that the throwing of stones is more constructive if there are clearly defined targets.

Like most research projects, this one was heavily influenced by other people. William H. Newman provided encouragement, insight, and excellent advice throughout the study. William K. Brandt, James M. Hulbert, and Michael L. Tushman also played major early roles in developing my interest in the subject and influencing the way I think about it. Numerous colleagues at New York University Graduate School of Business provided a scholarly and supportive environment for writing this book. Naturally, I alone am responsible for any errors and omissions, as well as for the specific views presented in this book. Lastly, I am grateful to the Strategy Research Center at Columbia University and the New York University Graduate School of Business for providing the research funds that supported this study.

1

INTRODUCTION

This is a book about organizational design in multinational corporations (MNCs). It also deals with selected elements of the international strategies and environments of MNCs and attempts to link organizational design to strategy and environment under the general approach that has come to be known as contingency theory. There are two broad purposes to this book: to review and extend conceptual theory about macro organizational design and strategic management and to integrate, test, and extend what is known about organizational design in MNCs.

A study such as this requires a number of introductions, and this is the purpose of the first chapter. At the outset, it is important to know the general state of a field at the time when a study is done. Although this tends to be the subjective assessment of the author, it provides the reader with a necessary context and background for understanding what follows. This is the subject of the first section of the chapter. In addition, a reader wants to know what broad conceptual frameworks will be used to orchestrate the masses of data and flood of ideas into something that is coherent and meaningful. The second section of this chapter presents a brief discussion of the population ecology and strategic choice theses and tries to show how these form a useful context for understanding a contingency theory study. Within this broad framework, the study uses an information-processing perspective of organizational design, that is introduced in Chapter 2.

THE GENERAL STATE OF ORGANIZATION THEORY

Views concerning the general state of organization theory seem to have become increasingly divided, and Astley and Van de Ven (1983:245) describe "a growing theoretical pluralism in the organizational literature." Adherents of rival approaches to a theory of structural functionalism in organizations appear to be raising their voices more loudly, if not more convincingly, against the structural contingency theories that have until recently dominated research about organizations (Silverman 1970; Heydebrand 1977; Burrell and Morgan 1979).

Donaldson (1985:9) carefully reviews the attacks on this traditional view of organization theory and groups them into two dominant themes:

1. That organization theory has been "too structural and not concerned with explanations in terms of the acts of individuals and the meanings that they attach to their social transactions";
2. That organization theory has been "too concerned with the organization per se, and insufficiently concerned with the larger set of social structures of society which shape and constrain the enterprise."

On the surface, this appears to be an attack on either the level of analysis or the unit of analysis selected by most structural contingency theories. Beneath the surface, however, such attacks and the seeming abandonment of the structural contingency theory perspective by many researchers may be saying that learning and understanding from this approach have bottomed out. Certainly, there is evidence to this effect.

Criticisms and frustrations with structural contingency theory can be grouped around two major problems. First, the various operational contingency models developed by Burns and Stalker (1961), Woodward (1965), Lawrence and Lorsch (1967), Hickson, Pugh, and Pheysey (1969), Stopford and Wells (1972), and dozens of additional researchers have not integrated well into grander, more abstract notions about organizations. For a paradigm to continue developing, later studies and models must encompass and explain earlier models and empirical results. Such has not been the case. Later studies reference earlier studies, but by and large they do not encompass their logics or provide more general and abstract explanations of their results.

A second major problem with structural contingency theory today is that research on it seems to be running in place. Recent empirical studies seem to alternatively confirm or contradict previous studies and models but no longer identify new, meaningful contingency variables or aspects of organizational design. In Kuhnian terms (Kuhn 1970), structural contingency theory seems to be in a "normal research" or consolidation stage, and, at least at present, efforts to break out of this stage appear to have abated. This by itself would not be regarded as bad, if meaningful consolidation were occurring. But as previously pointed out, structural contingency theory has shown little success in converging the conceptual and empirical diversity produced during the previous stage into a mainstream of paradigmatic thought. These problems have led to a fall-off of interest in a structural paradigm and a transfer of such interest to a wide variety of research streams that are still at relatively early stages of conceptual and empirical development.

Despite these negatives, it is important to remember that structural contingency theory has produced a considerable body of knowledge about organizations and their environments consisting of an elaboration of concepts and propositions. By and large, these concepts and propositions still stand; subsequent research has neither refuted nor replaced them. Instead, the field has become impatient with the pace of progress and bored by the lack of novelty that structural contingency theory affords. Because both are quite unattractive in the short run, researchers pursuing the structuralist approach must take a fairly long-term perspective. In the short run, the structuralist approach may survive and continue the debate (Donaldson's well-reasoned reply to the critics offers hope to this camp), or it may be forced into increasing obscurity, as a research topic. Most theoretical approaches contain some degree of truth or meaningful insight into what is considered reality at the time of conceptualization. Long-run truth about social phenomena can be determined only after (1) the attractiveness of novelty has worn away and (2) an approach has been accepted by people who are removed from its initial conceptualization because it seems to them a better representation of reality than alternative approaches.

This being the way things presently are in organization theory, an empirical researcher has a wide choice of conceptual approaches. The present study was conceived and executed within the traditional functional structuralist paradigm. Such an endeavor should be based on some belief that there is still considerable potential to extend this approach to capture more truth, more of the reality of organizations. At the same time, such an endeavor must be humbled by the knowledge that many have lost faith in it and seek, wherever reasonable, to respond constructively to their doubts and criticisms.

Although there is substantial convergence among some of the studies linking certain structural forms to certain elements of a firm's environment, this stream of research has provided only a limited understanding of how form might influence organizational behavior and what types of organizational behavior are required to successfully cope with specific environments. Thus, why certain empirically established fits between environment and form are important to organizational performance is not well understood. This situation describes contingency theory in general, prompting Aldrich (1979:57) to state: "Most research on contingency models is oriented more to designing than to understanding organizations and rests on incomplete conceptions of the environment. Little cumulation of the results of 'contingency' research is possible, because no commonly agreed upon theoretical scheme has been adopted." The lack of adequate taxonomy and systematics (McKelvey 1982) is an important contributor to this situation. Schoonhoven (1981) includes a similar criticism in her critique of contingency theory.

The problem lies with the design of most contingency research studies. Typically, data are collected about structural form and some set of contingency variables. When all significant associations between form and the contingency variables have been noted, explanations are sought as to why each association is important to the survival or performance of an organization. Where prior hypothesizing has occurred, its intent has generally been to replicate the findings of previous studies and not to test some general conceptual framework or theory capable of having generated the hypotheses. Although the present study seeks to extend present knowledge about the important fits between an MNC's structural form and elements of its environment, it also seeks to address the above problem by first developing and then empirically testing an information-processing model describing the relationship between environment, form, and organizational effectiveness.

A CONCEPTUAL BASIS FOR RELATING STRATEGY AND ENVIRONMENT WITH STRUCTURAL FORM

Two approaches in particular seem useful in better understanding the interactive roles of structural form and strategy in the survival and performance of an organization. These are the population ecology and strategic choice perspectives, which have frequently been considered alternative explanations of organizational change and survival (Child 1972). In a sense, these two perspectives bound the structural functionalist approach just discussed. Population ecology, on the macro side, seeks explanation of organizational performance in "the larger set of social structures which shape and constrain the organization." Strategic choice, on the micro side, attempts to explain organizational performance more in terms of "the acts of individuals and the meanings that they attach to their social transactions." (The quoted portions are from Donaldson's description, in the previous section, of the two primary criticisms being raised against structural functionalism.)

Our view is that these two need not be viewed as rival approaches to explaining organizational performance and survival, even though they employ different concepts and different levels of analysis. But before going further, we need to outline and understand the two perspectives.

The Population Ecology Perspective

Recently, the population ecology perspective has been used to explain structural change in organizations (Aldrich and Pfeffer 1976; Hannon and Freeman 1977; Aldrich 1979). This has provided new insight and promising conceptual underpinning to the relationship between organizational structure and organizational environment. Although different versions of the population ecology model exist, the general approach contains three phases. First, some structural change occurs in an organization, either accidentally or as the result of rational choice (the variation phase). Second, selection mechanisms in the environment judge whether the organization with the new structural form is more or less effective in terms of survival and growth than organizations lacking the new form. Because the organization and its competitors are assumed to be constrained by the available resources in the environment, organizations with structural forms most suited to exploiting these resources will tend to survive and grow, while organizations with other forms will tend to fail (the selection phase). Third, institutionalization and inertia cause the preferred structural form to be retained by organizations (the retention phase), until the variation and selection processes produce another structural form that is judged to be more effective in the then existent environment. Of course, variation in the environment can also lead to a new dominant structural form.

While empirical testing of population ecology models has been sparse (Aldrich 1979), there seems to be general support for the population ecology perspective. Its contribution to organization theory is a general logic for understanding the association between organizational structure and the environment that has been lacking in most contingency studies. It suggests that this association can be described and studied as a "fit" relationship, where fit has already been defined as that relationship which leads to the organization's being better able to exploit the resources in its environment.

Substituting Strategy for Environment

Before proceeding, it is necessary to argue that elements of an organization's strategy can be used to represent the organization's environment for purposes of applying the population ecology model to explain the evolution of structural form. The elements of strategy considered in the present study include such characteristics as foreign product diversity, product modification differences among foreign subsidiaries, the rate of product change, and the size of foreign operations. Previous studies that have considered the relationship between structural form and similar contingency variables have tended to describe them as elements of strategy or strategic conditions and the relationship as a strategy-structure relationship (Chandler 1962; Stopford and Wells 1972; Channon 1973). Mintzberg (1979:25) views an organization's strategy as "consistent patterns in streams of (significant) organizational decisions." The above elements fit this definition. They are patterns that have emerged from numerous organizational decisions. If an organization's strategy is viewed as "a mediating force between the organization and its environment" (Mintzberg 1979:25), then it should mirror or reflect the most critical or constraining elements of that environment. For example, if an organization pursues a strategy of product or market diversification, then it also faces a more heterogeneous and complex environment. Whether structural form is asked to fit a strategy of product/market diversity or a heterogeneous and complex environment is merely a matter of semantics, as far as a fit model is concerned.

Researchers such as Chandler (1962), approaching this issue from a strategy implementation paradigm, have tended to view it from a strategy and structure perspective, while organization theorists have tended to view it from an environment and structure perspective. Child (1972) helps to clarify the relationship between these two perspectives when he argues that many of the environmental conditions studied by organization theorists are, in fact, subject to the strategic choice of organizations (that is, organizations can strategically select their environments). This implies that structural fit can also be accomplished by strategically selecting an organizational environment that the organization's structure can properly exploit. Some recent empirical studies indicate that organizations actually do this (Miller and Friesen 1980; Snow and

Hrebiniak 1980). The opposing view is that most environmental conditions are relatively fixed and that structural fit is accomplished either by natural selection or by adaptation of an organization's structure to fit the environmental conditions (Pfeffer and Salancik 1978; Aldrich 1979).

Thus, there remains a debate whether the environmental conditions and structural forms included in this and other contingency studies should be viewed as strategic choices of the organization or environmentally determined. Although the distinction between these two views is important and clearly affects the degrees of freedom that a manager has to influence the success or failure of an organization, it does not affect our ability to apply the population ecology perspective when attempting to explain the survival and failure of structural forms in a population of organizations. Organizations that fail to structure properly to implement their strategies, or to fit the environmental conditions implied by these strategies, should find themselves at a relative disadvantage in exploiting the resources of their environments. Those who support the strategic choice argument will want to add that organizations can also select strategies and environmental conditions that fit their structures. This variation in structure or environment occurs at the level of the individual organization. Once an organization has made such a strategic choice, however, the environmental selection process of the population ecology model proceeds, at the population level, to select firms for relative success or failure. This selection process is indifferent to the sources of variation in either structure or the environmental conditions confronting an organization. Thus, strategic choice of structure or environment at the individual organization level need not be inconsistent with environmental selection of structural form at the population level.

This book generally refers to the contingency variables in this study as strategic conditions or elements of strategy. Depending on how the reader views the strategic choice issue, he or she may prefer to think of these as environmental conditions or simply contextual conditions. The real point is that the value of a contingency theory of organizational design is independent of where one stands on strategic choice or environmental determinism. The latter perspective would view the fits of a structural contingency theory as quite constraining and largely explaining the existence of structural form. The strategic choice perspective emphasizes a larger degree of human intervention in the development and selection of structural form.

Readers can certainly disagree over the degree of strategic choice that exists in organizations. Some will want to argue that many organizations exercise considerable choice over the nature and shape of their environments. For example, MNCs can generally choose in which countries they wish to operate foreign subsidiaries and whether they will sell certain product lines abroad (and, as a result, deal with certain customers and competitors), or not. Some may even see organizations choosing their own performance standards, although this degree of strategic choice requires some level of slack or lack of competitive pressure in the immediate environment. Others may largely want to confine strategic choice to the selection of structural form in an organization. Child (1972) suggests that organizations can, at least potentially, exert strategic choice over all three factors.

Although one's view about strategic choice influences the degrees of freedom that one perceives managers to have in negotiating relationships or fits between environment, structural form, and organizational performance, this in no way influences one's views about the consequences of these fits. And as Donaldson (1985) points out, it is the consequences of fit and misfit, not the causes, that are the rightful subject of a contingency theory of organizational design. Child (1972) seems to suggest that acceptance of a strategic choice perspective weakens the value of structural contingency theory and that research should shift to an examination of causes (such as political factors influencing choice) rather than consequences. Such advice needs to be seriously questioned. What kind of choice is there, if one is ignorant of its consequences? Such choice must be based on personal preferences and political pressures that are all largely ignorant of the consequences of such choice for the organization. This is hardly the notion of strategic management of the firm, which requires some significant attempt to foresee the consequences of alternative courses of action, not for the decision makers but for the organization, and demands that such foresight be used in guiding the organization. Efforts to build a contingency theory of organizational design are attempts to provide this kind of foresight. Thus, the strategic choice thesis should not be used to dissuade researchers from structural contingency research. This is not to say that such research should not be criticized for the way it has been done (Schoonhoven 1981; Van de Ven and Drazin 1985) or that research on the decisionmaking and political influences of strategic choice should not be encouraged.

The Problem of Evaluating Good Fit

A potential problem facing most empirical studies of organizations is that researchers tend to sample the population of surviving organizations. As a result, there has been a tendency to assume that all statistically significant relationships between structural features and contingency variables are important to the survival of the organization. Yet the environment is not everywhere constraining, and not all relationships may be critical. As Aldrich (1979) warns, if researchers wish to use the population ecology argument, it is important they define fits between structure and the environment independent of the fact that such fits tend to be found in surviving organizations. Some studies have attempted to use direct measures of organizational performance (profitability, sales growth) to evaluate the importance of certain contingency relationships (Lawrence and Lorsch 1967; Stopford and Wells 1972; Child 1975). This is one way to discriminate the relatively successful from the relatively unsuccessful in a sample of survivors. In general, however, differences in these measures cannot be strongly explained by structural fit, and the issue of how to directly measure organizational performance for the purpose of evaluating the effectiveness of organizational structure is still unresolved in the organizational design literature (House and Rizzo 1972; Steers 1975, 1977; Hitt and Middlemist 1979).

Another approach to establishing the importance of certain structural fits is to have an independent theory about what makes for goodness of fit in a contingency relationship (that is, what allows one structural form to exploit environmental resources better than another). If the theory is truly independent of our empirical observations of contingency relationships (that is, the theory can hypothesize effective strategy-structure relationships without first observing them), then empirical observation of a sample of surviving organizations will be a meaningful test of the theory. The population ecology argument states that surviving or successful organizations should exhibit a relatively high incidence of fit and a relatively low incidence of misfit between an organization's strategy and its structure. What is fit and what is misfit must, of course, be independently specified by the theory. The following chapters first discuss an information-processing perspective of organizations and then proceed to develop an information-processing model of organizational design that can be used to posit specific fits between MNC structure and MNC strategy.

2

AN INFORMATION-PROCESSING
PERSPECTIVE OF ORGANIZATIONAL DESIGN

A major problem for the population ecology perspective has been how to operationalize it in order to build specific theories about organizations—the kinds of theories that are necessary to support empirical research. It has been difficult to define which fits are important to organizational survival and growth and even more difficult to define these fits in a way that can be measured and evaluated.

Aldrich (1979:45) states: "we know the physics of air, water, and light to which flying, swiming and seeing creatures must conform. We need much better knowledge of organizational types and appropriate environments before we can do as well in understanding organizational change." The present study suggests that information processing may be the missing "physics" that can help us to better understand critical conformities between organizational types and environments.

This chapter develops the conceptual background needed to construct an operational model of organizational design and strategy in the next chapter. The first section traces the development of an information-processing view of organizations in organization theory. The second section reviews a number of different empirical studies that have used an information-processing perspective. The third section describes how information-processing concepts will be used to construct a model of organizational design and strategy for the present study.

THE ORGANIZATION AS AN
INFORMATION-PROCESSING SYSTEM

The general idea that it would be useful to view organizations as information-processing systems seems to have several sources. Quite a few theorists have sought to understand organizations by describing them as either communications systems, decisionmaking systems, or systems that have to cope with uncertainty. Although definitions of these concepts vary and for certain purposes the distinctions may be important, they can all be subsumed under the broader notion of information processing. Information processing in organizations is generally defined as including the gathering of data, the transformation of data into information, and the communication and storage of information in the organization (Galbraith 1973; Tushman and Nadler 1978).

At a very early date, when it was still fashionable to think of organizations almost solely in terms of formal authority relationships, Barnard (1938) observed that communications may be an even more important concept. In an oft-quoted passage (which probably overstates the point), Barnard (1938:91) strongly indicates that models of organizations should be built around the concept of intraorganizational communication:

> In an exhaustive theory of organization, communication would occupy a central place, because the structure, extensiveness, and scope of organization are almost entirely determined by communication techniques.

More important than this statement is the general reflection throughout Barnard's work that the communication and availability of information act as important constraining factors at all organizational levels. He fails, however, to link this important concept to the more formal aspects of an organization's design (that is, he does not state how such factors as structure or degree of centralization influence communications in an organization).

Katz and Kahn (1966:223) have also viewed the organization as a communications and information-processing system, and they have specifically noted the importance of information exchange at certain levels in the organization:

> The closer one gets to the organizational center of control and decision making, the more pronounced is the emphasis on information exchange. In this sense, communication—the exchange of information and the transmission of meaning—is the very essence of a social system or an organization.

Thus, Katz and Kahn state that the exchange and processing of information is the most important phenomenon taking place within the management levels of an organization. If true, it follows that when attempting to model these levels of the organization, information processing is potentially a powerful concept on which to base such a model.

Another group of organizational theorists has sought to understand organizations by focusing on the decisionmaking processes in organizations (Simon 1957; Cyert and March 1963). They have conceptualized the organization as a problem-solving system, facing an environment that does not provide all of the information required under the rules of classical decisionmaking. Also, the organization itself is pictured as a less than perfect decisionmaker, exhibiting limitations in both information-processing ability and storage capacity and influenced by the biases of its members. The major contribution of this group to a general information-processing view of organizations lies in explicitly identifying—really for the first time—information-processing limitations inherent in all organizations. This is a crucial step, for if the information-processing capabilities of organizations were perfect (that is, not limiting on organizational performance), it would make no sense to construct a contingency theory of organizations about this concept. As will be seen later, it is the differing information-processing limitations of different organizational designs that makes information processing such a useful contingency concept.

More recently, theorists interested in viewing the organization from an information-processing perspective have focused on environmental uncertainty and how organizations absorb uncertainty as the important contingency concept. Thompson (1967:10,13) presents the conceptual argument for the importance of uncertainty:

> we will conceive of complex organizations as open systems, hence, indeterminate and faced with uncertainty, but at the same time as subject to criteria of rationality and hence needing determinateness and certainty. . . .

> With this conception the central problem for complex organizations is one of coping with uncertainty. As a point of departure, we suggest that organizations cope with uncertainty by creating certain parts specifically to deal with it, specializing other parts in operating under conditions of certainty or near certainty. In this case, articulation of these specialized parts becomes significant.

> We also suggest that technologies and environments are major sources of uncertainty for organizations, and that differences in those dimensions will result in differences in organizations.

Thus, Thompson suggests that uncertainty arises from certain characteristics in the environment and technology facing an organization and that differences in uncertainty somehow lead to differences in the organization's design. For this reason, uncertainty is sometimes referred to as an intervening concept—intervening between the environmental and technological variables and the organizational design variables.

Galbraith (1969, 1973, 1977) added some additional conceptualization to Thompson's general framework and developed a much more operational framework and model that has generally been referred to as an information-processing approach to organizational design. He rigorously defined the concept of uncertainty in terms of information processing: "Uncertainty is the difference between the amount of information required to perform the task and the amount of information already possessed by the organization." This has also been expressed in equation form:

Uncertainty or information to be acquired and processed	=	Amount of information required for task performance	-	Amount of information possessed by the organization

A key assumption underlying this information-processing model is that organizations will attempt to close the information gap (uncertainty) by processing information (Tushman and Nadler 1978). This activity is likely to involve the gathering of additional data, transforming the data, and storing or communicating the resultant information. Thus, there is a relationship between the amount of uncertainty faced by an organization and the amount of information processing that must go on in an organization. Effective organizations are those that fit their information-processing capacities (for gathering, transforming, storing, and communicating information) to the amount of uncertainty they face. A more recent study by Daft and Macintosh (1981), however, casts doubt on the assumption that organizations always respond to uncertainty with information processing. They found that when task analyzability was poor, the equivocality of information processing was perceived to be high and this was associated with a reduced level of information processing in organizations.

Galbraith also specified the relative information-processing capacities of different organizational design features. These features are listed below, in order of increasing information-processing capacity (Galbraith 1973:15):

Rules and programs
Hierarchical referral
Goal setting
Vertical information systems
Lateral relations

Where conditions are routine and simple, rules and programs can be used to absorb the relatively small amount of uncertainty facing the organization. When uncertainty increases, exceptions must be referred up the hierarchical authority structure for decisionmaking. When information-processing requirements threaten to overload the management structure, goal setting and planning allow more decisions to be made at lower levels in the organization as long as they are within the plan. This relieves the information-processing load on the hierarchical structure.

When this is no longer adequate, various vertical information-processing systems can be attached to the hierarchical structure, which increase the organization's information-processing capacity. These frequently include computer-based information systems and staff groups and tend to increase the capacity for centralized information processing. When uncertainty and information-processing requirements are very great, the use of lateral relations allows more information processing to be decentralized so that the more limited information-processing capacity at higher levels of the organization is not overloaded. Lateral relations mechanisms include direct contact between individuals, liaison roles, task forces, teams, and matrix designs. Thus, Galbraith's model provides a relatively operational framework for linking quite a number of organizational design features to the level of uncertainty or information-processing requirements facing an organization.

Unfortunately, Galbraith's (1977:38) model provides less specific guidance on translating the contextual factors or strategic conditions of an organization into information-processing requirements than it did for translating organizational design into information-processing capacity:

> At the moment the information-processing load of a task and the information-processing capacity of an organization cannot be measured accurately. There exist measures for types of diversity and for the division of labor but no method for combining them into a measure of required information. This is due partially to the difficulty of operationalizing the measuring level of goal performance. Several researchers have developed measures of overall perceived task uncertainty. Rather than measuring each of the components discussed here, they aggregate them and measure the uncertainty perceived by the managers who must make the decisions.

Thus, researchers who view the organizational context as an important source of uncertainty and information-processing requirements have sought to operationally measure this in two different ways. Some researchers have used specific measures of environmental change and complexity and subunit interdependencies. By assuming certain relationships between these conditions and uncertainty or the requirement for information processing, they have sought to empirically link them to certain organizational design features that are assumed to provide certain information-processing capacities (Burns and Stalker 1961; Van de Ven, Delbecq, and Koenig 1976; Galbraith 1977; Tushman 1978). These research studies have used the intervening notion of uncertainty or information-processing requirements as an abstract concept (never actually measured) to relate contextual factors to an organization's design.

Other research studies have sought to build and employ comprehensive measures of uncertainty as it is perceived by members of an organization (Lawrence and Lorsch 1967; Duncan 1972). Efforts to validate these measures by replication have not been very successful and cast some doubt on whether uncertainty facing an organization can be operationally measured as an aggregate phenomenon (Tosi, Aldag, and Storey 1973; Downey, Hellriegel, and Slocum 1975). There is also some empirical evidence that perceived environmental uncertainty is not consistently related to perceived environmental change and perceived environmental complexity (Downey Hellriegel, and Slocum 1975). This has prompted Downey, Hellriegel, and Slocum (1975:614) to state: "perception of uncertainty can be considered as an individual psychological trait rather than simply as an environmental attribute." Downey and Slocum (1975) suggest that perceived uncertainty is influenced by an individual's cognitive processes, the variety of his experiences and his social expectations as well as attributes of the physical environment.

Thus, organizational theorists have not been consistent in their use of uncertainty as a concept. It ranges from viewing uncertainty as a personal trait and product of the "behavioral environment" (Duncan 1972; Downey and Slocum 1975) to one that views it as an abstract property of the physical environment, existing apart from the way it is perceived by anyone (Burns and Stalker 1961; Dill 1962; Galbraith 1977).

It is likely that different definitions of uncertainty are useful for different purposes. Researchers who want to study how individual differences influence the way the environment is perceived and consequently how they respond to uncertainty will not want to treat uncertainty as purely an environmental attribute. Researchers attempting to find general relationships between contextual contingency variables and organizational design features irrespective of individual differences within organizations, will want to conceptualize uncertainty as an objective trait of these contextual factors. If, in the latter case, the researcher is employing perceptual measures of uncertainty, he or she will want to control for individual differences so that the degree of uncertainty due to the contextual factors under study can be separated out.

Downey, Hellriegel, and Slocum (1975:622) present a summary of the state of the uncertainty concept that is still true today:

> Uncertainty concepts as presently used in organization theory involve much ambiguity. This does not mean all contingency theory need be restricted to one meaning for uncertainty. Moreover, it does not mean that contingency theory must wait for the development of the one meaning of uncertainty. These developments would reduce theory development to a pedantic exercise.

In a recent article, Milliken (1987), in fact, suggests that there are three different kinds of uncertainty.

Another issue that is sometimes confusing in the literature is the relationship between the concept of uncertainty and the concept of information processing. As observed above, Galbraith originally defined uncertainty in such a way that there is a one-to-one or equivalent relationship between the two concepts. Once he begins applying the concepts, however, he is not very rigorous in maintaining this one-to-one relationship. At one point, he states, "thus uncertainty and diversity create decision overloads" (Galbraith 1977:180), implying that diversity is influencing information-processing requirements, but not necessarily the level of uncertainty. Van de Ven, Delbecq, and Koenig (1976) define task uncertainty, task interdependence, and unit size as separate concepts that influence the information-processing requirements facing the unit. Tushman and Nadler (1978), on the other hand, indicate in their information-processing model of organizational design that task and environmental conditions first translate into uncertainty, which then translates into a requirement for information processing. Thus, once again, there is a lack of consistency in how these concepts are used in the literature.

Whether there is a one-to-one equivalency between uncertainty and information-processing requirements may well depend on what set of task and environmental factors one is working with. At the micro level, where the unit of analysis is the individual and environmental measures are often perceptual, it may be convenient to aggregate these under the concept of uncertainty. At more macro levels of the organization, however, where different measures of size and interdependency are often important contingency factors, it may be easier to think of these factors as influencing the requirements for information processing in an organization rather than the level of uncertainty.

Despite the present lack of conceptual unanimity, uncertainty and information-processing concepts have served as the basis for a substantial number of empirical studies. The next section reviews a number of these and attempts to provide a representative picture of the range of organizational design studies to which the information-processing approach has already been applied.

EMPIRICAL STUDIES THAT HAVE USED AN
INFORMATION-PROCESSING PERSPECTIVE

Burns and Stalker

In one of the earliest studies, which originally helped to establish the importance of the concept of environmental uncertainty, Burns and Stalker (1961) studied some twenty industrial companies located in the United Kingdom. They observed that companies with mechanistic structures (highly structured with more centralized decisionmaking and largely vertical information flows) tended to be effective under stable environmental conditions (with low uncertainty), while companies with organic structures (loosely structured with more decentralized decisionmaking and more lateral information flows) tended to be effective under changing environmental conditions (with higher levels of uncertainty). They noted, for example, that in effective companies, a higher rate of new product introductions was associated with a greater use of lateral relations and more influence for the product managers (instead of the hierarchical management). Since this was exploratory research, they did not establish any measurement criteria that would facilitate future study or replication.

Lawrence and Lorsch

In an ambitious study, Lawrence and Lorsch (1967) attempted to develop an instrument for operationally measuring environmental uncertainty in terms of the clarity of information, the uncertainty of cause and effect relationships, and the time span of definitive feedback. They not only measured environmental uncertainty between six companies in three different industries but also between different functional areas within a company. They observed that differences in environmental uncertainty were consistently related to differences in the organization's design and that these differences were most pronounced in high performing companies. As environmental uncertainty increased, structure was less formalized and the time orientation of organizational members was longer. Like Burns and Stalker, Lawrence and Lorsch also found that high environmental uncertainty requires the increased information-processing capacity associated with more lateral relations.

Galbraith

In a longitudinal case study, Galbraith (1970) found that a reduction in the time available for new product introductions led to an increase in the use of lateral relations between organizational subunits concerned with the development and introduction of the product. As the time was reduced and there was less slack in the process, information-processing requirements increased. After some delay, which was accompanied by a lower level of performance, the company responded by adding more lateral information processing capacity (liaison roles and task forces) as well as vertical information processing capacity (a PERT system). When information-processing requirements and capacity were again in balance, performance improved.

In another case study involving the data processing operations of a large company, Galbraith observed that the original project structure of these operations was associated with several problems (1977:197). Although projects tended to be completed on time, there were quality problems, accompanied by poor morale and a high turnover of personnel, especially near the end of a project. There was a need to improve information processing around functional expertise and the functional development of people and to preserve this expertise and development as old projects terminated and new ones began. The project structure did not provide this kind of information processing. These problems were significantly reduced when the data processing operations changed to a matrix structure involving both functional and project dimensions. After the change there was a better fit between information-processing capacity and information-processing requirements.

Duncan

In a study involving twenty-two decision groups in several manufacturing and research organizations, Duncan (1973) found that under conditions of high environmental uncertainty, the effective decision groups changed their style of decisionmaking for routine and nonroutine decisions. Duncan measured decisionmaking style, or what he termed its structural profile, in terms of the following dimensions, which were largely derived from a Weberian view of structure: (1) the hierarchy of authority, (2) degree of impersonality, (3) degree of participation, (4) degree of specific rules and procedures, and (5) degree of division of labor. Effective decision groups used a less structured profile for making nonroutine decisions than they did for routine decisions. The implication of the study is that the same organizational subunit will alter its information-processing capabilities to better fit changes in the information-processing requirements that it faces.

Van de Ven, Delbecq, and Koenig

In a study that focused on work groups in a state employment security agency, Van de Ven, Delbecq, and Koenig (1976) measured task uncertainty, task interdependence, and group size to determine their influence on the modes of coordination that were used within the groups. First, however, they identified three different modes of coordination, each possessing a different capacity to process information: impersonal coordination, personal coordination, and group coordination. The data revealed that as task uncertainty increased there was a substitution effect and that horizontal channels of communication and group meetings increasingly replaced impersonal modes of coordination. This increase in lateral information-processing capacity as uncertainty increased is consistent with the findings of all of the previously discussed studies.

As task interdependence increased, the use of impersonal and personal coordination modes remained the same while there was a significant increase in use of the group coordination mode. Thus, information-processing capacity increased in an additive manner as task interdependence increased. As size of the group increased, use of the impersonal coordinating mode increased, while the use of horizontal channels and group meetings remained unchanged. The use of the personal coordinating mode increased for a while and then declined as group size became larger than ten employees. Thus, task uncertainty, task interdependence, and group size are seen to influence the information-processing requirements facing a work group, which, in turn, meets these requirements by using different modes of intragroup coordination or information processing.

Tushman

An information-processing approach was also used by Tushman (1978) to study communications systems in R&D laboratories. Sociometric data were used to measure the level of information processing taking place within thirty research and technical service projects. As predicted, high performing research projects, which faced high uncertainty, had significantly higher levels of intraproject communication than did high performing technical projects, where there was less uncertainty. This difference was not observed for the low performing projects.

The influence of task interdependence, as another source of work-related uncertainty, was also explored. As predicted, high performing projects possessing high interdependency with organizationally distant areas of the wider organization had more communication with these areas than did low performing projects. Once again, this distinction was lacking among the low performing projects. Thus, it is important to fit the level of technical communication in R&D laboratories to the level of task uncertainty and task interdependence specific projects face.

Kmetz

In a detailed study of the workflow in aircraft electronics repair for the navy, Kmetz (1984) found a wide variety of informal information-processing mechanisms employed to compensate for breakdown and overload in the formal information-processing system. Information buffers, which decoupled an otherwise highly interdependent workflow, were found to be important mechanisms for adjusting to workflow problems. They allowed the organization to perform when the formal, hierarchical information-processing system failed to facilitate performance.

It would be misleading to emphasize too strongly the similarity among these and other researchers using some type of information-processing approach. They differ not only in their methodology and the way that they have operationalized concepts, but at times they also differ in their conceptual understanding of the uncertainty and information-processing concepts. What these studies do have in common is that each uses some aspect of information processing as the central concept for linking an organization's design to its contextual factors and strategic conditions. At the present time, there is probably some advantage in having the information-processing perspective rather loosely defined, for it facilitates new conceptualizations and the extension of information-processing concepts to other areas of organizational design. Given the present state of affairs, it is important that researchers explicitly state how they are conceptualizing uncertainty and information processing and how they are using these concepts in their theoretical frameworks.

HOW INFORMATION-PROCESSING CONCEPTS
ARE USED IN THE PRESENT STUDY

The proposed framework treats uncertainty as an intervening concept, which can be used to express the impact of certain strategic or environmental conditions on the information-processing requirements that confront an organization. In this sense, uncertainty is conceptualized as an attribute of the contextual environment and not a psychological trait of the individual perceiving or experiencing the uncertainty, as suggested by Duncan (1972) and Downey, Hellriegel, and Slocum (1975). It is also an abstract concept, not directly measurable in the study.

As has been the case in other studies (Galbraith 1970), the present study will tend to link strategic or environmental conditions directly to requirements for information processing, without explicitly indicating their impact on uncertainty. Although there is an implicit relationship between uncertainty and information-processing requirements, whether an operational model explicitly uses uncertainty as an intervening concept or not is largely a matter of convenience. Earlier, it was suggested that micro level studies, which often measure the contextual environment in terms of perceived uncertainty, will generally find it necessary to explicitly translate uncertainty into requirements for information processing. Macro level studies, however, when they do not use perceptual measures of contextual uncertainty, will generally find it as convenient to relate measures of size or subunit interdependence directly to information-processing requirements as to uncertainty.

Information processing is therefore the intervening concept that is explicitly used in the model. On the one hand, the impact on an organization of its strategy and the environmental factors that it chooses to deal with can be expressed in terms of the information-processing requirements they create. On the other hand, the potential of the organization to cope with these requirements can be expressed in terms of the information-processing capacities furnished by its organizational design. This use of the information-processing concept to relate an organization's strategy and environment to an organization's design is shown in Figure 2–1. The solid lines indicate that strategic and environmental conditions and organizational design features are directly measurable variables, while the broken lines indicate that information-processing requirements and information-processing capacities are abstract variables that can be derived only from measurable variables.

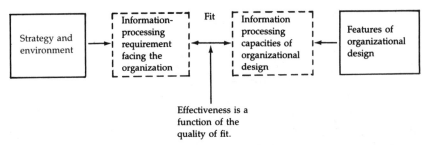

Figure 2–1. The General Information-Processing Approach to Organizational Design.

The strategic and environmental conditions include all those factors that are external to the organization's design and that influence the information-processing requirements of the organization. These include technology, size, environmental change, environmental complexity, subunit interdependency, and goals. Similarly, the different features of an organization's design (such as structure, degree of centralization, planning and control systems, interpersonal communication patterns) must also be measured or expressed in terms of the information-processing capacity they provide.

The more micro-level studies of organizations, where the units of analysis are either individuals or small groups, have managed to measure directly such aspects of information processing as the frequency of oral communications between work groups (Tushman 1978), the extent to which policies and procedures, work plans, personal contact, and meetings are used to coordinate members of work teams (Van de Ven, Delbecq, and Koenig 1976), and the structure of groups during decisionmaking (Duncan 1973). For more macro-level studies, such as the present one, the difficulty of directly measuring such detailed information-processing phenomena between very large subunits of an organization necessitates a different approach to operationalizing the information-processing perspective. Instead of attempting to directly measure information processing, the study uses information processing more as an abstract intervening concept to aid in positing relationships between directly measured characteristics of an organization's structure and strategy, both of which have identifiable information-processing implications.

It is important to stress that the relationship between strategic conditions and organizational design expressed by the general information-processing model in Figure 2-1 is one of fit and not causation. Consequently, it is important to remember that when structure is later referred to as the "dependent variable" and the strategic conditions are referred to as the "independent variables," we are merely applying conventional, if somewhat misleading, titles to these two sets of variables, without implying that either depends on the other in a causative sense. Many contingency studies have strongly implied that strategic or contextual conditions cause organizational design, and some longitudinal studies have found that organizations do change and adapt to changing environmental conditions (Terreberry 1968; Van de Ven 1977). This assumption is not required by a fit or congruence model of organizational design. Under the fit model being developed here, changes in strategic conditions may cause changes in organizational design, or changes in organizational design may lead to changes in certain strategic conditions, or neither may have any impact on the other. What is important in the present model is the relationship or fit, and not the forces that have created it.

How to measure fit between such dissimilar phenomena as strategic conditions and features of organizational design has troubled organization theory ever since it became contingency oriented. An information-processing perspective of organizational design calls for translating strategic conditions and organizational design features into their respective information-processing implications. Then it will be easy to measure fit between information-processing requirements and information-processing capacities, which are more comparable phenomena.

Galbraith (1977:39) indicates that the measurement or translating process is far from precise but potentially workable:

> These techniques do not permit the measurement of [information-processing] requirements and capacity so that adjustments can be made in the manner that organizations match supply and demand. However, organizations can detect changes in variables affecting information. Organizations know when they adopt strategies of product or market diversification, they know when the division of labor increases, and they know when they increase performance levels by pursuing shorter schedules, tighter quality tolerances, lower costs, higher productivity, etc.

Hickson, Pugh, and others working out of the tradition of the Aston Group have argued against using abstract intervening concepts to build organizational models (Hickson, Pugh, and Pheysey 1969). They want to directly link measurable contextual variables to measurable design variables. Despite the fact that their approach has not produced any overall or general organizational theory, their point is well taken. If researchers are allowed to loosely or arbitrarily translate measured strategic or contextual variables and measured organizational design variables into abstract information-processing concepts and then test their hypotheses by demonstrating fit at the abstract level, the results will be suspect and probably inconsistent from one study to the next. The weakness lies in the precision with which one can translate measured variables into abstract information-processing concepts.

A comparison of the Aston and information-processing approaches to organizational design introduces a fundamental dilemma of contingency theory. One can choose more limited contingency variables, where measurement is less open to criticism, but only limited theory development can occur. Or, one can choose richer and, unfortunately, more abstract variables that involve measurement problems but support more general theory development.

Considering the magnitude and extended period of the Aston-type studies, the fact that so little progress has been made toward building a general theory means that one is unlikely to come from this approach. The only way that it might proceed is to add more and more contingency variables to the model—a kind of "aggregating" versus the more parsimonious "integrating" approach of information processing. For the information-processing approach to advance, what is needed is a more precise translation of the measurable contextual and design variables into the information-processing concepts that are so useful for general theory building. This should be easier to accomplish if one first identifies the dimensions of information processing that are important to the type and level of organization being modeled and then constructs decision rules for mapping measurable contextual and design variables onto these dimensions. This is the approach that the present study attempts to follow.

3

A MODEL OF STRATEGY AND ORGANIZATIONAL DESIGN IN MNCs

The preceding chapter developed information processing as a conceptual basis for linking strategy and organizational design. This chapter proceeds to develop a model of strategy and organizational design in MNCs and identifies the specific features of organizational design and elements of international strategy that are to be considered.

A TWO-LEVEL MODEL OF STRATEGY AND ORGANIZATIONAL DESIGN

The focus of this study is on the organizational design of the parent-subsidiary relationship and not directly on the internal design of either the parent headquarters or the foreign subsidiary. The organizational design features that describe this relationship exist on two different levels. Certain organizational features, such as an international division structure, exist at the company level and are common to all parent-subsidiary relationships within a company. These are referred to as company-level organizational design features, meaning that they tend not to vary from subsidiary to subsidiary. Other features, such as the extent to which decisionmaking for a subsidiary is centralized or decentralized or the degree of control a parent exerts over a subsidiary, can more readily vary from subsidiary to subsidiary within the same company. These are referred to as subsidiary-level organizational design features. As Bartlett and Ghoshal (1985) point out, there has been a tendency for theory (and practice) to view all parent-subsidiary relationships within a company as homogeneous. Instead, they propose that MNCs should be studied (and managed) with a differentiated network model where parent-subsidiary relationships are allowed to be heterogeneous. The present study is consistent with this approach.

Figure 2-1, which described the general information-processing approach to organizational design, has been redrawn in Figure 3-1 to show this two-level view of the organizational design of the parent-subsidiary relationship. Included are the specific elements of strategy and the specific features of organizational design that were measured in the study. The general idea of fit between an organization's strategy and its organizational design has been further defined as three separate fits, each of which is sufficiently narrow that it can be measured and evaluated. Type One Fit expresses the relationship between company-level strategy and company-level organizational design. Type Two Fit expresses the relationship between the strategy of a specific foreign subsidiary and those design features that can vary from one subsidiary to another. Type Three Fit indicates that there is also a need for these subsidiary-level design features to be consistent with overall company-level strategy. The arrow between the company and subsidiary levels of organizational design means that the type of structure used by an MNC might also influence or constrain the degree of centralization, level of control, etc. that exists between the parent and its foreign subsidiaries. Figure 3-1 represents the skeleton of the model to be developed. It identifies the factors and relationships that are further specified and examined in the chapters that follow.

To date, there has been relatively little theory-driven research on multi-level organizational phenomena (Rousseau 1985). The need for multi-level theory and research stems from the complexity of modern organizations and their environments. Organizational behaviors and contingencies exist on multiple levels, and often there is considerable interdependency between these levels. Modeling such cross-level interdependency tends to be difficult, and Rousseau (1985) believes that stronger theory, rather than simply different methodology, is required to support effective cross-level research. The present study attempts to use an information-processing perspective or rationale to develop and test a cross-level theory of organizational design in MNCs.

ELEMENTS OF STRATEGY AND FEATURES OF ORGANIZATIONAL DESIGN TO BE INCLUDED IN THE MODEL

Elements of Strategy

Which elements of strategy should be considered when attempting to evaluate the quality of fit between an organization's strategy and its

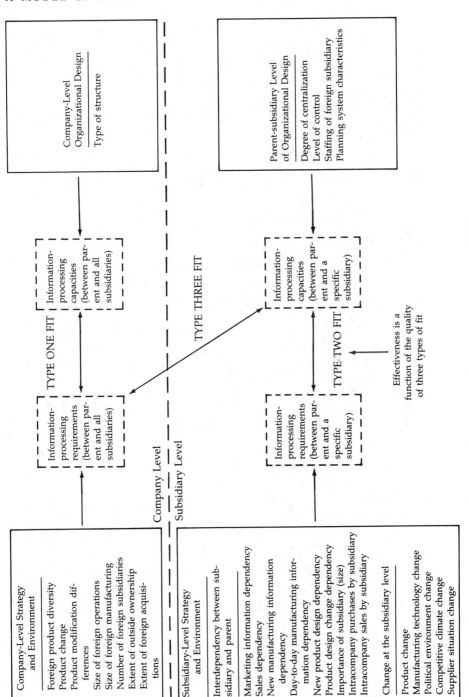

Figure 3–1. Two-Level Model of Strategy and Organizational Design in MNCs.

organizational design? Chapter 2 suggests an answer to this question. If one intends to take an information-processing perspective of organizational design, one must look at those elements of an MNC's strategy that most influence requirements for information processing between the parent and its foreign subsidiaries.

Below are the eight elements of company-level strategy that the study chose to measure:

1. Foreign product diversity
2. Product modification differences between subsidiaries
3. Product change
4. Size of foreign operations
5. Size of foreign manufacturing
6. Number of foreign subsidiaries
7. Extent of outside ownership in foreign subsidiaries
8. Extent of foreign acquisitions

How these elements were operationally measured is discussed in Chapter 4. Although four of the eight elements have appeared in previous contingency studies, these elements were selected primarily because they seem to have potentially important information-processing implications:

1. As *foreign product diversity* and *product change* increase, there is an increase in the requirement for product-related information processing between the centers of product knowledge in the parent and the foreign subsidiaries.
2. To the extent that *product modification differences* exist among foreign subsidiaries, the value of a center for product-related information processing and standardized approaches to such information processing is reduced.
3. As the *size of foreign operations* increases, the benefits associated with greater integration either among certain groups of subsidiaries or between foreign and domestic operations increase. This requires more information-processing capacity.
4. Whether an MNC uses *foreign manufacturing* or exports from the parent to support foreign sales influences the type of integration and information processing required between the parent and the foreign subsidiaries.

5. The *number of foreign subsidiaries* with which a parent must deal is directly related to the magnitude of the information-processing problem at the parent.
6. Significant *outside ownership* and growth through *foreign acquisitions* tend to constrain the level of control and the type of information processing that can exist between a parent and its foreign subsidiaries.

In Chapter 5 the information-processing requirements of each of the eight company-level elements of strategy will be more fully defined and matched with the appropriate information-processing capacity of an organizational structure. Defining information-processing requirements and capacities is laborious and qualitative in nature. Because such information is not readily retained by the mind, the practice will be to first define information-processing requirements and capacities at the point where they are first needed in order to hypothesize specific fits between features of organizational design and elements of strategy.

Listed below are the fourteen elements of subsidiary-level strategy measured in the study:

Measures of interdependency between subsidiary and parent:

1. Marketing information dependency
2. Sales dependency
3. New manufacturing information dependency
4. Day-to-day manufacturing information dependency
5. New product design dependency
6. Product design change dependency
7. Importance of subsidiary
8. Intracompany purchases by subsidiary
9. Intracompany sales by subsidiary

Measures of change at the subsidiary level:

10. Product change
11. Manufacturing technology change
12. Political environment change
13. Competitive climate change
14. Supplier situation change

Because there has been little previous research at the subsidiary level, there was little guidance about what factors might be important at this level. The study chose to measure elements that describe change, either within a subsidiary or its environment, and elements that define various types of interdependency between a subsidiary and the rest of the company. These elements were selected because it seemed they should influence the amount of information processing required between a subsidiary and the parent:

1. When an *organization and its environment change* more rapidly, there is usually an increased need for information processing between the subunits of the organization. Previous plans and decisions become out of date, and more communication and information exchange is required to update them.
2. When *interdependency between subunits* of an organization increases, more issues and decisions have to be coordinated, and this too increases the requirement for information processing between the subunits.

Listed below are six other factors that might be expected to have some influence on organizational design in MNCs:

1. Size of company
2. Age of company abroad
3. Size of subsidiary
4. Age of subsidiary
5. Nationality
6. Industry

Although these factors do not have as direct an implication for information processing across the parent-subsidiary relationship as the elements already described, previous studies have frequently found such factors to be related to significant differences in organizational structure, degree of centralization, and so forth. Although the present study will no doubt also find such relationships, the aim of the study is to explain such organizational variation in terms of the more specific elements of an organization's strategy. While factors such as nationality and industry may influence the strategies and environments of MNCs in general, this influence is seldom so binding that one will want to use it as a proxy for the actual set of strategic and environmental conditions faced by a particular company. This statement is subject to empirical testing, and leads to the first hypothesis of the study:

Hypothesis 3–1. Other factors, such as nationality, industry, size of company, age of company abroad, size of subsidiary, and age of subsidiary, will have no significant influence on the organizational design of an MNC, once the more specific elements of company-level and subsidiary-level strategy have been taken into account.

AN INTERACTION APPROACH TO MODELING FIT

Van de Ven and Drazin (1985) state that organizational researchers have employed three different types of fit models, generally without adequately identifying which type they were using. The three approaches to fit are a selection approach, interaction approach, and system approach. The present study primarily takes an interaction approach to fit. This view believes that structural form and environment or strategy interact to influence organizational performance. It further believes that one can identify and describe such interactions as a series of pair-wise fits. The systems approach also believes that interaction influences organizational performance but views the interaction pattern as far more complex than a series of pair-wise fits. A true systems model must describe the simultaneous interaction of numerous elements of strategy and environment with a variety of features of organizational design and relate such fit to performance.

The model to be developed in the present study is largely at the second level of fit, where interaction is represented by a series of pair-wise fits between individual elements of strategy and organizational design. In Chapters 5 and 6, which deal with type of structure, fits are combined into sets of fits for each type of structure. Multiple discriminant analysis is then used to simultaneously test the sets of fits, indicating some ability to approach a systems level of integration when modeling the strategy-structure relationship. In other chapters, the relative influence of company-level and subsidiary-level fit will also be investigated with multivariate analysis, but the fits themselves will be the result of a series of pair-wise analyses.

If the model to be developed in the study could be extended to become more of a systems model, it would undoubtedly be a better model. The underlying reality must surely involve simultaneous interactions. Some attempts were made at the end of the analyses to use canonical correlation analysis to uncover more of the equifinality, tradeoffs and simultaneous interactions that one suspects exist in the underlying phenomena. These efforts were largely unsuccessful, and the study must contend itself with describing fit at a level where its description can be supported by the empirical data. In Chapter 12, we want to return to this topic and discuss how some of the limitations of the present study might be overcome in future research studies.

4

METHODOLOGY

This chapter discusses the research design and the sample selection. Operational measures for the company- and subsidiary-level elements of strategy are also introduced and discussed.

THE RESEARCH DESIGN

Chapter 3 has outlined the general model that the study seeks to test. The elements of strategy and features of organizational design have been identified, but specific relationships among the variables will be developed in subsequent chapters, in parallel with the empirical testing. The model states that in order for an MNC to survive and be successful, it must possess good fit between its organizational design and its strategy. The research design to test this model contains the following steps:

1. Use the model and conceptual framework (that is, the information-processing implications of specific elements of strategy and specific features of organizational design) to generate a number of hypotheses about the relationship one would expect to find between strategy and organizational design in successful MNCs.
2. Select a sample of successful MNCs.
3. Analyze data collected from the sample of successful MNCs to determine whether or not they possess the hypothesized relationships.

To the extent that the sample data support the hypotheses, one can say that this constitutes empirical support for the information-processing model of organizational design in MNCs.

It is important to notice that this research design provides only a partial test of the model. The model also implies that if an MNC lacks fit between its organizational design and its strategy, it should be less successful at processing information and exploiting the resources in its environment. As a result, the organization's performance should suffer. Because the sample was selected to only contain successful companies, it cannot be used to directly test this second implication of the model.

ORGANIZATIONAL FIT AND PERFORMANCE

How to measure organizational performance and link it to organizational fit has been a major problem for structural contingency theory. Especially for large, complex organizations, there is a general lack of consensus as to what constitutes a meaningful measure of organizational performance or effectiveness (House and Rizzo 1972; Steers 1975, 1977; Hitt and Middlemist 1978). Zammuto (1982) points out that two of the deficiencies of current models of organizational effectiveness are that (1) they assume constituent preferences are both similar and static and (2) they do not consider the varying influences of environmental constraints on performance. Keeley (1984:1) states that effectiveness "does not simply denote degree of goal attainment, which is potentially a matter of fact; but it expresses a general and somewhat vague virtue of organizations, a matter of value."

From a very general population ecology perspective, effective organizations are organized for survivability, while ineffective ones are not. Within the broad parameters that determine survival and failure, organizations take specific actions aimed at realizing more narrow and specific definitions of effectiveness or performance. For example, a firm may install a computer system and establish an information-systems group to reduce administrative costs by eliminating people, improve manufacturing productivity via better scheduling, reduce inventories by better control, and improve customer service by increasing the reliability of shipping on time. The difficulties raised by Zammuto (1982) are relatively manageable at this level of organizing. Constituent preferences are specifically stated, and variance in environmental constraints can probably be identified and controlled for from one such project to the next. The effectiveness of such an action can be measured by and expressed in terms of how well it achieves these goals, a multidimensional measure of performance.

Macro organizational design and fit, however, are not directly aimed at satisfying any of these specific goals, and it seems unlikely there will be an empirical relationship between macro level fit and such goals. The problem is one of level of analysis. Specific goal-based measures of effectiveness may be suitable at more micro levels of analysis, where there is a clear causal link between action and goal. But the simple aggregation of such goal-based measures is unlikely to be a suitable measure of performance at more macro levels of analysis, where no such link between macro organizational design and the specific goals can be identified. If effectiveness measures cannot transcend levels of analysis, the search for a suitable measure should focus on operationalizing notions of effectiveness that are generally accepted as suitable for the level of analysis under study. Returning to the population ecology perspective, survivability versus failure of an organization is, perhaps, the most widely accepted notion of organizational performance at the macro level. It has both internal (management) and external (social) legitimacy as a measure of performance, and it also transcends both variety and change in constituent preferences.

Hannan and Freeman (1977:131) viewed the problems associated with measuring organizational performance as so great that they favored "dropping any pretext to scientific analysis of comparative organizational effectiveness." In a recent evaluation of the state of theory and research on organizational effectiveness, Zammuto (1982:26) writes:

> If, as these authors and others suggest, differences in perspectives or frames of reference for viewing performance lie at the heart of the problem, the search for a universal criterion or set of criteria is fruitless and ill-advised. No single set of criteria will be applicable to all organizations nor will they be viewed as applicable to all the participants judging a particular organization or action.

This being the case, profitability is probably a poor measure, especially across nationalities and industries, of the relative capabilities of firms to exploit the resources in their environments. It requires too many assumptions regarding the similarity of the firms' goals and the richness of their environments.

Relatively few studies of macro organizational design have successfully used performance measures to distinguish between organizational fit and misfit (Burns and Stalker 1961; Woodward 1965; Lawrence and Lorsch 1967), and frequently the measurement of either fit or performance has been open to criticism. Other studies have explicitly sought and failed to find such a link (Pennings 1975; Grinyer, Al-Bazzez, and Yasai-Ardekani 1980). Studies of organizational structure in MNCs by Franko (1973) and Hulbert and Brandt (1980) found that MNCs with direct reporting structures were less profitable (measured by ROI) than companies with other structures. But they provided no basis for determining whether these structures fit the strategies of these companies or not. Based on their sample findings, Stopford and Wells (1972) developed some fit criteria between type of structure and certain strategic conditions. Using sales growth and ROI, they found that firms with misfits performed more poorly, although frequently the difference was not great. The problem arises when there are many different organizational outputs that represent performance and effectiveness and there is no formal or consistent way to combine these together into a single measure of performance that can be compared across organizations.

The link between organizational fit and the performance measures used in most studies has been conceptually weak. As Aldrich (1979) has stated, studies tend to sample the population of survivors. In a sense, they attempt to explain differences in the degree of success more than they attempt to explain differences between success and failure. It is questionable whether such differences in degree of success (especially as reflected in relatively short-term profitability measures) are causally related to organizational fit and misfit. Such measures of success are frequently much more volatile than organizational fit and misfit, and this weakens the assumption that the latter is causing the former.

Although the present study sought to only sample successful MNCs, a variety of profitability and ROI measures were calculated from data that was readily available on the sample companies. None of these measures were meaningfully related to the measures of fit and misfit between strategy and type of organizational structure that are reported in Chapter 5.

The most convincing evidence that misfit between strategy and organizational design has a negative influence on organizational performance comes from an analysis by Donaldson (1984). Using data from Rumelt's (1974) study, Donaldson found that there were significant associations between prolonged fit/misfit and long-run performance. Organizational design or structure was represented by whether a firm had a functional division structure or a product division structure. Strategy was represented by degree of product diversity, and organizational performance by average sales growth over a ten-year period. Ninety-three firms had organizational fit across the entire ten-year period, while thirteen firms had misfit during the entire period. The difference between the two groups was significant and substantial. The group of misfits was estimated to have 3.35 percent per annum less sales growth than would have been attained under conditions of organizational fit. Although the analysis used a relatively simple, unidimensional operationalization of both the strategy and structure concepts, the findings provide direct support for the hypothesized relationship between fit/misfit and organizational performance.

The present study emphases the development and testing of a rather comprehensive information-processing theory about organizational fit. Thus, it will largely attempt to refine and extend structural contingency theory by responding to the criticisms that such theory has too often been atheoretical (Silverman 1968; Turner 1977; Burell and Morgan 1979). Given this emphasis, the research design focuses on identifying and measuring a broad array of hypothesized fits in a sample of some of the most successful MNCs. It will attempt to test many different dimensions of information-processing fit and evaluate which of the hypothesized fits tend to exist and are most important in a sample of successful organizations. This represents a partial rather than a complete test of the contingency model. The notion that unsuccessful organizations should exhibit a lower level of fit (or a higher level of misfit) cannot adequately be tested with the present sample.

As already mentioned, the attempt to use short-run profitability measures to distinguish between organizational fit and misfit was not successful. A measure of the quality of integration between parent HQ and foreign subsidiary, however, does appear to be related to fit and misfit in Chapter 5, providing some support for the misfit hypothesis. Quality of integration also appears to be more directly and causally related to information-processing fit than short-run profitability.

The present study uses the successful acquisition of scarce resources (in this case sales) in a competitive environment to measure and identify a sample of successful MNCs. This measure seems particularly appropriate for evaluating organizational design and information-processing fit because they are most critical and problematic in large, complex organizations. It is unlikely that MNCs could attain and maintain such prominent positions in competitive industries unless they had reasonably good organizational and information-processing fit. It is less clear how to identify a sample of ineffective organizations. Organizations that fail to survive are clearly ineffective in acquiring the necessary resources from the environment. Our fit model indicates that a sample of such firms should show a significantly higher incidence of organizational misfit than the previous sample. In between these two extremes, however, the link between organizational fit and effectiveness becomes less clear. This is because our measure of effectiveness is not necessarily a continuous scale. While it seems plausible that successful acquirers of resources must have reasonably good organizational fit, it does not follow that moderately less successful acquirers must have a poorer organizational fit. Differences in perceptions about effectiveness and environmental constraints could also explain this level of variation. Organizations that are ineffective as resource acquirers to the point where they fail to survive, are more likely to be associated with relatively poor organizational fit because differences in perceptions about effectiveness cannot account for this difference in performance.

Thus, the only clear definition of "unsuccessful" would be failure of the organization to survive (or perhaps its failure to survive as an MNC). There are, however, operational difficulties with this definition of an "unsuccessful" firm. It would be extremely difficult to identify a sufficient number of failed MNCs.[1] It would be even more difficult to go back and measure strategy and organizational design prior to failure with the kind of detail that is employed in the present study. The model suggests that such a sample of the unsuccessful would exhibit a significantly poorer level of fit between strategy and organizational design than one would find in a sample of successful firms. The problem is that failure is difficult to identify and data, with meaningful information-processing implications, is difficult to come by once failure has already occurred.

Thus, the present study takes a conservative approach toward operationalizing organizational performance. One that requires only the weakest of assumptions about the similarity and stability of constituent preferences. Survival as a large MNC is presumably desired by all such firms, and conceptually, such size and complexity should raise the importance of organizational and information-processing fit. Although it seems probable that the lack of such fit in large, complex organizations would cause poorer performance, this hypothesis will not be tested in the study. Neither will a more exact definition of what is meant by "poorer performance" (failure to survive, less profitability, less sales growth) be revealed. Because the link between organizational fit and performance remains a problematic issue, however, more will be said about research design in the final chapter.

THE SAMPLE

The sample was selected to represent the population of successful MNCs, where the population-ecology perspective would lead one to expect that important fits between strategy and organizational design are generally satisfied. The sample was almost evenly split between U.S. and European companies and was spread across several different industry groups. The following industry groups were selected because each was known to have been multinational for some time and to contain large, prominent MNCs: auto/truck, electrical/telecommunications equipment, industrial equipment, chemicals, pharmaceuticals, consumer packaged goods, and tires. From the *Fortune Directories of the 500 Largest U.S. Industrial Corporations* and the *500 Largest Industrial Corporations Outside the U.S.*, the fifty largest companies in these industries (including three not in these industries) were selected. The three companies not belonging to the above industry groups were included in the sample because they were such well known and highly regarded MNCs that it was considered desirable to include them in a sample of successful MNCs.

Yuchman and Seashore (1967) have argued that the only area in which the effectiveness of dissimilar organizations can be compared is on their success in acquiring scarce and valued resources (in this case, sales to customers) from their environments. Sales size should be a fairly robust and meaningful indicator of organizational success across cultures. Sales size is less influenced by different accounting and tax treatments than profit measures. Also, it would appear that sales are positively correlated with many different measures of organizational performance, including profits, security, employment, and so forth. The relative importance of such performances, no doubt, varies among companies, and certainly across nationalities.[2] Because the industries sampled were well established and competitive, sales represented an important and constrained resource for these firms. It is unlikely, in a competitive environment, that these firms could have achieved and maintained such prominent sales positions, without possessing reasonably good fit between their organizational designs and their strategies and environments. Furthermore, sales size implies success as a large, complex organization. Small, simple organizations can also be successful, but it is less likely that organizational design (or information processing) fit is as problematic or crucial as in large, complex organizations.

Companies with less than 15 percent foreign sales or with only mini-
mal foreign manufacturing were excluded from the sample for not
being sufficiently multinational. Company annual reports were used to
conduct the initial screening. Several companies were also excluded
because it was common knowledge that they were experiencing major
international operating problems. Eleven companies (three U.S. and
eight European) declined to participate in the study and were replaced
by other companies. The reasons given for declining either related to
company policies against participating in such studies or to the company's inability to make available the proper executives during the
interview period. Some general characteristics of the fifty companies
included in the sample are presented in Table 4–1.

MEASURES

The data were collected in 1977 and 1978 by structured interviews in
each company and from published company documents. In all but a
few cases, three interviews were conducted in each company. The first
dealt with companywide matters and the general relationship of the
parent to its foreign operations. The interviewee was usually a general
manager in charge of foreign operations (such as head of an international division) or, where this was not possible, a headquarters staff
executive who possessed the general manager viewpoint (such as direc-
tor of corporate planning).

The second interview dealt with a specific parent-subsidiary relationship (Brazil, or in a few cases, another developing country). The third
interview followed the same format as the second, except that it dealt
with a different parent-subsidiary relationship (a large European subsidiary). The interviewees for the second and third interviews tended to
be the individuals to whom the specific foreign subsidiary CEOs
reported. Where this was not possible, it was someone from this individual's headquarters staff, who was also very familiar with the specific
foreign subsidiary and its relationship to the parent HQ. The company-
level interview lasted a minimum of one hour and each subsidiary-level
interview lasted at least one and a half hours. The total interview time
spent in each company generally varied from five to eight hours. In the
end, data were obtained on fifty companies and ninty-four specific parent-subsidiary relationships.

Every effort was made to convey to a company ahead of time, the
kind of information required, so that interviews could be set up with
the most appropriate individuals. Multiple trips were frequently

Table 4–1. General Characteristics of the Sample Companies.

Total Company Sales (Millions of U.S. $)	
Less than 500	3
500–1,000	10
1,000–2,000	11
2,000–5,000	13
Greater than 5,000	13

Sales Outside of Parent Country (Percentage)	
Less than 25	2
25–50	19
50–75	20
Greater than 75	7
Missing values	2

Industry of Sample Companies	U.S.	UK	European	Total
Automobile and truck	2		6	8
Electrical and telecom. equipment	4	1	3	8
Industrial eq.	3		1	4
Chemicals	3		5	8
Pharmaceuticals	3	1	2	6
Consumer packaged goods	5	2	2	9
Tires	3	1		4
Other	1	1	1	3
	24	6	20	50

required to the same company HQ. In some cases, the general manager was located at corporate HQ (such as New York), while the interviewees for the two specific foreign subsidiary interviews were at geographical region HQs (such as Brussels for Europe, Coral Gables for Latin America). All of the interviews were taped, except in two companies, which objected to taping. From the tapes, the structured interview instruments were filled out and a substantial amount of additional information was written up. Specific measures and data from the interview instrument were then coded, and a computer data base was established to facilitate hypothesis testing.

Thus, all data were collected from parent HQ management. It would, of course, have been desirable to also collect the subsidiary-level data from each subsidiary management and compare it with the data collected from parent HQ management. Time and resource constraints precluded this. Measurement from the parent HQ perspective may introduce a certain bias into the data. There is some evidence from other studies, for example, that HQ managements tend to see decision-making as more centralized than subsidiary managements do. Yet such biases, or differences in HQ and subsidiary management perceptions, probably tend to be similar across all MNCs and therefore should not tend to distort comparisons between companies.

As a result of extensive pretesting of the interview instruments in several companies, two principles were adopted, which added to the quality of the data collection and measurement. First, questions that generated measures were phrased to be as specific and factual as possible. For example, respondents were not asked to judge how centralized or decentralized decision making for the German subsidiary was. Instead, they were asked which level (based on the company's own organization chart) would generally have to approve a given decision before action could be taken. As much as possible, the measures attempted to tap the respondents' knowledge or estimation of previous events or facts, rather than their judgment about some hypothetical or abstract situation. Second, the respondents were not asked to aggregate information to reach some broader generalization or categorization. The taping of the interviews meant that a great deal of data could be collected, coded, and aggregated later by the researcher according to a consistent set of rules.

The measurement of operational variables is frequently viewed as a mundane subject, but it is extremely important. One's ability to ultimately evaluate the merit of a conceptual framework—in this case, the information-processing model of organizational design—rests as much on the believability of the measures as on the strength of the deductive logic that comprises the framework and generates the testable hypotheses. At issue is not as much how fully an operational variable captures or represents the conceptual variable as it is how fairly or without bias it represents the conceptual variable. Weak operational measures will tend to produce weak or insignificant results, but biased operational variables will tend to produce erroneous or misleading results. The remaining three parts of this section describe and discuss how the eight elements of company-level strategy, the fourteen elements of subsidiary-level strategy, and the six other factors were measured. Measurement of each feature of organizational design (structure, centralization, planning, control, staffing) will be described in the chapter that develops and tests hypotheses involving that feature.

Company-Level Strategy

Foreign Product Diversity. This variable was measured by the number of broad product lines a company offered for sale in two designated foreign countries. One country was a major European country and the second was Brazil. Because both tended to be large, actively developed markets for most companies in the sample, the product offerings in these two markets were considered representative of the company's total foreign product offering. Correlation between the two measures was $R = .87$. The highest of these two measures was used to represent the company's foreign product diversity.

The number of broad product lines in a subsidiary was measured during the subsidiary-level interviews. In order to be considered a separate broad product line, products had to have either a different manufacturing technology (that is, cannot be made with the same manufacturing facility) or different customers and end uses, or both. For example, in a pharmaceutical company, pharmaceuticals, veterinary supplies, and cosmetics are considered separate broad product lines. This approach led to eight categories of foreign product diversity, where the final category was "eight or more" broad product lines (four companies fell into this final category).

The concept of product diversity as an important contingency variable for organizational structure was first defined and operationalized by Chandler (1962). Although he did not develop a quantitative measure of product diversity, he identified its impact on organizational structure in terms of the different kinds of technical knowledge and customer characteristics with which the organization had to cope. The present study's attempt to measure product diversity in terms of technological and market differences is consistent with Chandler's original notion about why product diversity creates pressures for new forms of organizational design.

Other studies (Stopford and Wells 1972; Franko 1976; Daniels, Pitts, and Tretter 1984, 1985) have used a different operational measure of foreign product diversity, based on the number of two-digit SIC codes that were represented by a company's foreign manufacturing or, in some studies, a company's foreign sales. Generally, it appears the SIC codes also reflect technology and market differences, although the linkage has not been made as explicit as with the broad product line measure.

Product Modification Differences. Product modification differences among foreign subsidiaries was measured on a five-point scale, which the interviewer used to rate the MNC following a discussion with the respondent of product differences across subsidiaries. On the scale, 1 indicates "identical products, parts are interchangeable world-wide"; 3 indicates "substantial cosmetic differences, but share same basic technology engineering"; and 5 indicates "basic technology differences, require separate basic technology engineering."

Product Change. This variable was measured by the percentage of company sales spent on R&D. The same measure was also used by Stopford and Wells (1972).

Size of Foreign Operations. This variable was measured by the percentage of a company's sales occurring outside of the parent country. In instances where a U.S. company's Canadian operations were organizationally treated as a part of U.S. operations and management for the two was integrated, Canadian sales were considered to be domestic rather than foreign. The Stopford and Wells study treated all Canadian sales as domestic sales for U.S. firms.

Some have also wondered whether the European countries should not be treated as a part of the domestic market for European MNCs. This is a debatable issue, but at the present time we think that European managers tend not to view Europe as a single national market. Although European MNCs often treat neighboring countries as markets that they understand very well and can depend upon, both strategically and organizationally they tend to respect and distinguish between the national differences more than U.S. or Canadian firms generally do with the North American market. Among the sample companies, the only exception was the way some German MNCs tended to treat the Austrian market.

Size of Foreign Manufacturing. This variable was measured by the percentage of foreign sales accounted for by foreign manufacturing rather than exports from the parent country. This was calculated by dividing the value of foreign manufacturing (adjusted by the gross profit margin to make it equivalent to sales volume rather than cost of goods sold) by foreign sales. In a few instances, where this information was not available, it was calculated by using foreign manufacturing assets to estimate the percentage of total company manufacturing occurring outside of the parent country, which was then divided by the percentage of foreign sales.

Number of Foreign Subsidiaries. This variable was measured by the number of foreign countries in which the company had either resident marketing or manufacturing operations. This is a measure of the number of parent-subsidiary relationships for which organizational design must provide information-processing capacity.

Extent of Outside Ownership. The extent of outside ownership in a company's foreign subsidiaries was measured by the percentage of a company's foreign sales accounted for by subsidiaries with greater than 30 percent outside ownership. This variable was measured by categories (such as 0 to 5 percent, 5 to 10 percent) with the final category open-ended (more than 20 percent).

Extent of Foreign Acquisitions. This variable was measured by the percentage of a company's foreign sales accounted for by acquisitions made within the past ten years. This variable was measured by categories (such as 0 percent, 0 to 5 percent) with the final category open-ended (more than 25 percent).

Subsidiary-Level Strategy

Interdependency between subsidiary and parent was measured by nine different variables.

Marketing Information Dependency. This variable was measured by the extent to which a subsidiary depended on the parent for technical information relating to its marketing and distribution activities (training, sales techniques, distribution methods, advertising). It was measured on a five-point scale that varied from "insignificant" to "daily and significant." The scale was completed by the interviewer, based on the extent and frequency with which the subsidiary required such information.

Sales Dependency. Sales dependency was measured by the percentage of a subsidiary's sales that were booked by the parent (excluding intracompany transfers). For example, some tire companies will supply an auto company with tires at numerous locations worldwide. Such sales are negotiated by the parent, although they are made by a local subsidiary. This variable measures this kind of dependency and was estimated or looked up by the respondent.

New Manufacturing Information Dependency. This variable was measured by the extent to which a subsidiary was currently dependent on the parent for new manufacturing technology (that is technology that did not presently exist in the subsidiary). It was measured on a five-point scale that varied from "insignificant" to "daily and significant." This scale was completed by the interviewer following a discussion of technology transfer with the respondent. The variable tends to identify those parent-subsidiary relationships that at the time were involved in the transfer of new technology from the parent to the subsidiary.

Day-to-day Manufacturing Information Dependency. This variable was measured by the extent to which a subsidiary depended upon the parent for day-to-day or routine technical and manufacturing information (such as production schedules and changes, technical advice on operating problems). This kind of day-to-day operating information was distinguished from new manufacturing technology information during the pretest. Measurement was based on a discussion of how frequently the subsidiary requested this kind of information. It was recorded on a five-point scale, which varied from "insignificant" to "daily and significant."

New Product Design Dependency. This variable was measured by the percentage of a subsidiary's new product designs that came from the parent. It was estimated by the respondent.

Product Design Change Dependency. This variable was distinguished from the previous variable during the pretest. It was measured by the percentage of a subsidiary's changes to existing product designs that came from the parent. This variable was estimated by the respondent.

Importance of Subsidiary. This variable was measured by expressing subsidiary sales as a percentage of total foreign sales.

Intracompany Purchases by Subsidiary. This variable was measured by the percentage of a subsidiary's sales that were purchased from some other part of the company. It was either estimated or looked up by the respondent.

Intracompany Sales by Subsidiary. This variable was measured by the percentage of a subsidiary's sales that went to other parts of the company. It was either estimated or looked up by the respondent.
Change at the subsidiary level was measured by five different variables.

Product Change. The degree of product change inherent in the strategy of a foreign subsidiary was measured by the percentage change in the number of products offered for sale by the subsidiary over the last five years. This percentage was estimated by the respondent.

Manufacturing Technology Change. This variable was measured by the extent to which the production technology of a subsidiary had changed over the past five years. It was measured on a five-point scale varying from "not at all" to "large and significant change." This scale was completed by the interviewer following a discussion with the respondent about changes in the degree of automation, vertical integration, and manufacturing methods that had occurred over the previous five years.

Political Environment Change. The degree of change inherent in the political environment of a subsidiary was measured by the extent to which change in government policies and regulations had affected the subsidiary over the past three years. It was measured on a five-point scale varying from "to a very little extent" to "to a very great extent." This scale was completed by the interviewer following a discussion about changes in import and export policies and regulations, business taxes, currency restrictions, local employment policies, and relevant government licensing or permissions (such as the approvals needed for the sale of pharmaceuticals).

Competitive Climate Change. This variable was measured by the extent to which the competitive climate of a subsidiary had changed over the past three years, in terms of competitors entering, leaving, changing position, and changes to the basis of competition. It was measured on a five-point scale varying from "to a very little extent" to "to a very great extent." The scale was completed by the interviewer, who aggregated the number of these changes that had occurred.

Supplier Situation Change. This variable was measured by the extent to which the supplier situation of a subsidiary had changed over the past three years, in terms of sources of supply, quality of supplies and services, and the existence of alternative sources of supply. It was measured on a five-point scale varying from "to a very little extent" to "to a very great extent." The scale was completed by the interviewer, who aggregated the number of these changes that had occurred.

Other Factors

Six other factors, without specific information-processing implications, were also measured because they have appeared as important contingency variables in other studies. The overall quality of parent-foreign subsidiary relationships in a company was also measured. It is used in Chapter 5 to determine if poor strategy-structure fit results in a poorer quality of parent-subsidiary relationship.

Nationality. This variable measured the nationality of the parent company, using three groups: U.S., UK, and European. The UK companies were broken out as a separate group, when analysis of variance of the strategic and environmental conditions revealed that there were significant differences between the UK companies and the other European companies. No such difference was found among the other specific European nationalities (Germany, Switzerland, Sweden, France, and Italy).

Industry. This variable was measured by the primary industry group in which the company operated.

Size of Company. This variable was measured by the total number of employees in the company.

Age of Company Abroad. This variable was measured by the number of years since the company began its first significant overseas expansion, beyond exporting. It was estimated by the respondent, using a number of categories.

Size of Subsidiary. This variable was measured by the number of employees in a subsidiary.

Age of Subsidiary. This variable was measured by the number of years since a subsidiary was founded or acquired by the company.

Quality of Parent-Subsidiary Relationship. This variable was measured during the company-level interview with the following instrument, which was based on the Lawrence and Lorsch (1967) instrument for measuring the quality of integration between organizational subunits:

> We would like to know about the relationship between the parent here in [parent country] and the foreign subsidiaries as a whole. Listed below are eight descriptive statements. Each of these might be thought of as describing the general state of the relationship between the parent and the foreign subsidiaries. We would like you to select the statement that you feel is most descriptive of each of the relationships shown below and to enter the corresponding number to the right of it.

Parent-subsidiary relationship in the area of:

    a. Marketing matters_____

    b Manufacturing matters_____

    c. Financial matters_____

Relationship between parent and foreign subsidiaries is:

1. Sound—full unity of effort is achieved.
2. Almost full unity.
3. Somewhat better than average relations.
4. Average—sound enough to get by even though there are many problems of achieving joint effort.
5. Somewhat of a breakdown in relations.
6. Almost complete breakdown in relations.
7. Couldn't be worse—bad relations—serious problems exist which are not being solved.

Validity of the Data

The validity of the data, or how well the measured variable represents the conceptual variable, is frequently a problem when measuring conditions at the macro organizational level. The conceptual variables, such as product complexity and change and the associated requirement for information processing capacity tend to be rich and complex. At best, the operational measure only taps a part of the conceptual meaning. Although the operational measures used in the study have face

Table 4–2. Means, Standard Deviations, and Correlation Matrix of Strategic and

	Mean	S.D.	1	2	3	4	5
Company-Level Conditions (N = 35 to 50)							
1. Foreign product diversity	3.8	2.3					
2. Product modification differences	2.7	1.2	.07				
3. Product change	4.1	2.5	.05	-.13			
4. Size of foreign operations	52.2	20.9	.27	-.05	.34*		
5. Size of foreign manufacturing	66.7	25.3	.04	.38***	-.30	-.09	
6. Number of foreign subsidiaries	51.5	29.6	.20	.16	.14	.06	.25
7. Extent of outside ownership	2.4	1.6	.31**	-.04	.08	.11	-.13
8. Extent of foreign acquisitions	1.7	.9	.19	.20	.05	.23*	.07
Subsidiary-Level Conditions (N = 67 to 94)							
9. Marketing information dependency	2.2	1.1	-.06	.19*	.23*	.14	-.01
10. Sales dependency	4.0	15.3	.13	-.01	-.04	-.07	-.02
11. New manufacturing information dependency	.9	.2	.20	-.25**	.14	-.05	-.35**
12. Day-to-day manufacturing information dependency	2.0	1.0	.14	-.24**	.22	-.02	-.36***
13. New product design dependency	86.6	24.1	.24*	-.38***	.18	.06	-.32**
14. Product design change dependency	58.2	35.5	-.01	-.43***	.13	.07	-.34**
15. Importance of subsidiary	11.8	12.9	-.23*	-.02	-.20	-.03	.17
16. Intracompany purchases by subsidiary	24.8	26.4	.12	-.39***	.20	.17	-.46***
17. Intracompany sales by subsidiary	7.4	12.2	-.23*	.06	-.02	-.22*	.18
18. Product change	28.0	40.1	-.15	.03	-.17	-.12	.13
19. Manufacturing technology change	2.9	1.4	.06	-.04	-.12	-.05	-.12
20. Political environment change	3.0	1.5	0	-.15*	.05	-.05	-.05
21. Competitive climate change	2.5	1.1	-.19	.02	-.22	-.15	-.06
22. Supplier situation change	2.2	1.3	.10	-.08	-.04	.08	-.36***

* $p < .05$ (two-tailed test); ** $p < .01$; *** $p < .001$.

Note: Correlations involving variables 2, 7, and 8 are Kendall's tau because these variables are only assumed to be ordinal. The remainder are Pearson correlations.

validity (that is they appear to be related to the conceptual variable), the best support for validity comes from having a conceptual framework that is used to develop prior testable hypotheses between operational measures of the dependent and independent variables. Unless the operational measures appropriately represent the conceptual variables, the chance that these hypotheses will be confirmed is small.

RELATIONSHIPS AMONG THE INDEPENDENT VARIABLES

Table 4–2 shows the means, variances, and intercorrelations for all of the company and subsidiary-level strategic conditions, as well as the

Environmental Conditions.

6	7	8	9	10	11	12	13	14	15	16	17	18	19	20	21
-.09															
.11	.39**														
.15	-.05	-.18													
-.13	.12	.09	.15												
.18	.12	-.18	.11	.07											
.10	.14	.02	.37***	.09	.20										
.14	-.01	-.19*	.17	.10	.73***	.21*									
-.08	-.06	-.16	.17	.06	.36***	.27*	.52***								
-.22	-.13	-.19*	-.07	-.07	-.48***	-.20	-.43***	-.28*							
-.19	.10	-.06	.02	-.03	.22*	.18	.32**	.34**	-.13						
.05	-.19*	.03	.04	.04	-.26*	-.07	-.27*	0	.28*	-.10					
-.20	-.07	.02	.18	0	-.06	.04	-.09	.12	.18	-.11	.18				
.11	-.01	-.12	.22	-.02	.09	.33**	.16	.15	-.22	-.20	-.08	.18			
0	0	-.06	.23*	.19	.11	.14	.17	-.03	-.20	-.14	-.21*	.19	.22*		
-.22	-.13	-.13	.14	.10	-.09	.19	-.07	.08	-.17	-.09	.12	.14	.26*	.15	
-.07	-.03	.10	.07	.01	.13	.22*	.22*	.16	-.27*	.01	-.11	.17	.38***	.32**	.17

four quantifiable other factors. While there are a number of significant correlations among these variables, the levels are sufficiently low that each variable can still be viewed as representing a different aspect of a firm's international strategy and environment. As indicated in the table, several of the independent variables had a relatively high number of missing values. In no case was any of this data intentionally withheld. Its availability seemed to be largely a function of which individuals in the company the researcher had access to and how readily available the data were to them. It is reasonable to assume that the data are randomly missing as far as any of the hypotheses are concerned.

Table 4–3 shows that eight of the twenty-two strategic and environmental conditions vary in a significant way across the three nationality groups.

Table 4–3. How Strategic and Environmental Conditions Vary by Nationality.

	U.S.	UK	Europe	F
Company-Level Conditions (N = 35 to 50)				
Foreign product diversity	3.33	4.17	4.35	1.1
Product modification differences	2.75	4.00	2.35	4.7*
Product change	3.46	4.02	5.70	3.1
Size of foreign operations	37.69	68.20	66.31	22.4***
Size of foreign manufacturing	74.54	85.17	53.60	6.0**
Number of foreign subsidiaries	59.56	48.80	43.31	1.3
Extent of outside ownership	1.91	1.67	3.10	4.0*
Extent of foreign acquisitions	1.36	2.00	1.95	2.5
Subsidiary-Level Conditions(N = 67 to 94)				
Marketing information dependency	2.19	1.83	2.39	1.3
Sales dependency	3.73	1.42	5.28	.3
New manufacturing information dependency	.89	.71	.96	5.7**
Day-to-day manufacturing information dependency	1.97	1.58	2.14	1.2
New product design dependency	86.09	65.25	94.79	7.7***
Product design change dependency	53.83	40.25	69.82	3.9*
Importance of subsidiary	12.59	11.88	10.70	.2
Intracompany purchases by subsidiary	18.98	5.08	38.11	10.7***
Intracompany sales by subsidiary	9.43	7.67	4.92	1.3
Product change	25.89	29.36	30.31	.1
Manufacturing technology change	2.99	2.92	2.80	.2
Political environment change	3.11	2.62	3.01	.5
Competitive climate change	2.58	2.50	2.39	.3
Supplier situation change	1.97	1.92	2.56	2.3

* $p < .05$; ** $p < .01$; *** $p < .001$.

UK MNCs tend to have higher levels of product modification difference across foreign subsidiaries than do U.S. or European MNCs. As might be expected, U.S. firms tend to have a smaller percentage of their sales abroad. European MNCs have the lowest percentage of foreign manufacturing and rely more than U.S. or UK MNCs on exports from the parent country. Outside ownership also tends to be higher in the subsidiaries of European MNCs. The significant differences involving subsidiary-level strategic conditions all show that foreign subsidiaries in

UK MNCs tend to be less dependent on the parent for new manufacturing technology, new product designs and design changes, and exports than subsidiaries in European and U.S. MNCs. In the case of exports, subsidiaries in U.S. MNCs also receive significantly fewer exports than do subsidiaries in European MNCs.

NOTES

1. Large organizations do not go out of existence very often. More often, the strategy and top management of a firm are changed, but the organization itself continues to exist. This occurs because forces in the firm's environment (governments, unions, lenders) are willing to save it for the sake of employment, international competitiveness, and so forth. This intervention by environmental forces complicates the problem of identifying organizational failure for large, complex organizations.

2. The difficulty associated with using a profitability measure as a performance criterion across all companies can be illustrated by the fact that the mean ROI was 13.6 percent for the U.S. companies and only 7.5 percent for the European companies (using before tax earnings and total assets). Because profitability is frequently a less important performance criterion in European companies, however, it would be inappropriate to conclude their performance and organizational designs were less successful.

5

ORGANIZATIONAL STRUCTURE—ELEMENTARY FORMS

The most important feature of organizational design at the company level is the type of structure to be used for managing foreign operations. The study of fifty MNCs revealed twelve different types of structure. Table 5–1 lists the types of structure by industry and nationality.

The first four types of structure (along with the direct reporting structure) will be referred to as elementary structures, because the reporting or authority relationship takes place along a single dimension. The worldwide functional division structure implies that the functional activities in a foreign country (such as marketing and manufacturing) report back to their respective functional divisions in the parent, as do the domestic operations of the company. The international division structure separates foreign operations from the domestic functional or product divisions. Typically, the head of the international division reports to the parent CEO as do the heads of the domestic divisions. The geographical region structure divides the world into regions, each with its own headquarters. The region is responsible for all of the company's products and business within its geographical area. The worldwide product division structure extends the responsibilities of the domestic product divisions to cover their product lines on a worldwide basis. A direct reporting structure means that the subsidiary CEO reports direct to the CEO of the parent. Because only one example of this structure appeared in the sample, it will not be discussed further.

Major portions of this chapter are reprinted from "Strategy and Structure in Multinational Corporations: An Information-Processing Approach" by William G. Egelhoff, published in *Administrative Science Quarterly* Volume 27, Number 3 by permission of *Administrative Science Quarterly*. Copyright 1982 by Cornell University.

Table 5–1. Type of Structure by Industry and Nationality.

	Elementary Structures							
	Functional Divisions	International Division	Geographical Regions	Product Divisions	Matrix Structures	Mixed Structures	Other[a] Structures	
Industry								
Auto	4	2	1				1	8
Elec. and tele. equip.			1	5	1	1		8
Industrial equipment	1		1	1			1	4
Chemical			2	4	1	1		8
Pharmaceutical		2			3	1		6
Consumer pkgd goods		2	4	1	2			9
Tires		1				3		4
Other			1	1		1		3
Total	5	7	10	12	7	7	2	50
Nationality								
U.S.	1	6	8	2	2	5		24
UK			2	2	1	1		6
European	4	1		8	4	1	2	20
Total	5	7	10	12	7	7	2	50

a. Includes one direct reporting structure and one based on size of foreign subsidiary.

These five elementary types of structure may be combined in one of two different ways to form more complex structures. These are called matrix structures and mixed structures. Under a matrix structure, a subsidiary simultaneously reports to the parent along two of the elementary dimensions already discussed. Any two of the elementary dimensions can be combined in a matrix. Only the international division and geographical regions are mutually exclusive dimensions that cannot appear together at the same organizational level.

In a mixed structure, each foreign operation reports to the parent along a single dimension, but it is not the same dimension for all subsidiaries. For example, the Brazilian subsidiary might report to the international division while operations in Germany report to their respective worldwide product groups. The same pairs of combinations are available under the mixed structures as with matrix structures. Organizational structure will be dealt with in two chapters. This chapter will deal with the elementary forms, and Chapter 6 will deal with the matrix and mixed forms of structure.

MEASUREMENT OF STRUCTURE

The classification of organizational structure was done by either obtaining or in some cases constructing, with the help of organizational members, organization charts for each company. At least half an hour was spent with organizational members directly discussing the structure and how it worked. The classification of structure was based on the formal reporting relationships or identified lines of authority between the parent and the foreign subsidiaries. This variable represents the operating structure, which can be different from the legal structure of an MNC.[1] The reporting relationships also differ from purely advisory relationships and lines of influence. The latter constitute another potentially important source of information-processing capacity between parent and subsidiary, but this is not the variable that has been defined as structure.

Our experience is that macro structure is one of the most difficult concepts to accurately and consistently measure, for complex organizations. Formal organization charts can represent legal rather than operational structures. Descriptions of structural forms are not always consistent across organizations, and this was especially true for matrix and mixed structures. The present study relied on the first-hand collection of information about structure and sought to validate this across three respondents in a company and against a large amount of additional organizational information. For example, the organization charts were subsequently used to measure centralization, which involved identifying which organizational level and subunit would have to approve certain decisions for a subsidiary. If the organization chart did not suffice, it was discussed further and reconstructed. This kind of checking especially helped to distinguish between reporting relationships and advisory or consultative relationships.

Every complex organization has exceptions to its general pattern of organization. One or two subsidiaries may report differently, or a small product area may be organized differently. Where such deviations were clearly exceptions to a general pattern, they were excluded from the classification scheme. Where deviations from some pattern were significant and no longer an exception, the structure was categorized as a mixed structure. As a result of this data collection method, the present study identified twelve unique forms of structure in a sample of fifty firms. Generally these forms should not be further combined because each represents a uniquely different set of information-processing capacities.

STRATEGY AND STRUCTURE STUDIES

The first empirical work that sought to relate structure to the strategy of an organization was Chandler's (1962) study of seventy large U.S. corporations. It tended to show that as a company's product-market strategy changed, it was important that the organization's structure also change to support implementation of the new strategy. Additional studies by Pavan (1972), Channon (1973), Rumelt (1974), and Dyas and Thanheiser (1976) further demonstrated that certain strategies need to be supported by certain structures. A number of empirical studies have also attempted to describe the relationship between strategy and structure for multinational corporations (Fouraker and Stopford 1968; Brooke and Remmers 1970; Stopford and Wells 1972; Franko 1976; Hulbert and Brandt 1980; Daniels, Pitts, and Tretter 1984, 1985). Of these, the Stopford and Wells study was the largest and most comprehensive, and it also developed the most explicit theory linking strategy and structure in MNCs.

In their book on strategy implementation, Galbraith and Nathanson (1978) credit Stopford and Wells with having extended the earlier strategy-structure models of Chandler (1962) and Scott (1971) to include international strategy and structure. Figure 5–1 shows the critical variables and relationships of the Stopford and Wells model. Whether an MNC possesses an international division, worldwide product division, or area division structure was observed to be largely a function of the firm's foreign product diversity and the relative size of its foreign sales. The Stopford and Wells study took place in U.S. MNCs, but subsequent research by Franko (1976) in European MNCs tended to confirm the relationships shown in Figure 5–1. Although recent research has raised some questions about the validity of the international division boundary (Bartlett 1979, 1983; Davidson 1980; Davidson and Haspeslagh 1982; Daniels, Pitts, and Tretter 1984), the other relationships have essentially gone unchallenged and remain intact. In fact, with the exception of a recent study by Daniels, Pitts, and Tretter (1985), the upper and right sides of the model (those portions associated with relatively high

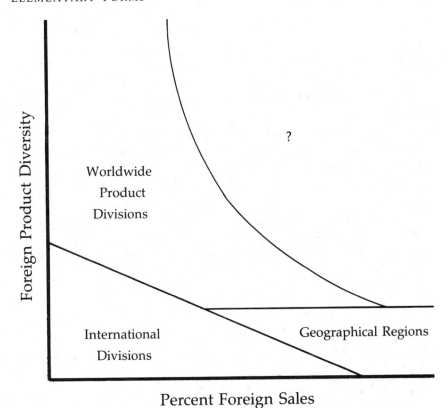

Figure 5–1. The Stopford and Wells Model of the Relationship between Strategy and Structure in Multinational Corporations.

levels of foreign sales and/or foreign product diversity) have remained largely untested since the original research by Stopford and Wells and Franko. These portions of the model (and especially the portion represented as a question mark) are of growing significance, however, because the strategies of more and more MNC's are moving in this direction.

Recent literature has also tended to raise a number of specific questions about strategy-structure relationships in the more strategically complex portions of the model. First, Galbraith and Nathanson (1978) ask what international strategy fits the matrix structure, because both they and Davis and Lawrence (1977) noted a probable trend toward matrix structures in MNCs. Stopford and Wells had suggested that matrix (and mixed) structures might be appropriate for firms in the upper right corner of the model (where both foreign sales and foreign product diversity are high), but their data provided only weak support for this relationship. Because the widespread move to matrix structures expected by Davis and Lawrence has not occurred despite the fact that many MNC strategies today contain relatively high levels of foreign sales and foreign product diversity, the question about what international strategy fits a matrix structure would still seem to be an open one.

A second issue with strategy-structure implications seems to be raised by Hout, Porter, and Rudden (1982). They believe that the increasing growth in global interdependency can best be exploited by global strategies, where the appropriate unit of analysis for strategic planning and management is the global market for a product instead of multiple domestic markets. They point out that global strategies require new, more centralized forms of structure that can integrate managerial decisionmaking across many domestic markets that were heretofore dealt with in a decentralized manner.

A third issue that seems to be influencing international strategy is increasing host government pressure for more national responsiveness in the strategies of MNCs (Doz 1980; Doz and Prahalad 1980). This pressure is generally reflected in calls for more local manufacture and R&D, a balance between exports and imports, and sometimes products and technologies that are consistent with national interests. This trend obviously runs counter to the previous trend for global strategies.

These trends toward global strategies and more national responsiveness have largely come to prominence since the Stopford and Wells study, and subsequent research has not really attempted to integrate these developments into the existing set of strategy-structure relationships for MNCs. This is perhaps not surprising, because the new issues in international strategy seem to be still in the exploratory research phase, while research done under the strategy-structure paradigm has evolved to the point where it requires clearly defined concepts and operational measures. Yet it is important that attempts start to be made to integrate some understanding of the new issues and trends in international strategy into the established set of strategy-structure relationships. Otherwise, the understanding of strategy will increasingly outstrip our understanding of how to organize to implement such strategy.

AN INFORMATION-PROCESSING MODEL FOR RELATING STRATEGY AND STRUCTURE

In this study, the organization is viewed as an information-processing system, and information processing between organizational subunits is considered an important aspect of macro organizational behavior and performance. Each of the various types of structure available to an MNC is seen as facilitating certain types of information processing between the subunits of the organization—in this case the parent and foreign subsidiaries—while at the same time restricting other types of information processing.

The elements of a firm's strategy, on the other hand, are seen as posing different requirements for information processing between the parent and the foreign subsidiaries. If strategies can be measured in terms of the kind and amount of information processing required to implement them, then one can create a general framework for hypothesizing fit or congruence between structure and strategy. There is good fit between structure and strategy when the information-processing requirements of a firm's strategy are satisfied by the information-processing capacities of its structure.

The information-processing approach calls for translating strategic conditions and organizational structure into information-processing requirements and information-processing capacities respectively, which are more comparable phenomena. Generally, information processing needs to be measured along several dimensions to be a useful intervening concept for comparing the information-processing requirements of an organization's strategy with the information-processing capacities of its structure. Deciding which dimensions to use to measure information processing requires some judgment, but the general criterion should be to select dimensions that best reflect the information-processing limitations of the different structures for the strategic context in which they must operate.

The present study focuses on the purpose and perspective of information processing (whether it is strategic or tactical) and the subject or content of information processing (whether it deals with product matters or company and country matters). Ansoff (1965) refers to operating, administrative, and strategic decisions in organizations. Tactical information processing combines the first two categories and deals with the large volume of relatively routine day-to-day problems and situations confronting an organization. The decisionmaking perspective required to handle these situations tends to be relatively narrow, and it usually exists at the middle and lower levels of management. Strategic information processing attempts to deal with a much smaller volume of relatively nonroutine, and usually more important, problems and situations. These problems deal with the fundamental position of the organization in its environment and usually involve changing this position. Thus, strategic information processing has a different purpose and requires a different perspective than tactical information processing. It addresses higher-level organizational goals, is broader in scope, and usually has a longer time horizon.

Research suggests that different levels of an organization process different kinds of information and have different purposes for processing information (Landsberger 1961; Thomason 1966). Mintzberg (1979:54) states that "the issues each level addresses are fundamentally different" and notes that strategic decisions generally involve members of the "strategic apex" or top management of an organization. Because the majority of tactical decisions do not involve members of the strategic apex, tactical and strategic information processing tend to occur at different levels of an organization.

The study also considers the subject or content of information processing and distinguishes between information processing for product matters (product and process technology, market information) and information processing for company and country matters (finance, tax, legal, government relations, purchasing, personnel). Subject knowledge or specialization tends to vary horizontally across organizations. Different organizational structures tend to cluster it into different subunits and provide for different linkages between these subunits. Using these distinctions, four types of information processing are developed, as shown in Figure 5–2. The four types are generally not substitutes for each other because they tend to address different problem areas that require different types of knowledge and different perspectives of the organization and its goals.

THE INFORMATION-PROCESSING CAPACITIES
OF STRUCTURE

There is considerable empirical evidence that macro organizational structure exerts a strong influence on information flows in organizations (Aguilar 1967; Brooke and Remmers 1970; Galbraith 1977; Scharpf 1977). These studies show that organizational structure acts to constrain and channel information flows to follow the formal reporting channels expressed by a particular structure. Aguilar's (1967:112) study of environmental scanning and related information processing in chemical companies concluded: "More striking than the inducements to communication provided by spatial and organizational proximity are the barriers erected by spatial and organizational distance. The most severe and

SUBJECT OF INFORMATION PROCESSING
Company and Country Matters   Product Matters

	Company and Country Matters	Product Matters
Tactical	Tactical information processing for company and country matters Example: Evaluating how and when to raise money in international money markets	Tactical information processing for product matters Example: Deciding on a routine change in the price of a product
Strategic	Strategic information processing for company and country matters Example: Deciding on the company's position vis-à-vis foreign government pressures for local ownership in foreign subsidiaries	Strategic information processing for product matters Example: Deciding on the long-range level of R&D support for a major product line

PURPOSE AND PERSPECTIVE OF INFORMATION PROCESSING

Figure 5–2. Typology for Categorizing Information Processing.

repeated failures of communication were noted between divisions of a company." Albaum (1964) also found that there was little horizontal communication of external information between the divisions of a diversified manufacturing company. Scharpf's (1977:163) study of ministries of the German government concluded that organizational boundaries "seem to create semi-permeable walls which impede the flow of information (on the demand side as well as on the supply side) and which reduce the capacity for conflict resolution."

Consistent with the above, this chapter considers the four elementary types of structure commonly used by MNCs: worldwide functional divisions, international divisions, geographical regions, and worldwide product divisions. It then uses relative organizational distance (or closeness) through the formal organization structure to define where communication will be facilitated and where it will be hindered between organizational subunits. In addition to organizational distance (which specifies interconnected subunits), macro structure also influences what type of information (in terms of subject and perspective) can be processed between interconnected subunits. Horizontal differentiation (or specialization) largely determines in which subunits certain types of knowledge reside, just as vertical differentiation largely determines at what levels tactical and strategic perspectives of the business can be taken. How parent headquarters are differentiated and which subunits are directly linked through the hierarchy largely determines how much of each of the four types of information processing a structure will provide.

Next, the four types of information processing are used as a four-dimensional framework to help describe and distinguish between the information-processing capacities provided by the four different MNC structures. These capacities are summarized in Table 5–2.

Table 5–2. Type and Level of Information-Processing Capacity Provided by Different Types of Structure.

	Level of Informaiton-Processing Capacity			
	For Company and Country Matters		For Product Matters	
	Tactical	Strategic	Tactical	Strategic
Functional divisions	High[a]	Low	High[a]	Low
International divisions	High[b]	High[b]	Low	Low
Geographical regions	High[c]	High[c]	High[c]	High[c]
Product divisions	Low	Low	High	High

a. Only within a functional area. Low across functions.
b. Only between subsidiary and international division.
c. Only between subsidiary and regional headquarters.

A worldwide functional division structure means that the functional activities in a foreign subsidiary report directly to their respective functional divisions in the parent. Because none of the functional subunits could operate as a separate business (that is, individually survive in the environment), the formulation of business strategy requires a cross-functional perspective. In a functional division company a cross-functional or general management perspective only exists at one level, at the top or strategic apex (Mintzberg 1979) of the parent HQ. Subunits in foreign subsidiaries cannot participate in or make direct inputs to the strategy-formulation process, for nearly all information processing within a subsidiary or between it and the parent takes place within a functional area. Consequently, this structure provides almost no strategic information-processing capacity between foreign subsidiaries and the parent. The centralization of strategic information processing means that processing capacity is limited (only a few people at one level of the parent are involved), and it is difficult for new information about the environment to enter the process. The functional structure should be most suitable when the information required to formulate strategy already exists in the strategic apex of the parent and when strategy can be formulated more on a worldwide than a subsidiary-by-subsidiary basis (for example, where a product tends to sell more in a uniform worldwide market than in differentiated, local markets).

The functional structure should facilitate tactical information processing between the parent and foreign subsidiaries as long as the processing can take place within a functional area. Tactical information processing across functions, however, will be low because the structure does not facilitate communication between divisions at either the subsidiary level or the tactical levels of the parent. Functional division companies should ideally have strategies that both minimize and routinize the demands for information processing across functions. For an MNC, this might mean a homogeneous and stable line of products as well as a relatively homogeneous and stable worldwide environment.

With an international division structure, all foreign subsidiaries report to an international division that is separate from the domestic operations. Brooke and Remmers (1970) found that this structure tends to facilitate information processing between the parent and foreign subsidiaries, while at the same time it hinders information processing at the parent level between the international division and the domestic operations. Product knowledge tends to be centered in the domestic divisions, while knowledge about such company and country matters as international finance and foreign political conditions is centered in the international division. Consequently, parent-subsidiary information-processing capacity is relatively high for company and country matters and relatively low for product matters. There is a general management or strategic apex at both the subsidiary and international division levels. Thus, strategic as well as tactical information processing can take place between a subsidiary and the international division, but it will center around company and country matters rather than product matters. This structure would seem to fit international strategies that do not rely on transferring domestic marketing and manufacturing strengths to the foreign operations. It should be well suited to implementing international and domestic strategies that are more different than they are similar.

A geographical region structure divides the world into regions, each with its own HQ. Each HQ is responsible for all of the company's products and business within its geographical area. The regional HQ is the center of the company's knowledge about company and country matters within the region. Most regional HQs also contain either product or functional staffs to provide coordination for product matters across subsidiaries in the region (Williams 1967). There is a general management or strategic apex at both the subsidiary and regional HQ levels. As a result, this structure facilitates a high level of all four types of information processing between a subsidiary and its regional HQ. The information-processing capacity between a foreign subsidiary and domestic operations or a subsidiary in another region is low. The only mechanism for coordinating across regions is the corporate HQ, and for the companies in the sample, most of the staff tended to be at the regional rather than the corporate level. This structure should be most suitable when operations within a region are relatively large, complex, and sufficiently different from other regions that opportunities for specialization and economies of scale are greater within a region than they are along worldwide product lines.

A worldwide product division structure extends the responsibilities of the domestic product divisions to cover their product lines on a worldwide basis. Under this structure, there is a tendency to centralize product-related decision making at both the strategic and tactical levels in the parent product groups and decentralize all nonproduct decision-making to the foreign subsidiaries (Brooke and Remmers 1970). Consequently, the capacity for processing information between the parent and foreign subsidiaries for company and country matters tends to be low because much of it has been decentralized to the local subsidiary level and parent management has a product orientation. Product-related tactical and strategic information-processing capacities, on the other hand, tend to be high. The foreign product divisions in the subsidiaries are connected to the centers of product knowledge in the parent. For each product line, there is a strategic apex at both the subsidiary and parent product-division levels. This structure should fit situations where product-related information processing between parent and subsidiary is most important to implementing strategy.

The four structures differ widely when measured by the four dimensions of parent-subsidiary information processing. Although the capacities seem to be consistent with previous research findings concerning the influence of formal structure on information flows in organizations, they remain largely assumptions that have not as yet been directly tested. The present study will, however, test these assumptions indirectly, by using them to formulate hypotheses about strategy and structure that can then be directly tested.

THE INFORMATION-PROCESSING REQUIREMENTS
OF STRATEGY

Implicit in an organization's strategy are requirements for information processing between its subunits. The purpose of this section is to define these requirements for MNCs in terms of the four types of information processing. The eight elements of company-level strategy introduced in Chapter 3 were selected as potentially important contingency variables because conceptually they should exert a strong influence on parent-subsidiary information-processing requirements. Four of the elements (product modification differences among foreign subsidiaries, the size of foreign manufacturing, the extent of outside ownership in foreign subsidiaries, and the extent of foreign acquisitions) have not appeared in previous studies. They were included in the study because preliminary discussions with multinational executives indicated that these strategic conditions are currently open to change in many MNCs and that the implications of such change for organizational structure are poorly understood. The other four elements of strategy (foreign product diversity, rate of product change, size of foreign operations, and number of foreign subsidiaries) have been found to have significant associations with structure in earlier studies, but the relationships have not been defined from an information-processing perspective.

Foreign Product Diversity

Numerous studies have confirmed the importance of product diversity to the choice of appropriate macro structure (Chandler 1962; Stopford and Wells 1972; Franko 1976; Pitts 1977; Daniels, Pitts, and Tretter 1985). As product diversity increases, there is an increase in both market diversity (environmental complexity) and manufacturing and technical diversity (technological complexity). Several studies have found that, as environmental and technological complexity increase, requirements for information processing between interdependent subunits also increase (Lawrence and Lorsch 1967; Galbraith 1977). Consequently, as product diversity increases, there is a greater need for tactical and strategic information processing for product matters; for example, there will be more technical operating problems and a greater number of strategic product decisions. There is no associated increase in the complexity of nonproduct matters. The structure providing the most product-related information-processing capacity between the centers of product knowledge in the parent and the foreign subsidiaries is the worldwide product division structure. It utilizes several separate information-processing channels between a subsidiary and the parent, one for each product division in the subsidiary. If new product lines are introduced in a subsidiary, it is the only structure that provides for an increase in the number of information-processing channels with the parent.

> *Hypothesis 5–1.* MNCs with product division structures will tend to have more foreign product diversity than MNCs with other structures.

The functional division structure also provides a high level of tactical information-processing capacity for product matters, but it does so along functional channels. Marketing and manufacturing matters come together and are first integrated at the parent level. This kind of centralization is manageable only if there is a narrow line of products that tend to be similar around the world. If product diversity were introduced, it would quickly overload both the limited strategic information-processing capacity at the top of the parent HQ and the limited cross-functional capacity at the tactical level of the parent HQ.

> *Hypothesis 5–2.* MNCs with functional division structures will tend to have less foreign product diversity than MNCs with other structures.

Product Modification Differences

The degree to which products are locally modified or differ from one foreign subsidiary to another specifies yet another type of product complexity or heterogeneity. Although no research exists on the effects of such heterogeneity at such a macro level, it has been studied within manufacturing or operating subsystems. Woodward (1965) associated this kind of product and process heterogeneity with unit or batch production systems, Harvey (1968) with technological diffuseness, and Perrow (1967) with task variability. All found that this kind of heterogeneity led to more decentralized decisionmaking and communication patterns.

To the extent that a product is the same around the world, it is efficient and economical to centralize knowledge and management of the product at a single point in the parent. Under such conditions, product-related information processing can be standardized with all product subunits, and product planning can be integrated to achieve global economies of scale. To the extent that product characteristics and uses vary from subsidiary to subsidiary, opportunities to realize these advantages decline and the costs of maintaining and disseminating product knowledge from a central point increase. Consequently, as product modification differences increase, one would expect MNCs to use structures that decentralize product-related information processing. Centralization appears to be greatest in the functional and product division structures because both structures centralize all of the parent's knowledge and information-processing capacity for a product in a single parent subunit.

> *Hypothesis 5–3.* MNCs with functional and product division structures will tend to have lower levels of product modification differences across foreign subsidiaries than will MNCs with other structures.

The geographical region structure, on the other hand, has several focal points for each product line (one in each regional HQ) and provides relatively decentralized product-related information processing. Because the centers of product knowledge are relatively disconnected from foreign operations under an international division structure, there is no structural reason for hypothesizing any particular level of product modification difference for this structure.

> *Hypothesis 5–4.* MNCs with geographical region structures will tend to have higher levels of product modification difference across foreign subsidiaries than will MNCs with other structures.

Product Change

Researchers have generally found that higher rates of product and process change require more information processing between interdependent subunits (Burns and Stalker 1961; Emery and Trist 1965; Lawrence and Lorsch 1967). High rates of product change require that an MNC have the ability to transfer new technology as well as the ability to reformulate product strategy on a frequent basis. Technology transfer requires product-related information-processing capacity of a tactical nature. It takes place between the centers of technical knowledge in the parent and the corresponding subunits in the subsidiary. The need to reformulate product strategy means that there is a concurrent requirement for strategic information-processing capacity.

The structure that provides both tactical and strategic processing capacity between the subsidiary and the centers of product technology and product planning in the parent is the product division structure. The functional division structure also provides a high level of tactical information-processing capacity for product matters (such as technology transfer), but it does not provide any strategic information processing between subsidiary and parent. The latter is centralized in the parent. Thus, a functional division structure should fit a high level of technology transfer but not a high level of product change.

Hypothesis 5–5. MNCs with product division structures will tend to have a higher level of product change than MNCs with other structures.

Size of Foreign Operations

In their study of U.S. MNCs, Stopford and Wells (1972) found that as the percentage of foreign sales in a company increased, there was a tendency for MNCs to abandon international division structures and adopt a geographical region structure. From an information-processing viewpoint, this finding makes sense. As the relative size of foreign operations increases, the opportunities for increased integration either across subsidiaries or between foreign and domestic operations increases. Thus, as the relative size of the foreign sector increases, product interdependency either within this sector or between it and the domestic sector should also increase as effective MNCs seek to realize synergies and economies of scale on either a regional or worldwide basis. This requires more product-related information-processing capacity. As developed above, all of the structures except the international division can provide a high level of product-related information-processing capacity either between foreign and domestic operations or among groups of foreign subsidiaries. Because the international division structure does not provide the kind of information processing required to realize product-related synergies and economies of scale, it tends to fit strategies with relatively small foreign operations, where these opportunities are not present.

Hypothesis 5–6. MNCs with an international division structure will tend to have a lower percentage of foreign sales than MNCs with other structures.

Size of Foreign Manufacturing

A company's foreign operations can be split into the percentage of foreign sales exported from the parent and the percentage manufactured by the foreign subsidiaries. Exports from the parent to the foreign subsidiaries create numerous interdependencies that increase the requirement for product-related information processing between the two. Because geographical region structures provide relatively low information-processing capacity between foreign and domestic operations, this structure will not support a high level of parent-subsidiary exports.

Instead, it supports a high level of foreign manufacture and product exchange within a region (Such as Europe). Because the worldwide functional and product division structures can provide high levels of product-related information-processing capacity between domestic and foreign operations, they can support either high levels of parent exports or high levels of foreign manufacture. However, when the level of foreign manufacturing becomes very large and parent exports very small, opportunities for synergy and economies of scale will generally be more intraregional than global, and the advantages of the geographical region structure will tend to outweigh those of the functional or product division structures. Because the international division structure does not provide a high level of product-related information processing either between parent and foreign subsidiary or among foreign subsidiaries, there is no basis for associating either a high level of parent exports or a high level of foreign manufacture and intraregional exchange with this structure.

> *Hypothesis 5–7.* MNCs with geographical region structures will tend to have higher levels of foreign manufacturing than MNCs with other structures.

Number of Foreign Subsidiaries

As the number of foreign subsidiaries increases, requirements for all four types of information-processing capacities at the parent level will increase. Under such conditions, decentralized structures are likely to better fit the larger number of parent-subsidiary relationships than the more centralized structures. The functional division structure centralizes information processing for both foreign and domestic operations in the same parent HQ. The international division structure also centralizes information processing for all foreign operations in a single subunit, the international division, but separates it from domestic operations. Thus, information processing is less centralized than under the worldwide functional division structure. Both the geographical region and product division structures have foreign operations reporting to several different focal points in the parent, the separate regional or product division HQ. From the parent's point of view, parent-subsidiary information processing is less centralized under these structures. Structures with multiple focal points in the parent for parent-subsidiary information processing should be able to accommodate more parent-subsidiary relationships.

> *Hypothesis 5–8.* MNCs with functional division structures will tend to have fewer foreign subsidiaries than firms with international division structures,

which, in turn, will tend to have fewer subsidiaries than firms with geographical region or product division structures.

Extent of Outside Ownership

Significant outside ownership in foreign subsidiaries places additional constraints on the way that subsidiaries can be managed. Almost certainly, outside owners will oppose decisions that reduce subsidiary profits for the sake of maximizing total company profits. Because outside owners are only interested in the goals and performance of an individual subsidiary, this condition should be easiest for an MNC to accommodate when its structure favors setting goals and developing strategies for the subsidiary at the subsidiary level (that is, strategies of subsidiaries can be relatively independent of each other). A functional division structure centralizes strategic information processing near the top of the parent HQ, and this leads to establishing goals and making decisions that are based more on optimizing total company performance than on optimizing any subunit's performance. Consequently, organizations with functional structures should find it extremely difficult to accommodate the subsidiary-level interests of outside owners.

The situation should be less severe in geographical region and product division companies because subsidiaries can participate in strategy formulation with the parent, and greater variability at the subsidiary level can be accommodated. Yet geographical region and product division structures will attempt to optimize regional or product division performance as much as subsidiary performance. The international division structure, however, does not provide the product-related information-processing capacity required to realize regional or global synergies and economies of scale across foreign subsidiaries. Because there is largely a pooled interdependency (Thompson 1967) among the individual subsidiaries, this structure should be the most consistent with setting strategy for the subsidiary at the subsidiary level.

> *Hypothesis 5–9.* MNCs with worldwide functional division structures will have the lowest levels of outside ownership in their foreign subsidiaries, followed by firms with geographical region and product division structures. Firms with international division structures will have the highest levels of outside ownership.

Extent of Acquisitions

Most acquisitions are themselves multifunctional organizations. They contain subunits that already engage in manufacturing, marketing, and financial activities and possess some kind of organizational structure and information-processing system linking these subunits together. Multinational structures that can absorb a foreign acquisition while leaving the acquisition's existing structure and its associated information-processing system intact should be able to accommodate a higher rate of growth by acquisition. Macro structures that require substantial reorganization of an acquisition's structure and information-processing systems to make them consistent with those of the parent should tend to discourage acquisitions.

Worldwide functional division structures should have the most difficulty accommodating foreign acquisitions. Separate functional information-processing systems must be constructed between subsidiary and parent and many existing interfunctional systems within the subsidiary dismantled. None of the other structures should require such significant change. In most cases, the internal structure and information-processing systems of the acquisition can remain relatively unchanged while the external, or boundary-spanning, relationships and activities absorb the change required to fit the new parent-subsidiary information-processing system.

> *Hypothesis 5–10.* MNCs with worldwide functional division structures will tend to make fewer and smaller acquisitions than MNCs with other structures.

TESTING THE HYPOTHESES

Thirty-four of the sample companies had one of the four elementary types of structure described above. This is the sample that is used to test the hypotheses developed in the previous section. The companies with various forms of matrix and mixed structures are considered in Chapter 6.

Table 5–1 showed the distribution of the fifty sample firms by industry, nationality, and type of structure. Although companies in an industry may favor certain international structures over others, the variance is too great for the type of industry to have any meaningful predictive value. Past studies have confirmed the lack of an important contingency relationship between type of industry and the structure of international operations (Brooke and Remmers 1970; Stopford and Wells 1972; Brandt 1978).

Although nationality is clearly related to the type of structure used by a company, the conceptual model and hypotheses are meant to be true across cultures because the information-processing implications of both strategy and structure are thought to be similar across cultures. European MNCs may tend to face different environments and possess different goals than U.S. MNCs, and, as a result, the elements of their strategies may also tend to differ in a consistent manner from those of U.S. firms. Nevertheless, if a European MNC faces a high level of product diversity, this product diversity creates the same requirement for information processing that it would in a U.S. MNC. Similarly, if a European MNC uses a worldwide product division structure, this structure tends to possess the same capacity for parent-subsidiary information processing that it would in a U.S. company.

Two types of analyses were used to examine the fit relationships between strategy and structure. First, bivariate ANOVA contrasts were used to test separately each relationship expressed by the hypotheses. Then a multivariate discriminant analysis was used to examine simultaneously the relationships between structure and all of the contingency variables (elements of strategy). Table 5–3 contains a summary of each hypothesis and the results of the associated ANOVA contrasts. Except for a few fits involving two of the elements, the sample data showed significant support for the hypotheses. Those not fully supported included hypotheses 5–3 and 5–4, dealing with product modification differences across subsidiaries. Although all three relationships expressed in the hypotheses were directionally supported, only one, the low level of product modification differences in companies with functional division structures, was statistically significant.

Hypothesis 5–9, concerning the level of outside ownership in foreign subsidiaries, also failed to receive much support from the data. Only the low level of outside ownership in the functional division companies followed the hypothesized fits. The mean level of foreign sales derived from subsidiaries with greater than 30 percent outside ownership was only 5 percent for functional division companies. This figure was calculated using category midpoints to represent a category (such as 2.5 percent to represent 0 to 5 percent) and is an accurate representation only for this group; since none of these companies fell in the open-ended, greater-than-20-percent category. Thus, the empirical data clearly support part of the hypothesis—namely, that worldwide functional division structures fit strategies containing low levels of outside ownership in foreign subsidiaries. The other two relationships expressed by this hypothesis (that is a low level of outside ownership in product division MNCs and a high level in international division MNCs) were clearly not supported by the data.

Table 5–3. Hypotheses and Results of Bivariate ANOVA Contrasts.

Hypothesis	Mean Values of Elements of Strategy				Differences
	FD	ID	GR	PD	
1. Product diversity greatest in PD 2. Lowest in FD	1.4^a	1.7	3.4	5.8^b	[a]Different from GR at $p <$ .01 and PD at $p <$ .001. [b]Different from GR at $p <$ .01 and FD and ID at $p <$ .001.
3. Product modification differences lowest in FD and PD. 4. Highest in GR	1.8^a	2.9	3.4	2.7	[a]Different from GR at $p <$ .05 and from other structures at $p <$ .10, based on Mann-Whitney U test.
5. Product change highest in PD	3.2	2.9	2.9	5.4^a	[a]Different from other structures at $p <$ .05.
6. Size of foreign operations lowest in ID	58	34^a	47	61	[a]Different from GR at $p <$ .05 and from FD and PD at $p <$ .01.
7. Size of foreign manufacturing higher in GR than in FD and PD	42	76	91^a	61	[a]Different from FD and PD at $p <$ .001.
8. Number of foreign subsidiaries fewest in FD; next fewest in ID	12^a	41^b	55	58	[a]Different from ID and PD at $p <$ .001 and from GR at $p <$ .01 [b]Different from GR at $p <$ .10 and from PD at $p <$ .05.
9. Level of outside ownership lowest in FD; next lowest in GR and PD; highest in ID	1.8	1.9	1.9	3.0	No difference between structures at $p <$ .10, based on Mann-Whitney U test.
10. Level of foreign acquisitions lowest in FD	$.8^a$	1.3	2.1	2.2	[a]Different from GR and PD at $p <$ .025, based on Mann-Whitney U test.

Note: FD = Functional divisions; ID = International divisions; GR = Geographical regions; PD = Product divisions.

A MULTIVARIATE TEST OF FIT BETWEEN
STRATEGY AND STRUCTURE

Thus far, the study has dealt with fit between strategy and structure in a bivariate manner. This was done because it is easier to model a complex situation as a collection of independent bivariate relationships. The model is admittedly much simpler than the real situation, in which an organization must select one structure and attempt to satisfy as many of the crucial bivariate fits as it can simultaneously. Thus, while there is obvious support for the bivariate fits from central tendencies in the entire sample of MNCs, the question remains how useful the model is in a situation in which an organization must, by itself, achieve good fit between its structure and all the elements of its strategy.

While the information-processing framework has been useful for positing a series of bivariate relationships between structure and elements of strategy, it does not allow one to add up or accumulate the total information-processing requirements placed on an organization by its strategy. In order to test how well successful MNCs actually do achieve simultaneous fit between structure and the various elements of their strategy, multivariate analysis was required. Since structure was measured as a nominal variable, a step-wise multiple discriminant analysis was run using the four types of structure as the groups and the eight elements of strategy as the independent variables. The results appear in Table 5–4. Five of the independent variables had sufficient discriminating power to enter and remain in the discriminant model. The standardized discriminant coefficients indicate the relative contribution of an independent variable to the discriminant function. Only the first two discriminant functions are statistically significant.

Table 5–5 shows how successful the discriminant functions were in predicting the type of structure for each company, given measures of the elements of its strategy. In 76 percent of the cases, the discriminant model could predict the actual structure of a company, which is significantly better than the chance probability of predicting only 27 percent of the cases correctly. Product diversity and size of foreign manufacturing provide the most discriminating power, followed by size of foreign operations. Each of these three variables was hypothesized to be an important element of strategy for type of structure to fit. The multivariate analysis confirms that companies in the sample generally realize a high level of simultaneous fit with these three pivotal elements.

Table 5–4. Multiple Discriminant Analysis of the Elements of Strategy on Type of Structure.

Independent Variable	Discriminant Function			F-value
	1	2	3	
Product diversity	-.90[a]	-.38	.13	7.96***
Product modification differences	-.33	-.12	-.19	2.34
Product change	-.55	-.48	.75	2.12
Size of foreign operations	-.51	.20	-.73	4.45**
Size of foreign manufacturing	.26	-.99	-.01	7.98***
Canonical correlation	.86	.74	.33	
Wilks Lamda	.10***	.39**	.89	

** $p < .01$; *** $p < .001$.
Note: Type of structure is the dependent variable.
[a] All values under the three functions are standardized discriminant coefficients.

Table 5–5. Predicted Type of Structure from Coefficients of Discriminant Functions.

Actual Group Membership	Predicted Group Membership			
	FD	ID	GR	PD
Functional divisions (FD)	4	1	0	0
International divisions (ID)	2	5	0	0
Geographical regions (GR)	0	3	6	1
Product divisions (PD)	0	0	1	11

Note: Structures of MNCs correctly classified = 76 percent.

Table 5–6 shows the centroids of each of the four groups (types of structure) measured along the three discriminant functions. Clearly, the first function, which largely measures product diversity, discriminates Group PD (Product Divisions) from the other three groups. Hypothesis 5–1 predicted that product diversity would be higher in companies with product division structures than it would in companies with other structures. The second discriminant function, which is based on the size of foreign manufacturing, discriminates Group GR (Geographical Regions) from Group FD (Functional Divisions) and to a lesser extent Group PD. Hypothesis 5–7 specified that MNCs with geographical region structures would tend to have a higher percentage of foreign manufacturing than companies with functional or product division structures. The third discriminant function, based on the size of foreign operations and product change, does a poorer job of discriminating Group ID (International Divisions) from the other groups. Hypothesis 5–6 states that MNCs with international division structures would tend to have a lower percentage of foreign sales than firms with other structures. In a sense, the discriminant model has selected three of the elements of strategy and their associated fit hypotheses and used them to construct its classification scheme. This provides some evidence that successful companies do in fact achieve considerable simultaneous fit between their structures and important elements of their strategies.

Table 5–6.   Centroids of the Four Structural Groups Measured along the Discriminant Functions.

	Discriminant Function		
Group	1	2	3
Functional divisions	.95	3.19	-.33
International divisions	2.05	-.13	.46
Geographical regions	.56	-.79	-.37
Product divisions	-1.85	.07	.14

Finally, the study attempted to check whether those companies that seemed to have poorer fit between strategy and structure (that is, the eight deviant cases in the discriminant analysis) also suffered from poorer quality information processing, as the framework would suggest. The instrument that Lawrence and Lorsch used to measure the quality of integration between subunits was used to measure the quality of the parent-foreign subsidiary relationship (see Chapter 4 for measurement). Although information processing was not explicitly mentioned in the instrument, at the macro level of analysis what is processed or exchanged between the parent and the foreign subsidiaries is information. Hence, the relationship can be viewed as primarily an information-processing relationship as opposed to a physical or social one. Data on quality of integration were available on seventeen of the thirty-four companies in the sample. The reason for so many missing cases is that this was the last question asked in the interview, so that when the allotted interview time ran out the question frequently was omitted.

Table 5–7 shows the mean scores for the quality of the parent-foreign subsidiary relationship measured for marketing, manufacturing, and financial matters. The lower the score, the better the quality of the relationship. While the low N is unfortunate and hinders statistical significance, there is no reason to believe that running out of interview time (frequently a function of external interruptions) has any biasing association with the quality of the parent–foreign subsidiary relationship. Although only one of the differences approaches statistical significance, the results are consistent and provide additional support for (1) the general argument that strategy and structure can be related through their information-processing implications and (2) the assumptions used in the model to specify this relationship operationally.

Table 5–7. Quality of Relationship between Parent and Foreign Subsidiaries.[a]

	Good fit cases (N = 13)	Deviant cases (N = 4)	t
Marketing matters	2.6	3.8	2.06[*]
Manufacturing matters	2.5	2.9	.76
Financial matters	2.2	2.6	.73

[*] $p = .028$ (single-tailed test).

[a] Lower scores denote better quality relationship.

DISCUSSION

The study has attempted to develop a more complete model than had previously existed of the strategy-structure relationship in MNCs. One way that the model extends previous work is through the addition of more contingency variables. While the bivariate testing replicated a number of findings from earlier studies, the four new elements of strategy appearing in the model extend the concept of international strategy to include areas that are of growing importance to MNCs (such as modifying products to fit local conditions, foreign manufacturing, outside ownership, and foreign acquisitions). Figure 5–3 summarizes the hypothesized fits that are supported by the sample data.

TYPES OF STRUCTURE

ELEMENTS OF STRATEGY	Functional Divisions	International Divisions	Geographical Regions	Product Divisions
Foreign product diversity	Low foreign product diversity			High foreign product diversity
Product modification differences between subsidiaries	Low product modification differences between subsidiaries			
Product Change				High rate of product change
Size of foreign operations		Relatively small foreign operations	Relative large foreign operations	Relative large foreign operations
Size of foreign manufacturing			High level of foreign manufacturing	
Number of foreign subsidiaries	Few foreign subsidiaries	Low to moderate number of foreign subsidiaries	Large number of foreign subsidiaries	Large numbers of foreign subsidiaries
Extent of outside ownership in foreign subsidiaries	Low level of outside ownership in foreign subsidiaries			
Extent of foreign acquisitions	Few foreign acquisitions			

Figure 5–3. Important Fits between Elements of Strategy and Types of Organizational Structure.

Five fits are important for firms with worldwide functional division structures: a narrow and highly consistent worldwide product line, a limited number of foreign subsidiaries, a low level of outside ownership, and few foreign acquisitions. This structure is the least flexible of the multinational structures. It requires more fits between structure and the elements of strategy than any of the other structures. The great advantage of a worldwide functional division structure is that it allows foreign operations to lean heavily on the technological and product-related strengths of the parent. Because organizational capabilities are centralized at one point and need not be duplicated at other locations in the organization, this structure should be the lowest cost of the high product-integration structures. (Product integration refers to the extent to which the product-related matters of foreign subsidiaries are integrated or coordinated on either a regional or global basis.) The other two high product-integration structures are geographical regions and worldwide product divisions. Offsetting the economies of highly centralized capabilities in the functional division structure are the costs of the information-processing system required to link the operating subunits to the center. Clearly, the strategic conditions that fit this structure attempt to minimize these costs by providing the organization with a relatively homogeneous and stable environment.

The international division structure has a single dominant fit with the firm's international strategy. It is appropriate when foreign operations are relatively small. It is a low product-integration structure that economizes on the amount of information-processing capacity that it provides between the parent and the foreign subsidiaries. Unlike the functional division structure, it is a very tolerant structure, capable of operating under a wide range of strategic conditions. The international division is also a low-cost structure. It centralizes international expertise at a single point in the organization and thus does not require a large cadre of internationally experienced management. It also allows management in the rest of the company to devote all its attention to domestic opportunities. The primary thing that a company gives up with this structure is the opportunity for foreign operations to take full advantage of the technological and product-related strengths of the parent. When foreign operations are relatively small, this loss is more than offset by the low cost and flexibility of the structure.

For companies with geographical region structures, the most important fits are a sufficiently large foreign operation and a high percentage of foreign manufacturing. The geographical region structure is a high-cost structure. It requires considerable information-processing capacity at several regional HQs for both product matters and company and country matters. Thus, from an economic viewpoint, it requires sufficient size and potential for regional optimization to offset this cost. Companies with worldwide product division structures also have large foreign operations and are distinguished from other structures by higher levels of product diversity and product change. The product division structure is a high-cost structure with separate marketing, manufacturing, and, frequently, research capabilities for each product division. The cost of maintaining several separate worldwide information-processing systems (one for each product division) generally requires sufficient size, product diversity, and product change to justify organizing around product knowledge.

A second way that the study attempts to extend previous work on the strategy-structure relationship is by using a better conceptual framework for modeling and understanding the relationship. Although the population-ecology perspective provides a general basis for relating structure and environment, it lacks an operational means to measure fit between an organization's structure and an organization's ability to exploit its environment. The argument presented here has been that this general fit can be accurately represented by the fit between the information-processing capacities of an organization's structure and the information processing required to implement its strategy or cope with its environment.

The information-processing model seems to be able to explain those fit relationships found in previous studies and also to generate new relationships that empirical testing tends to support. There are several advantages to using such a model. Since one can never empirically relate all of the variants of strategy and structure, the model provides a basis for predicting, a priori, the probable impact on the organization of new elements of strategy or new forms of structure by simply describing their impact on information processing. Another advantage is that one can predict when the general fits presented in Figure 5–3 might have to be modified. It is important to notice that the hypotheses were formulated and fit was evaluated at the population and not the individual organization level. At the individual level, organizations may violate some of the structural fits in Figure 5–3 and compensate for this by using other information-processing mechanisms.

Research on the strategy-structure issue has focused on the structural configuration aspect of an organization's design. Yet fit between strategy and structure must be influenced by other design features (such as planning and control systems, an MIS, the use of staff groups) that also influence the information-processing capacities of an organization. The general information-processing framework underlying the present model provides the basis for extending the model to include the effect of these other features of an organization's design on the basic strategy-structure relationship. To date, such integration has occurred only within case studies, and it has been difficult to combine these to produce a general model of organizational design and strategy implementation.

As discussed in Chapter 3, the present study has not attempted to measure information processing directly but, rather, to formulate hypotheses based on using information processing as an abstract intervening concept. Empirical testing of these hypotheses has failed to disconfirm either the general argument that information processing can be used to explain the relationship between strategy and structure or the specific assumptions about the information-processing capacities of structure used in the study. The multivariate analysis attempted to examine how well successful MNCs are able to satisfy simultaneously the many fits contained in the model. If companies were not able to satisfy most important fits simultaneously, the model would still be valid but probably not as useful. Instead, it would appear that the simultaneous demands for multiple fits often present an unsolvable problem and that companies can realize only some fits while failing to satisfy many others. The results of the multiple discriminant analysis, however, indicate that successful companies seem to satisfy many of the fits simultaneously and that the need to tradeoff fit in one area for fit in another is not that severe.

NOTES

1. Formal organization charts of some companies (especially European MNCs) showed all foreign subsidiaries reporting direct to the parent CEO or, on other occasions, all of the boards of directors of foreign subsidiaries were depicted as responsible to the parent board of directors. Such charts tend to reflect the legal, shareholder relationship and are especially useful in representing to critics of MNC power, the autonomy of local subsidiaries. Only if the company has a holding company structure, will these charts actually represent the operating structure of the company. A researcher must, clearly, penetrate this web and uncover the actual operating structure. Respondents sometimes had another set of organization charts (usually marked "company confidential") that reflected this relationship, or they could readily construct one (which interviews with subsequent respondents tended to validate).

6

ORGANIZATIONAL STRUCTURE—MATRIX AND MIXED FORMS

This chapter attempts to extend the strategy-structure model developed in the previous chapter to include matrix and mixed structures. Except for a number of case studies, very little empirical research has focused on the fit between matrix and mixed structures and strategy. One reason for this is that survey research samples generally include too few matrix and mixed structures to support meaningful exploratory analysis. Another reason seems to be the lack of a conceptual basis for relating matrix or mixed structures to the various contingency variables or elements of strategy that researchers have studied—and especially, a conceptual basis that can be operationalized and tested.

The types of organizational structure available to MNCs include worldwide functional divisions, international divisions, geographical regions, and worldwide product divisions. In the previous chapter, these were referred to as elementary structures because authority and communications tend to flow along a single primary hierarchy or dimension. Matrix structures can be viewed as an overlaying of two of the elementary structures. Under a matrix structure, a foreign subsidiary simultaneously reports to the parent along two of the elementary dimensions (for example, it might report to a geographical region HQ and to a number of product division HQs). This is a "multiple command" or "two-boss" structure (Davis and Lawrence 1977). A mixed structure, on the other hand, has some foreign subsidiaries reporting to the parent along one dimension (for example geographical regions) and other subsidiaries along another dimension (for example product divisions). This is still a unitary command or one-boss structure because the two hierarchies or primary dimensions do not overlap.

MATRIX AND MIXED STRUCTURE STUDIES

Formal matrix structures first appeared in the aerospace industry during the 1960s, where the traditional functional dimension was matrixed or overlaid by a project dimension. A considerable literature exists on this form of project matrix structure (Cleland and King 1968; Marquis 1969; Galbraith 1971; Butler 1973). The second application area for matrix structures has been business corporations and especially large, complex corporations, such as MNCs. In their book on matrix designs, Davis and Lawrence (1977:193) raise the question whether there is "some organizational imperative towards a matrix form in multinational firms." Most researchers seem to think that there is (Stopford and Wells 1972; Prahalad 1976; Davis and Lawrence 1977; Galbraith and Nathanson 1978). The reason for this is the belief that multiple diversity (product and geographic) will continue to increase in MNCs and that matrix structures provide the best fit with these characteristics.

Davis and Lawrence (1977) have developed the most extensive conceptual framework for relating matrix structures to contextual factors and strategic conditions. From a number of case studies, they identified three conditions that seem to be necessary to the adoption of matrix structures:

1. Outside pressure for dual focus (such as equal pressure to organize around functional specialities and products).
2. Pressures for high information-processing capacity (stemming from high uncertainty, complexity, or interdependency).
3. Pressure for shared resources (such as people and physical facilities).

Davis and Lawrence state that since matrix structures are so difficult and costly to manage, a company should not adopt one unless all three conditions apply.

Two survey research studies that have explored the relationship between strategy and structure in MNC's have included matrix and mixed structures. The Stopford and Wells (1972) study included three matrix and twenty-two mixed structure MNCs in a sample of 162 U.S. MNCs. They found that both structures seemed to be associated with strategies involving a high level of foreign product diversity and large foreign operations (high foreign sales as a percentage of total company sales). The Franko (1976) study contained six matrix and mixed structure MNCs (not separated) in a sample of seventy European MNC's. He found that such complex structures tended to be associated with high foreign product diversity and extensive foreign manufacturing (all had manufacturing in more than ten countries).

These specific MNC fit criteria appear to be consistent with the more general fit criteria subsequently developed by Davis and Lawrence (1977). High foreign product diversity and a high level of foreign sales or foreign manufacturing clearly encourage a dual focus (around products and regions). They also increase complexity (of the product line) and interdependency (among subsidiaries within a region), both of which increase information-processing requirements. While the pressure to share resources across products or regions is not explicitly represented in the MNC criteria, it implicitly exists for all organizations operating in a competitive environment (including MNCs). In a competitive environment, survival requires low cost, and this is accomplished through specialization and economies of scale, both of which involve the efficient sharing of resources (Williamson 1981).

The present study seeks to extend current understanding of matrix and mixed structures and their relationships to MNC strategy. More specifically, it attempts to develop and test a stronger conceptual framework for relating specific types of matrix and mixed structure to specific elements of an MNC's strategy, than currently exists from the Stopford and Wells (1972) and Franko (1976) studies. Because the proposed conceptual framework is consistent with the general criteria specified by Davis and Lawrence (1977), it also can be viewed as an attempt to more specifically operationalize and test their criteria. The conceptual framework is based on an information-processing perspective of the strategy-structure relationship. In Chapter 5, this perspective was used to develop a specific model of the strategy-structure relationship for the four types of elementary structure. The following section attempts to conceptually extend the model to include matrix and mixed structures. Subsequent sections then empirically test and evaluate the extended model.

EXTENDING THE MODEL TO MATRIX AND MIXED STRUCTURES

The model for elementary structures rests on being able to distinguish between the various structures by virtue of their differential information-processing capacities (Table 5–2). In order to extend the model to matrix and mixed structures, similar distinctions must be developed for these types of structure. Matrix structures are considered first.

Matrix Structures

Existing conceptual frameworks for understanding matrix structures and their relationships to strategy are lacking in two ways: (1) They are too general to be meaningfully operationalized, and (2) they cannot be readily integrated with the far stronger conceptual frameworks that already exist for understanding elementary structures and strategy. Focusing on the first shortcoming, neither Davis and Lawrence (1977), Stopford and Wells (1972), nor Franko (1976) distinguishes between the various types of matrix structure that can occur when any two of the four different types of elementary structure are overlaid. Because previous research and theory have clearly established significant differences between the elementary structures (and their relationships to strategy), it is reasonable to expect equally significant differences between various matrices of these elementary structures. Similarly, matrix structures have not been linked to very many contingency variables. Stopford and Wells (1972) explain the existence of matrix structures with two contingency variables (high levels of foreign sales and foreign product diversity). Franko (1976) also uses only two contingency variables (high levels of foreign sales and substantial foreign manufacturing). Davis and Lawrence (1977) stop after linking matrix structures to the three general contingency requirements described in the introduction. When one considers that elementary structures have been linked to at least eight different contingency variables in MNCs, it becomes apparent that existing contingency models for matrix structures are probably under-defined.

The second shortcoming with existing models is that they do not integrate well with the existing models that define strategy-structure fit for elementary structures. This is important if matrix structures are to be conceptually viewed as overlays of elementary structures and specific matrix structures must be evaluated against specific elementary structures. The fact that it seems to be difficult to empirically study large samples of matrix organizations further argues for building off of the empirically supported understanding that already exists for the elementary structures. The present study, in fact, argues that its results are meaningful largely because the admittedly small sample of matrix companies is used to test an a priori model that was derived from the empirically supported knowledge that already exists for elementary strategy-structure relationships.

A number of in-depth case studies have provided some understanding of how important organizational processes and organizational behavior tend to be different within companies possessing matrix structures (Galbraith 1971; Goggins 1974; Prahalad 1976; Davis and Lawrence 1977). An important difference is that matrix structures tend to provide communication and information flow along multiple channels, while elementary structures tend to largely use single channels. For example, the annual planning process in an MNC with a geographical region x product division matrix structure would reveal substantial information flows between a foreign subsidiary and its geographical region HQ as well as between the subsidiary and the various product division HQs in the parent. Both regional and product division HQs are responsible for developing annual planning with regard to the same foreign subsidiary. In an elementary structure MNC, only one type of headquarters exists and information flow and responsibility follow a single hierarchy.

Another key difference between matrix and elementary structure companies is that with a matrix structure, important decisions about a subsidiary's operations are made by two separate hierarchies of managers, each with a different set of goals and objectives. Returning to the annual planning process as an example, decisions made along the geographical region hierarchy will tend to maximize performance of the region. At the same time, decisions made along the product division hierarchy will tend to maximize performance of the product line on a worldwide basis. Although multiple goals also exist in elementary structure MNCs, goal consistency is likely to be greater. Also, when the tradeoffs between multiple goals are made within a single hierarchy, the process is likely to be different than when such tradeoffs occur between two hierarchies. In the latter case, conflict resolution must be the outcome of successful confrontation rather than hierarchical forcing (Lawrence and Lorsch 1967; Davis and Lawrence 1977). In fact, Sayles (1976:4) points out that the matrix form is a structural approach to the same problem that has been addressed by OD consultants with other techniques— that problem being how to improve "cooperation and coordination between departments, managers, and subsystems."

It is apparent that matrix structures provide more types of communication and information flow between the parent and a foreign subsidiary than an elementary structure. Decisionmaking in a matrix structure will also tend to encompass a wider range of goals and objectives and is more likely to involve confrontation between multiple perspectives. These characteristics tend to increase the information-processing capacity of a matrix structure over that of an elementary structure. In fact, the information-processing capacity of a matrix structure can be viewed as the combined information-processing capacity of the two elementary structures that are included in the matrix. The combination should probably be viewed more as qualitative than quantitative addition. Thus, an international division x product division matrix structure should provide a high level of tactical and strategic information-processing capacity for company and country matters (such as minimizing foreign exchange losses, balancing political risk, and coping with changing tariff policies) along its international division dimension. At the same time, the product division dimension should provide a high level of tactical and strategic information-processing capacity for product matters (such as how to counter a competitor's new product launch, deciding when to introduce the latest model into a market, and dealing with recurrent quality control problems in a subsidiary).

There seem to be two principal costs associated with the increased information-processing capacity provided by matrix structures. The first is the cost of duplication. This occurs because matrix structures create multiple communication and decisionmaking hierarchies between the parent and the subsidiary, and each tends to process a good deal of common as well as unique information. This requires additional resources (subunits, people) both in the parent and the subsidiary. The second cost associated with matrix structures is a higher level of conflict centered around the parent-subsidiary relationship. This conflict stems from the difference in goals of the separate decisionmaking hierarchies and the need to ultimately reconcile these decisions when they impact on the same subsidiary operation. As a result, more resources have to be devoted to conflict resolution and achieving unity of effort. Both of these factors will generally cause a matrix structure to be a higher cost structure than an elementary structure.

To offset its higher cost, matrix structures should provide better fit with the company's strategy than either of the two elementary structures represented in the matrix. Otherwise, a successful MNC in a competitive environment would tend to use one of the less costly elementary structures. Strategies that fit matrix structures should therefore require the joint information-processing capacities of both of the elementary structures represented in the matrix. From this conceptual framework, the following general hypothesis can be drawn:

Matrix structure hypothesis. MNCs with matrix structure A x B will tend to have strategies that contain some of the strategic fit characteristics that are critical to elementary structure A and some that are critical to elementary structure B and cannot be completely satisfied by either elementary structure.

Operational hypotheses for each of the four types of matrix structure found in the sample are developed and tested in the next section.

Mixed Structures

Under a mixed structure, two different structures exist side by side for managing parent-subsidiary relationships. A subsidiary falls under one or the other but not both. Virtually no research or literature exists on these structures or when to use them. They have either been lumped with matrix structures (Franko 1976) or treated very generally as some other form of global structure suitable for coping with multiple diversity in a firm's environment or strategy (Stopford and Wells 1972). Thus, there seems to be a need to both conceptually and empirically establish a meaningful distinction between mixed structures and matrix structures.

Mixed structures should be most appropriate where there is a wide difference between subsidiaries with regard to the type of parent-subsidiary information processing required. This would allow one to divide the subsidiaries into two more similar groups and then fit an appropriate structure to each group. The basis for dividing subsidiaries into groups or deciding which structure a specific subsidiary will come under will vary from company to company. Subsidiaries may be considered similar when they are the same size or handle a certain product line or lie in a certain geographical region. Thus, small subsidiaries may tend to report to the international division. Certain product activities may always report to a parent product division. Or all operations in Europe may report to a regional headquarters, while operations elsewhere report to their product divisions.

One would expect successful companies with mixed structures to have some subsidiaries fitting one structure and some the other. The most thorough way to empirically test this would require dividing all the subsidiaries in a company up according to the structures of their reporting relationships, and testing each group separately to determine how well its elementary structure fit the strategic conditions facing the group. Because this would involve measuring all the parent-subsidiary relationships within a company, this approach was too ambitious for the present study. If, however, one group of subsidiaries fits a certain set of strategic conditions (such as those associated with an international division structure) and a second group of subsidiaries another set of strategic conditions (such as those associated with a product division structure), then one would expect the values of such strategic conditions for an international division & product division mixed structure MNC to lie between the values usually associated with the two elementary structures. Such values will, in fact, tend to be some weighted average of the values associated with the two elementary structures.

For example, assume that half of a company's foreign operations involve product lines that have a small percentage of foreign sales and that the foreign subsidiaries of these product lines report to the company's international division. The other half of the company's foreign operations involve product lines that have a high percentage of foreign sales, and the foreign subsidiaries of these product lines report to worldwide product divisions. Then one would expect the percentage of foreign sales for the company to be the 50–50 weighted average of the percentages of foreign sales for the international division group (the mean for all elementary international division structure MNCs in the sample is 34 percent) and the worldwide product division group (the mean for all elementary product division structure MNCs in the sample is 61 percent). The expected percentage for a mixed structure company would be .5 X 34 percent + .5 X 61 percent = 47.5 percent. With this line of reasoning, company-level data can be used as a kind of proxy for group-level data (which are not available from the study), in order to test strategy-structure fit for mixed structure companies. This leads to the following general hypothesis:

> *Mixed structure hypothesis.* MNCs with mixed structure A and B will tend to have strategies that will approximate some weighted average of the strategic fit conditions associated with elementary structure A and elementary structure B.

Operational hypotheses for each of the two types of mixed structure found in the sample are developed and tested in the next section.

DEVELOPMENT AND TESTING OF HYPOTHESES

Table 6–1 shows the distribution of the matrix and mixed structure companies in the sample by industry and nationality. Once again, there is no discernible contingency relationship between type of industry and type of structure. Although nationality seems to be more related to type of structure (five of the seven matrix structure MNCs are European or

Table 6–1. Types of Matrix and Mixed Structure by Industry and Nationality.

	Matrix Structures				Mixed Structures	
	ID x PD	GR x PD	FN x PD	FN x GR	ID & PD	GR & PD
Industry						
Auto						
Elect. and tele. equip.				1		
Industrial equipment	1					
Chemical	1				1	
Pharmaceutical		1	1	1	1	
Consumer pkgd goods		1		1		
Tires					1	2
Other						1
Total	2	2	1	2	4	3
Nationality						
U.S.	2				3	2
UK				1		1
European		2	1	1	1	
Total	2	2	1	2	4	3

Note: FD = Functional divisions; ID = International division; GR = Geographical regions; PD = Product divisions.

UK, and five of the seven mixed structure MNCs are U.S.), the conceptual model and hypotheses are meant to be true across cultures. As discussed in Chapter 5, the reason for this is that the information-processing implications of both strategy and structure are thought to be similar across cultures.

In addition to measuring structure and the eight elements of strategy already described, the interviews included several open-ended questions about management's perceptions of the company's international strengths, weaknesses, and objectives and whether there was any need

Table 6–2. Supplementary Information on International Strengths, Weaknesses,

	International Division x Product Division		Geographical Region x Product Division
	Company 1	*Company 2*	*Company 1*
International strengths	Great products	Great products	Great products
International weaknesses	Top parent management lacks an international perspective	Unwillingness on the part of parent management to invest a higher percentage overseas	Lacks good marketing (not good in reacting to external events)
International objectives	?	Past—introduce new products and increase share for existing lines	Past—retain market position and share
		Future—consolidation and profit improvement	Future—?
Need for structural change	An overall plan exists to change toward more of a product orientation and such change is in progress	Need for more product division involvement in international business is apparent, but no convergence yet on plan for change	No apparent need or plans to change

or plan for structural change. This information is summarized in Table 6–2. While such information cannot be used to directly test strategy-structure hypotheses, it can be used to help broaden our interpretation of the strategy-structure relationship found in the data. Subsequent interpretations of the analyses refer back to this information.

The format for testing each of the four types of matrix structure and two types of mixed structure found in the sample is to (1) use the conceptual framework already presented to develop an operational hypothesis relating the structure to specific elements of strategy, (2) use the sample data to test the hypothesis, and (3) discuss the critical strategy-structure fits for the specific structure. A broader discussion of the

Objectives, and the Need for Structural Change.

Geographical Region × Product Division	Functional Division x Product Division	Functional Division x Geographical Region	
Company 2	Company 1	Company 1	Company 2
1) Great products 2) Great international management team	1) Great technology 2) Great marketing organization in all markets	1) Great technology 2) Good management style and practices	Great technology
Faces mature markets (with low growth and high competition)	Lack of efficient international coordination to get new products introduced to all markets	Maturing products	Top parent management lacks an international perspective
Past—develop and expand in U.S. market	Past—educate and develop people to go with rapid expansion	Past—exploit groundwork laid in prior years (get profits from prior technology and product work)	?
Future—same	Future—more effective coordination of effort on an international basis	Future—same	
No apparent need or plans to change	No apparent need or plans to change	No apparent need or plans to change	No apparent need or plans to change

strategy-structure relationship and the key issues that pertain to matrix and mixed structures is left to the final section of the chapter.

International Division x Product Division Matrix

The primary strategic conditions that fit an international division structure are relatively small foreign operations with a low to moderate number of foreign subsidiaries. These were developed in Chapter 5 and are summarized in Figure 5–3. The primary strategic conditions that fit a worldwide product division structure are high foreign product diversity, a high rate of product change, and relatively large foreign operations with many foreign subsidiaries. These fits are also summarized in

Figure 5–3. These two sets of fits can be combined to produce the following hypothesis about the strategy which best fits an international division x product division matrix structure.

> *Hypothesis 6–1.* MNCs with an international division x product division matrix structure will tend to have strategies that contain relatively small foreign operations and few subsidiaries but high levels of foreign product diversity and product change.

The development of this hypothesis is summarized in Table 6–3. This kind of strategy would not fit either of the elementary structures but would require the dual information-processing capacities of the matrix.

Table 6–3. Development of Hypothesized Strategic Fits for International Division x Product Division Matrix.

	Important Fits for: [a]		
	International Division Structure	*Product Division Structure*	*Hypothesized Fits for International Division x Product Division Matrix*
Foreign product diversity		High	High
Product change		High	High
Size of foreign operations	Small	Large	Small
Number of foreign subsidiaries	Low to moderate	Large	Low to moderate

[a]These fits are taken directly from Figure 5–3.

It is most important that the reader examine Table 6–3 and Figure 5–3 together, in order to observe that the critical fits that are used to hypothesize an appropriate matrix strategy come from the previously established elementary structure fits. Matrix structures and the strategies that they fit need to be understood in terms of the same elementary strategy-structure fits employed in Chapter 5. Only now they are combined (overlaid) in a more complex manner.

Table 6–4 shows that the two international division x product division matrix companies in the sample do tend to have the hypothesized kind of strategy. They have strategies that call for managing a high level of foreign product diversity across relatively small foreign operations with relatively few foreign subsidiaries. The high level of foreign product diversity fits a worldwide product division structure, while the relatively small size of foreign operations and number of foreign subsidiaries fit an international division structure. In this case, the rate of product change does not help to explain structure because it does not fit the high rate of product change that would require a product division structure and product change is not an important fit criterion for an international division structure.

It is apparent that the matrix structure provides a better fit with the strategies of these companies than would either the elementary international division or product division structures. These companies have a requirement for more specialization and coordination around product lines and more product-related information processing between the parent and foreign subsidiaries than companies with simple international division structures. They face almost as much foreign product diversity as MNCs with worldwide product division structures (that is, an average of five product groups versus 5.8 for MNCs with product division structures and 1.7 for MNCs with international division structures). Yet if they adopted a worldwide product division structure, they would violate another important fit between strategy and structure. The relative size of their foreign operations is too small to justify the high cost of multiple global managements and information-processing systems that are associated with the worldwide product division structure. On average, these companies derive only 34 percent of their sales abroad and have thirty-three foreign subsidiaries. This is similar to the MNCs with international division structures (also 34 percent of sales abroad and forty-one foreign subsidiaries) and quite different from MNCs with worldwide product division structures (61 percent of sales abroad and fifty-eight foreign subsidiaries).

The resultant matrix structure is an appropriate response to the two-way pull exerted by these firms' strategies. For purposes of economy, they centralize communication and decisionmaking capacity for non-product matters (such as finance, personnel, government relations) in the international division. At the same time, product-related information processing is differentiated along product lines and decentralized to the various product divisions. This allows the foreign operations to lean upon the product and technical strengths of the parent while at the same time using an international division to achieve specialization and economies of scale for nonproduct or international matters.

In order to statistically test how well the strategic fits can be used to distinguish the matrix structure from either of the elementary structures, a step-wise multiple discriminant analysis was used, with the three structures as the groups and the four elements of strategy as the independent variables. The results are shown in Table 6–5. The

Table 6–4. Testing of Hypothesized Strategic Fits for International Division x Product Division Matrix.

	Important Fits for		Hypothesized Fits for International Division x Product Division Matrix	Actual Fits for International Division x Product Division Matrix (N = 2)
	International Division Structure (N = 7)	Product Division Structure (N = 12)		
Foreign product diversity	(1.7)	High (5.8)	High	High (5.0)
Product change	(2.9)	High (5.4)	High	Medium (3.6)
Size of foreign operations	Small (34)	Large (61)	Small	Small (34)
Number of foreign subsidiaries	Low to (41) moderate	Large (58)	Low to moderate	Low to (33) moderate

Note: Values in parentheses are mean values of the element of strategy for each type of structure.

Table 6–5. Multiple Discriminant Analysis of the Elements of Strategy on Type of Structure (Distinguishing International Division x Product Division Matrix).

	Discriminant Function		
Independent Variable	*1*	*2*	*F-value*
Foreign product diversity	1.48	.91	5.87*
Product change	1.32	.79	1.49
Size of foreign operations	.28	-.73	9.20**
Number of foreign subsidiaries	-.23	-.82	2.89
Canonical correlation	.92	.63	
Wilks lamda	.09**	.60	

* $p < .05$ ** $p < .01$

Note: The following types of structure are the dependent variable: International division, Product division, International division x Product division Matrix. All values under the two functions are standardized discriminant coefficients

Classification Table

	Predicted Group Membership		
Actual Group Membership	*ID*	*PD*	*ID x PD*
International division (ID)	7	0	0
Product division (PD)	0	9	3
International division x Product division matrix	0	0	2

Note: Structures of MNCs correctly classified = 86 percent.

univariate F-values show that both foreign product diversity and size of foreign operations vary significantly across the three types of structure. The conceptual model emphasized both foreign product diversity and size of foreign operations as important discriminators. The discriminant model emphasizes foreign product diversity and product change but reflects the two size variables only in the nonsignificant second discriminant function. Looking at the classification table, the model has some trouble discriminating between the matrix structure and the product division structure, misclassifying three product division companies as matrix companies. This is understandable, given that size of foreign operations and number of subsidiaries are the primary discriminating factors between these two structures. Nevertheless, the model is able to correctly classify 86 percent of the cases, including the two matrix companies.

The supplementary information in Table 6–2 provides additional insight into the strategy-structure relationships of these companies. Both firms see a lack of top management understanding or commitment to international operations as the company's primary international weakness. One of the companies was already involved in long-term organizational change that was increasing the role of the product divisions in international operations. The second company recognized the need for similar change but had not developed any plan for such change. This information suggests that the international division x product division matrix may not be a very permanent structure for either company.

Both companies seemed to be experiencing some pressure to strengthen the product division dimension of the matrix at the expense of the international division dimension. Indeed, as the size of foreign operations and number of foreign subsidiaries increase, the strategies of these companies will increasingly gain fit with the product division dimension and lose fit with the international division dimension. Davis and Lawrence (1977) have suggested that matrix structures may be transitional structures, which are used as a company moves from one elementary structure to another. Although these companies seem to currently fit an international division x product division matrix, the additional information provided by management suggests they may be passing through a matrix phase as they evolve toward worldwide product division structures.

Geographical Region x Product Division Matrix

The strategic conditions that fit a geographical region structure are relatively large foreign operations, a high level of foreign manufacturing, and many foreign subsidiaries (summarized in Figure 5–3). The strategic conditions that fit a product division structure are high foreign product diversity, a high rate of product change, and relatively large foreign operations with many foreign subsidiaries (also summarized in Figure 5–3). These two sets of fits can be combined to produce the following hypothesis about the strategy that best fits a geographical region x product division matrix structure:

Hypothesis 6–2. MNCs with a geographical region x product division matrix structure will tend to have strategies that contain relatively large foreign operations with many subsidiaries, a large amount of foreign manufacturing, and high degrees of foreign product diversity and product change.

The development of this hypothesis is summarized in Table 6–6. This kind of strategy would require high degrees of product knowledge specialization and parent-subsidiary product coordination (to cope with high foreign product diversity and product change) and a high level of regional specialization and coordination (to handle the interdependencies associated with sourcing foreign sales from foreign manufacturing instead of parent country exports).

Table 6–6. Development of Hypothesized Strategic Fits for Geographical Region x Product Division Matrix.

	Important Fits for:		
	Geographical Region Structure	*Product Division Structure*	*Hypothesized Fits for Geographical Region x Product Division Matrix*
Foreign product diversity		High	High
Product change		High	High
Size of foreign operations	Large	Large	Large
Size of foreign manufacturing	Large		Large
Number of foreign subsidiaries	Large	Large	Large

Table 6–7 shows that the two geographical region x product division matrix companies in the sample do have the hypothesized strategy. The high levels of foreign product diversity (six product groups) and product change (7.7 percent of sales spent on R&D) fit a worldwide product division structure, while the high level of foreign manufacturing (86 percent) fits the geographical region structure. The large size of foreign operations and number of foreign subsidiaries fit both of the elementary structures.

Foreign product diversity and product change increase the requirement for product-related information processing between the foreign subsidiaries and the centers of product knowledge in the parent. The product division dimension provides this kind of information-processing capacity, while the geographical region dimension does not. The high percentage of foreign manufacturing, on the other hand, creates a different kind of information-processing requirement. It increases opportunities for rationalizing and integrating manufacturing, distribution, and other activities on a regional basis. The regional HQ provides the information-processing capacity between subsidiaries in a region to accomplish this. Its costs are offset by the economies of scale realized from planning and integrating across subsidiaries and product lines within the region. Thus, the strategies of these MNCs require the dual information-processing capacities that neither of the elementary structures could provide but that are provided by the matrix structure.

Table 6–7. Testing of Hypothesized Strategic Fits for Geographical Region x Product Division Matrix.

Important Fits for			
Geographical Region Structure (N = 10)	Product Division Structure (N = 12)	Hypothesized Fits for Geographical Region x Product Division Matrix	Actual Fits for Geographical Region x Product Division Matrix (N = 2)
Foreign product diversity	(3.4)	High (5.8)	High	High (6.0)
Product change	(2.9)	High (5.4)	High	High (7.7)
Size of foreign operations	Large (47)	Large (61)	Large	Large (92)
Size of foreign manufacturing	Large (91)	(61)	Large	Large (86)
Number of foreign subsidiaries	Large (55)	Large (58)	Large	Large (78)

Note: Values in parentheses are mean values of the element of strategy for each type of structure.

Table 6–8 shows that only two of the elements of strategy had sufficient discriminating power to enter and remain in the discriminant model when a step-wise procedure was used. The conceptual model used size of foreign manufacturing, foreign product diversity, and product change as the discriminating factors among the three structures. The discriminant model confirms that size of foreign manufacturing is the most important discriminator. It fails, however, to reflect differences in foreign product diversity and product change because these differences are less significant than those found in size of foreign operations (which was not hypothesized to be an important discriminator). There is also a meaningful correlation between size of foreign operations and degree of foreign product diversity ($R = .30$). When foreign product diversity and product change are substituted for size of foreign operations in the model, there is no significant change in the discriminating power. The model was able to successfully classify 75 percent of the cases, including the two matrix companies.

Table 6–8. Multiple Discriminant Analysis of the Elements of Strategy on Type of Structure (Distinguishing Geographical Region x Product Divsion Matrix).

	Discriminant Function		
Independent Variable	1	2	F-value
Size of foreign operations	-.82	.67	3.95*
Size of foreign manufacturing	.91	.55	5.67*
Canonical correlation	.84	.31	
Wilks lamda	.27**	.91	

* $p < .05$; ** $p < .01$.

Note: The following types of structure are the dependent variable: Geographical region, Product division, Geographical region x Product division Matrtix. All values under the two functions are standardized discriminant coefficients

Classification Table

	Predicted Group Membership		
Actual Group Membership	GR	PD	GR x PD
Geographical region (GR)	9	1	0
Product division (PD)	2	7	3
Geographical region x Product division matrix	0	0	2

Note: Structures of MNCs correctly classified = 75 percent.

The supplementary information in Table 6–2 presents a picture of stability in strategy and structure for both of the companies with a geographical region x product division structure. Conceptually, it is also difficult to view this particular matrix form as a transitional structure. Both the geographical region and product division dimensions are already global structures (Stopford and Wells 1972). The former fits a strategy emphasizing large foreign operations and sizable foreign manufacturing; the latter, large foreign operations and high levels of foreign product diversity. It is unlikely, in a successful MNC, that any of these elements of strategy will regress toward lower levels. In a sense, this form of matrix already fits the most complex and mature of international strategies.

Functional Division x Product Division Matrix

The strategic conditions that fit a worldwide functional division structure are low foreign product diversity, low product modification differences across subsidiaries, few foreign subsidiaries, and low levels of outside ownership and foreign acquisitions (summarized in Figure 5–3). Functional division structures have more critical fits than any other elementary structure. Because the elementary functional division structure is so confining, it is not surprising that some MNCs have matrixed it with another elementary dimension in order to gain more flexibility in terms of the range of strategic conditions the organization can cope with. Once again, the strategic conditions that fit a product division structure are high foreign product diversity, a high rate of product change, and relatively large foreign operations with many foreign subsidiaries (also summarized in Figure 5–3). Two of the conditions—high foreign product diversity and many foreign subsidiaries—overlap the opposite and much more confining fits of the functional division structure.

The reason why elementary functional division structures require low product diversity and few foreign subsidiaries is because they cannot provide high level of cross-functional information processing. And requirements for cross-functional information processing are largely proportionate to both the number of product lines and the number of foreign subsidiaries. Yet in the matrix structure, the product division dimension provides virtually all of the cross-functional coordination or information processing (for example, strategic product planning for a subsidiary and preparing the annual budget would both be done under the direction of the product divisions). This means the matrix structure can handle a higher level of foreign product diversity and more foreign subsidiaries than the elementary functional division structure. Within the matrix, functional divisions can support a higher level of foreign product diversity and more foreign subsidiaries, as long as information processing takes place within functional channels. If product diversity becomes too great, however, functional specialization becomes less useful to a company. When manufacturing technologies or marketing distribution systems differ radically within a company, there is little to be gained from having a central unit attempt to understand and cope with such differences (Chandler 1962). For this reason, the functional dimension in the matrix requires a lower level of foreign product diversity than a worldwide product division structure. This level has been referred to as "medium" in Table 6–9, because it lies somewhere between the "low" level required by an elementary functional division structure and the "high" level associated with an elementary product division structure.

Table 6–9 shows how these two sets of conditions might combine to create a strategy that would best fit the dual information-processing capacities of a functional division x product division matrix structure. The strategy should retain enough of the environmental and technological homogeneity and stability to still fit a meaningful level of functional

Table 6–9. Development of Hypothesized Strategic Fits for Functional Division x Product Division Matrix.

	Important Fits for:		
	Functional Division Structure	*Product Division Structure*	*Hypothesized Fits for Functional Division x Product Division Matrix*
Foreign product diversity	Low	High	Medium
Product modification differences	Low		Low
Product change		High	High
Size of foreign operations		Large	Large
Number of foreign subsidiaries	Low	Large	Large
Extent of outside ownership	Low		Low
Extent of foreign acquisitions	Low		Low

specialization and coordination (low product modification differences and low levels of outside ownership facilitate this). Yet the strategy needs to reflect the higher levels of product diversity and product change that require and justify the added specialization and coordination capacities provided by the product division dimension. This line of reasoning leads to the following hypothesis:

Hypothesis 6–3. MNCs with a functional division x product division matrix structure will tend to have strategies that contain relatively large foreign operations with many subsidiaries, high levels of product change, a medium amount of foreign product diversity, and low levels of product modification differences, outside ownership, and foreign acquisitions.

As Table 6–10 shows, the functional division x product division matrix company in the sample largely supports the hypothesized fits, although data for two of the elements of strategy were missing. A low level of product modification difference across subsidiaries supports rather centralized, functional information processing between the parent and foreign subsidiaries for technical matters. The low level of outside ownership also minimizes the need for cross-functional information processing at the subsidiary level. Both are important fits for the functional division dimension of the matrix. Without them, any appreciable parent-subsidiary coordination or information processing along functional channels would be difficult.

Table 6–10. Testing of Hypothesized Strategic Fits for Functional Division x Product Division Matrix.

	Important Fits for			
	Functional Division Structure (N = 5)	Product Division Structure (N = 12)	Hypothesized Fits for Functional Division x Product Division Matrix	Actual Fits for Functional Division x Product Division Matrix (N = 1)
Foreign product diversity	Low (1.4)	High (5.8)	Medium	Medium (3.0)
Product modification differences	Low (1.8)	(2.7)	Low	Low (2.0)
Product change	(3.2)	High (5.4)	High	?
Size of foreign operations	(58)	Large (61)	Large	?
Number of foreign subsidiaries	Low (12)	Large (58)	Large	Medium (39)
Extent of outside ownership	Low (1.8)	(3.0)	Low	Low (1.0)
Extent of foreign acquisitions	Low (.8)	(2.2)	Low	HIgh (2.0)

Note: Values in parentheses are mean values of the elements of strategy for each type of structure.

The outstanding misfits between the international strategy of this firm and an elementary functional division structure are the extent of foreign product diversity, the number of foreign subsidiaries, and the extent of foreign acquisitions. There is too much product diversity and there are too many subsidiaries for a worldwide functional division structure, where all cross-functional information processing is centralized at the top of the parent. No elementary functional division MNC has product diversity greater than two or more than eighteen foreign subsidiaries. The product division dimension in the matrix, however, can readily satisfy both strategic conditions, because it allows considerable information processing across functions to occur at both the subsidiary and product division HQ levels. The relatively high extent of foreign acquisitions would also be difficult to accommodate under an elementary functional division structure, because each acquisition would have to be internally reorganized to fit the worldwide functional structure. Under the matrix structure, new acquisitions can report to the appropriate product division without significant internal reorganization. Coordination between the functional sectors of the parent and the subsidiary then can be developed over time.

It is important to notice that while three of the strategic conditions fail to fit an elementary functional division structure, none of the strategic conditions represents a real misfit with an elementary product division structure. Yet the conditions are somewhat different from those of the typical MNC with an elementary product division structure. Foreign product diversity is only three instead of 5.8 and the number of subsidiaries is only thirty-nine instead of fifty-eight. Although information on product change and size of foreign operations was missing, they are not as important in discriminating between functional division and product division structures as are product diversity and number of subsidiaries. It would appear that this company has lost fit with an elementary functional division structure and is approaching fit with an elementary product division structure.

If foreign product diversity and number of foreign subsidiaries were to increase further, the strategy would strongly fit an elementary product division structure and make functional information processing at the parent-subsidiary level more difficult. At present, however, there is no basis for saying that either the functional division x product division matrix or the elementary product division structure provides a better fit with the set of strategic conditions than the other.

Table 6–11 shows that four of the elements of strategy had sufficient discriminating power to enter and remain in the discriminant model. The conceptual model emphasized foreign product diversity, product modification differences, number of foreign subsidiaries, extent of outside ownership, and extent of foreign acquisitions as potentially important discriminating variables for the three structures. The statistically significant first function contains four of the five variables, excluding product modification differences. The classification table shows that the model could correctly classify 89 percent of the cases, including the matrix company.

Table 6–11. Multiple Discriminant Analysis of the Elements of Strategy on Type of Structure (Distinguishing Functional Division x Product Division Matrix).

Independent Variable	Discriminant Function		F-value
	1	2	
Foreign product diversity	.83	.10	10.62**
Number of foreign subsidiaries	.59	.07	14.42***
Extent of outside ownership	-.55	1.03	1.10
Extent of foreign acquisitions	.80	-.72	3.97*
Canonical correlation	.93	.36	
Wilks lamda	.11**	.87	

$*\ p < .05;\ **\ p < .01;\ *** < .001.$

Note: The following types of structure are the dependent variable: Functional division, Product division, Functional division x Product division Matrix.

Variables Product change and Size of foreign oeprations were omitted from the analysis, since data for these variables was missing for the Functional division x Product division Matrix case.

All values under the two functions are standardized discriminant coefficients

Classification Table

Actual Group Membership	Predicted Group Membership		
	FD	PD	FD x PD
Functional division (FD)	5	0	0
Product division (PD)	0	10	2
Functional division x Product division matrix	0	0	1

Note: Structures of MNCs correctly classified = 89 percent.

The supplementary information in Table 6–2 shows that the company tends to describe its strength more in terms of technology than products. This may be consistent with the fact that the company was generally regarded as the most research-oriented company in its industry. Further investigation reveals that the functional dimension of the matrix exists only for the research and manufacturing areas of the company. Marketing and sales groups report only to the product divisions. Management also indicated that it had recently increased the central control of research and development across the company in an effort to speed up the worldwide diffusion of new product technology. Without this supplementary information, one might well have concluded that this is another example of a matrix structure being used as a transitional structure (that is, a matrix structure being used to move from a functional division structure to a worldwide product division structure as foreign product diversity, the number of foreign subsidiaries, and so forth increase). Yet as long as technological leadership remains a key element of the company's strategy, it would appear that the functional dimension will remain a stable part of the company's structure.

Functional Division x Geographical Region Matrix

As in the previous section, matrixing a functional division structure with another dimension tends to relax some of the constraints associated with an elementary functional division structure. The strategic conditions that fit a functional division structure are low foreign product diversity, low product modification differences across subsidiaries, few foreign subsidiaries, and low levels of outside ownership and foreign acquisitions (summarized in Figure 5–3). These conditions are important because they keep the environment and technology of a company homogeneous and stable, and this minimizes the need for cross-functional information processing. While the above fits tend to keep a company's strategy simple, the fits associated with a geographical region structure emphasize large, complex foreign operations. Large foreign operations, a high level of foreign manufacturing, and many foreign subsidiaries are the strategic conditions that fit a geographical region structure (also summarized in Figure 5–3).

Combining these two strategies, Table 6–12 shows the hypothesized strategic conditions that would require a functional division x geographical region matrix structure. This strategy calls for large foreign operations with high levels of regional interdependency but with relatively low complexity in other areas (that is, low levels of product diversity, modification differences, outside ownership, and foreign acquisitions). The former conditions require regional specialization and decentralized coordination for certain matters (such as market plans and sales promotions, production scheduling), while the latter conditions still allow functional specialization and centralized coordination on a global basis for other matters (such as product design, manufacturing process technology). This line of reasoning leads to the following hypothesis:

> *Hypothesis 6–4.* MNCs with a functional division x geographical region matrix structure will tend to have strategies that contain relatively large foreign operations with many subsidiaries, a large amount of foreign manufacturing, and low levels of foreign product diversity, product modification differences, outside ownership, and foreign acquisitions.

Table 6–12.   Development of Hypothesized Strategic Fits for Functional Division x Geographical Region Matrix.

	Important Fits for:		
	Functional Division Structure	*Geographical Region Structure*	*Hypothesized Fits for Functional Division x Geographical Region Matrix*
Foreign product diversity	Low		Low
Product modification differences	Low		Low
Size of foreign operations		Large	Large
Size of foreign manufacturing		Large	Large
Number of foreign subsidiaries	Low	Large	Large
Extent of outside ownership	Low		Low
Extent of foreign acquisitions	Low		Low

As Table 6–13 shows, the functional division x geographical region companies provide only partial support for the hypothesis. It is interesting that all three of the fits associated with the geographical region dimension are supported, while only one of the fits associated with the functional dimension is supported. The matrix companies have large foreign operations with many foreign subsidiaries (on average, 68 percent of sales are foreign and there are fifty-two foreign subsidiaries). They also have a high level of foreign manufacturing (on average, 79 percent of foreign sales are sourced with foreign manufacturing). These conditions fit the kind of regional specialization and coordination provided by the geographical region dimension of the matrix.

Table 6–13. Testing of Hypothesized Strategic Fits for Functional Division x Geographical Region Matrix.

	Important Fits for			
	Functional Division Structure (N = 5)	Geographical Region Structure (N = 10)	Hypothesized Fits for Functional Division x Geographical Region Matrix	Actual Fits for Functional Division x Geographical Region Matrix (N = 2)
Foreign product diversity	Low (1.4)	(3.4)	Low	Medium (3.0)
Product modification differences	Low (1.8)	(3.4)	Low	High (3.0)
Size of foreign operations	(58)	Large (47)	Large	Large (68)
Size of foreign manufacturing	(42)	Large (91)	Large	Large (79)
Number of foreign subsidiaries	Low (12)	Large (55)	Large	Large (52)
Extent of outside ownership	Low (1.8)	(1.9)	Low	Low (2.0)
Extent of foreign acquisitions	Low (.8)	(2.1)	Low	Medium (1.5)

Note: Values in parentheses are mean values of the element of strategy for each type of structure.

The strongest fit with a functional division structure is the low level of outside ownership. Otherwise, the levels of foreign product diversity and foreign acquisitions are above those of the typical functional division company and the extent of product modification differences between subsidiaries is nearly as high as it is in geographical region companies (which tend to have the highest levels of product modification difference). These companies exhibit very little fit with the functional division dimension of the matrix. All of these conditions, however, can be readily handled by the geographical region dimension of the matrix.

Table 6–14 shows that five of the elements of strategy had sufficient discriminating power to enter and remain in the discriminant model. The conceptual model viewed all seven elements of strategy as potential discriminators between the three types of structure. The statistically significant first function of the discriminant model uses four of these variables (most significantly, the size of foreign manufacturing). The model succeeds in correctly classifying 76 percent of the cases, with all of the mis-classification occurring between the geographical region and of the mis-classification occurring between the geographical region and matrix structure groups. This is not surprising because the strategic conditions associated with the matrix companies seem to fit an elementary geographical region structure as well as they do a matrix structure. The supplementary information in Table 6–2 reveals that managements of both companies tend to describe their strengths in terms of technology. As was the case with the previous matrix form, the functional dimension of the matrix exists only for the research and manufac-

Table 6–14. Multiple Discriminant Analysis of the Elements of Strategy on Type of Structure (Distinguishing Functional Division x Geographical Region Matrix).

	Discriminant Function		
Independent Variable	1	2	F-value
Foreign product diversity	.76	-.04	2.68
Product modification differences	.71	0	4.14*
Size of foreign operations	.36	.92	1.85
Size of foreign manufacturing	.99	-.14	27.71***
Number of foreign subsidiaries	.70	.48	8.24**
Canonical correlation	.97	.53	
Wilks lamda	.04**	.72	

* $p < .05$; ** $p < .01$; *** $p < .001$.
Note: The following types of structure are the dependent variable: Functional division, Geographical region, Functional division x Geographical region Matrix. All values under the two functions are standardized discriminant coefficients.

Classification Table

	Predicted Group Membership		
Actual Group Membership	FD	GR	FD x GR
Functional division (FD)	5	0	0
Geographical region (GR)	0	7	3
Functional division x Geographical region matrix	0	1	1

Note: Structures of MNCs correctly classified = 76 percent.

turing areas of the company. The rationale seems to be the same as in the previous case. All three companies with a functional division dimension in the matrix are European and have strong central research and manufacturing divisions in the parent. Despite the fact that they have had to organize with product division or geographical region dimensions to handle a large number of foreign subsidiaries, a high level of foreign acquisitions, and a high level of foreign manufacturing, their apparent desire to also retain functional authority in the technical and manufacturing activities has forced them into a matrix structure. There is no corresponding matrix effect over the marketing or sales activities of the foreign subsidiaries.

Although insufficient information was available to determine whether these companies at some point moved away from an elementary functional division structure, such is probably the case. All stages of growth models (Chandler 1962; Scott 1971) show companies passing from a functional division structure to other elementary or complex structures. Franko (1976) also reports that movement from a functional division structure to either a matrix structure or a product division structure is the normal pattern for most European companies. Yet the fact that the functional dimension remains only in the technical and manufacturing areas should not suggest that these are merely transitional structures along the path to an elementary product division or geographical region structure. Although these companies seem to already fit such structures, supplementary information indicates a potential reason for continuing to retain the functional dimension. Each of these companies perceives technological leadership to be a key component of its strategy, and the functional dimension of both matrices strongly supports this less formally measured component of strategy.

Mixed Structures

Under a mixed structure, two different structures exist side by side for managing parent-subsidiary relationships. A subsidiary falls under one or the other, but not both. In four companies in the sample, some foreign subsidiaries report to an international division while others report to the parent's product divisions. Thus, the type of information-processing capacity provided varies widely from one parent-subsidiary relationship to another. For subsidiaries reporting to product divisions, there is a high level of product-related information-processing capacity, while for those reporting to the international division, information processing is largely around company and country matters.

Actually, there is no meaningful total company strategy for mixed structure companies. Instead, there is a strategy for one group of foreign subsidiaries and another strategy for the other group of foreign subsidiaries. What the study has measured is some averaging together of these two strategies or sets of strategic conditions. Two fits are important for those operations organized under an international division structure: relatively small foreign operations and few subsidiaries. Four fits are important for those operations organized under a worldwide product division structure: high foreign product diversity, high product change, relatively large foreign operations, and many foreign subsidiaries. Employing the logic developed earlier in this chapter, one can make the following hypothesis about the values these four elements of strategy should have for the mixed structure companies:

Hypothesis 6–5. MNCs with an international division & product division mixed structure will tend to have levels of foreign product diversity, product change, size of foreign operations, and number of foreign subsidiaries that are some weighted average of the levels of these elements for an elementary international division and an elementary product division structure (that is, the values associated with the mixed structure will lie between the values associated with the two elementary structures).

Three companies in the sample used mixed geographical region & product division structures. Again, there are two distinctly different parent-subsidiary relationships in these companies. Three fits are important for those operations organized under a geographical region structure: relatively large foreign operations, large amounts of foreign manufacturing, and many subsidiaries. As noted above, four fits are important for those operations organized under a worldwide product division structure: high foreign product diversity and product change, relatively large foreign operations and many foreign subsidiaries. Employing the same logic used above, one can make the following hypothesis about the values these five elements of strategy should have for the mixed structure companies:

Hypothesis 6–6. MNC's with a geographical region & product division mixed structure will tend to have levels of foreign product diversity, product change, size of foreign operations, size of foreign manufacturing, and number of foreign subsidiaries that are some weighted average of the levels of these elements for an elementary geographical region and an elementary product division structure (that is, the values associated with the mixed structure will lie between the values associated with the two elementary structures).

Figure 6–1 shows the key elements of strategy that are required to test the two hypotheses. Except for number of foreign subsidiaries, data for both structures tend to support the hypotheses. In each each case, the set of strategic conditions associated with the mixed structure can be approximated by a weighted averaging of the strategic conditions associated with the two elementary structures. A comparison of this pattern with those shown for the matrix structure companies clearly indicates the difference in the two patterns. The values associated with the matrix companies tend to lie at the two extremes, fitting (equaling) some of the strategic conditions of one of the elementary structures and some of the other elementary structure. The values associated with the mixed structure companies tend to lie between the two extremes, not fitting either but representing a weighted average of the conditions associated with the two elementary structures.

Both types of mixed structure companies tend to have a higher number of foreign subsidiaries than either of the associated elementary structures. Although this violates the hypotheses, it does not produce any misfit with the information-processing capacity of either of the mixed structures. The product division dimension can readily handle a large number of foreign subsidiaries, as can the geographical region dimension. It is probably apparent to the reader that the problem with this particular variable (number of foreign subsidiaries) lies not with the data but with the hypotheses. The total number of foreign subsidiaries in a mixed structure company is not going to be the weighted average of the number of subsidiaries organized under each of the two elementary structures but the sum of the two. Because, conceptually, mixed structure strategies are a simple averaging together of the two elementary structure strategies, a discriminant analysis, such as was used with the matrix structure companies, would not be very meaningful. This has not been a rigorous test of fit between mixed structures and strategy. Such a test would have to consider groups of subsidiaries rather than the entire company as the unit of analysis. Still, the above test has presented a considerable opportunity to reject the hypothesized notion of fit, and the sample data have clearly failed to support such a rejection.

DISCUSSION

This study has attempted to develop a more complete model of how matrix and mixed structures need to be related to the international strat-

	International Division & Product Division			Geographical Region & Product Division		
	International Division Structure	Mixed Structure	Product Division Structure	Geographical Region Structure	Mixed Structure	Product Division Structure
Foreign Product diversity	1.7	4.8	5.8	3.4	4.3	5.8
Product change	2.9	4.1	5.4	2.9	3.3	5.4
Size of foreign operations	34	43	61	47	52	61
Size of foreign manufacturing				91	82	61
Number of subsidiaries	41	115	58	55	72	58

Figure 6-1. Mean Values of the Key Elements of Strategy for the Two Types of Mixed Structure and Their Associated Elementary Structures.

egies of MNCs. Given the relatively small number of matrix and mixed structure MNCs in the sample and the variety of structural forms, there is a need to carefully consider the evidence for extending the information-processing model to matrix and mixed structures. Previous empirical studies dealing with this subject have been essentially exploratory (that is, looking at samples of MNCs, they have discovered a number of recurrent relationships between matrix and mixed structures and a few elements of strategy). A posteriori, they have been able to attribute some importance or rationale to the relationships (Stopford and Wells 1972; Franko 1976). Relatively small samples of matrix and mixed structures, however, have hindered such refinements as distinguishing between different types of matrix and mixed structures.

Although not employing a large sample, the present study appears to be a significant extension of existing empirical research on matrix and mixed structures. It goes beyond the case studies in sample size and objectivity of measurement, while at the same time retaining more detail than can be found in previous survey research studies (that is, the elementary structures contained in the matrix or mixed structure are specifically identified, and a significantly greater number of strategic conditions are meaningfully related to type of structure). It is also important to notice that the present study is not really exploratory analysis, in the sense that the Stopford and Wells and Franko studies were exploratory. Instead, it seeks to extend an existing model (the set of elementary strategy-structure fits) and underlying conceptual framework to explain how matrix and mixed structure companies should be related to their international strategies if they are to survive and succeed. With this kind of a priori logic and specifying of strategy-structure fits, the small N is far less a drawback than in pure exploratory analysis (with an a posteriori explanation). Given the apparent low density of matrix and mixed structures in the population of structural types and the impossibility of selectively sampling only matrix and mixed structure companies, this approach has a certain advantage over pure exploratory analysis.

There seems to be a good level of empirical support for the model. The hypothesized fits for the four types of matrix structure are generally supported by the data. The discriminant analyses provide statistical significance for a number of the hypothesized fits and further support the distinctions made between matrix structures and both of the elementary structures associated with each type of matrix. This is especially impressive when one considers that the discriminant models tend to concentrate on discriminating between the two types of elementary structure (where the group N's are much larger).

Earlier, this chapter described two important deficiencies of existing theories about matrix structures: (1) They are too general to be meaningfully operationalized, and (2) they cannot be readily integrated with the much stronger theory that already exists for understanding elementary structures and strategy. The new model represents a significant improvement in both areas. It conceptually distinguishes between the different types of MNC matrix structure by describing the capacities of each type for providing different kinds of specialization and coordination within an MNC. Empirical testing tends to support these distinctions. The new model is also more complete in terms of the number of contingency variables employed. All eight of the MNC contingency variables previously used to characterize the strategy-structure relationship for elementary structure companies are also required to characterize strategy-structure relationships for matrix companies.

The new model can also be integrated with existing theory about elementary strategy-structure relationships. In fact, it grows out of an understanding and overlaying of these relationships. This integration with existing knowledge tends, to some extent, to compensate for the complexity of the matrix relationships shown in the model. This complexity is, unfortunately, necessary. As strategies and environments become more complex (heterogeneous), the notion of requisite variety should lead one to expect an appropriate increase in the complexity of the organizational response. Matrixing is a way of raising the level of organizational complexity. When working with complex systems, however, it is important to be able to decompose the system into subsystems that are familiar. This is the argument for growing matrix models out of our considerable understanding of elementary strategy-structure relationships.

The new model also can be viewed as an important complement to the more process-oriented theorizing about matrix designs that has been done by Davis and Lawrence (1977), Sayles (1976), and others. Such work has described the dual pulls and goals existent in matrix organizations, the increased needs for communication and coordination across subunits, and the higher levels of conflict. The new structural model defines more precisely the nature of dual pulls under a variety of different international strategies. It shows how structural fit is needed not only to facilitate the increased levels of communication and coordination but to provide the right kinds of coordination and information processing between parent and foreign subsidiary. Although coping with organizational conflict is a process issue, the structural model provides additional understanding about the kinds of conflict that are most likely to occur in a specific matrix form, based on differences in the goals and concerns of the two managerial hierarchies (structural dimensions). Since so many of the coordination and conflict problems reported in matrix designs are structurally determined, a more defined structural model is a necessary complement to the more behavioral and process-oriented models.

In addition to providing a means for coping with relatively permanent increases in the complexity of a firm's international strategy, the study suggests that matrix structures may at times serve two somewhat different purposes. First, the supplementary information indicates that the international division x product division matrix structure may be being used as a transitional structure for moving from an elementary international division structure to an elementary product division structure as strategic conditions change. Davis and Lawrence (1977) found that some firms have used a matrix for this purpose. In this case, the matrix could be an effective bridge for moving from an international division structure to a worldwide product division structure. Simply changing the formal reporting relationships from an international division to a worldwide product division structure will not immediately provide a company with the information-processing capacities usually associated with a worldwide product division structure. Considerable time will usually be required for the former domestic product divisions to become internationalized so that they can understand and manage their product lines on a global basis.

In the meantime, however, the firm has already destroyed the capacities of the old structure to manage its foreign operations, so that during the transition period the firm will be vulnerable to coordination or information-processing failure. Passing through a matrix, however, tends to retain the old capacities while the new ones are being developed. The price for this mode of change is more duplication (of people and subunits) and conflict (between the two hierarchical systems and their differing goals). There may also be more behavioral reasons why a firm should not use a matrix structure. Yet, the quality of fit between information-processing requirements and capacities is likely to be better with more evolutionary structural change (such as that provided by the matrix bridge) than with revolutionary structural change (where generating new capacities requires the prior destruction of existing capacities).

The study also suggests a second purpose for using a matrix structure that has not been specifically identified in previous research. This is using a matrix structure across a more limited portion of a company's activities in order to emphasize or support a unique capability. In our sample, the functional dimension seems to be matrixed with worldwide product divisions in one case and geographical regions in another for this purpose. By matrixing only across the research and manufacturing operations of the foreign subsidiaries, these companies avoid the costs associated with a fully developed matrix. Yet they provide special support for technological leadership, which the supplementary information suggests is a key component of each of these firms' strategies. This kind of flexibility in using matrix structures is especially interesting for firms where one function (marketing, manufacturing, research) captures most of the competitive advantage of the firm, and this advantage tends to work in a similar way around the world.

There is considerable need for more research on matrix structures. Future research needs to be especially careful to measure the substantial variety of matrix types that exist and not aggregate across types that possess different capabilities and were very possibly designed for different purposes. There is also a need for longitudinal study to more fully describe the use of matrix structures as transitional structures to bridge from one elementary structure to another. Because major structural change is a dangerous and destablizing event for most companies, it would be valuable to know if the matrix bridge offers any significant advantage over more abrupt structural change. The present study suggests that the matrix may be especially useful when making the transition between two very dissimilar structures, such as moving from an international division structure to a worldwide product division structure.

Instead of overlaying strategies and structures, a mixed structure company attempts to operate two strategies and two structures in parallel. Some foreign subsidiaries operate under one strategy and its associated structure, while other subsidiaries fall under the other strategy and structure. At the parent-subsidiary level of analysis, the problem of good fit between strategy and structure is the same as it is for an elementary structure company. There will, of course, be two sets of strategy-structure fits for each company, but they are largely independent of each other, and only the highest level of parent HQ management need concern itself with two strategies and two structures.

Empirical evidence supporting the notion of strategy-structure fit for mixed structure MNCs is less direct than it was for the matrix structure firms. Such fit really needs to be evaluated at the group (that is, the group of subsidiaries organized under one of the elementary structures) rather than the total company level of analysis. To date, no empirical study has attempted to do this. Instead, the present study has attempted to use company-level data as a proxy for group-level data. As hypothesized, the two types of mixed structure MNCs in the sample face strategic conditions that appear to be some weighted average of the conditions that would fit each of the elementary structures represented in the mixed structure. While this is not a rigorous test of strategy-structure fit, it supports the hypothesized relationship and rather clearly illustrates that strategy-structure fit is quite different for matrix and mixed structures.

Mixed structures obviously provide more flexibility than an elementary structure. A given foreign subsidiary can now be managed under one of two different types of structure, each possessing different information-processing capacities. MNC managers can choose which structure best satisfies the information-processing requirements associated with a given parent-subsidiary relationship. Matrix structures provide even more flexibility because they provide the joint information-processing capacities of both elementary structures. Because mixed structures have neither of the disadvantages or costs associated with matrix structures (that is, duplication and more conflict), they should be considered before a firm adopts a matrix structure.

The empirical data seem to support extending the existing information-processing model to matrix and mixed structures. It is important to realize that the N's supporting this claim are not as small as the individual tests might indicate. Because the underlying information-processing characteristics of strategy and structure and the elementary strategy-structure fits were previously tested in Chapter 5, the N supporting this part of the model is forty-eight (both the thirty-four elementary structure MNC's and the fourteen matrix and mixed structure MNCs and all the hypotheses about their strategy-structure relationships rely on the same conceptualization and set of elementary strategy-structure fits). The notion of how the elementary strategy-structure fits (and their associated information-processing capacities and requirements) combine for matrix and mixed structures is only tested in this chapter, and therefore the N supporting this part of the model is fourteen.

The conceptual extension of the information-processing model to encompass matrix and mixed structures and the subsequent successful testing of the hypotheses derived from this extension provide a second test of the underlying information-processing characteristics associated with the elementary types of structure and the elements of strategy. This second test is largely independent of the first test, which was described in the previous chapter and involved only elementary structure MNCs. One of the vulnerabilities of the information-processing model of strategy-structure fit is the fact that there are no direct measures of the information-processing implications of strategy or structure. The role that information processing plays as a useful abstract intervening concept between strategy and structure has been only indirectly tested by the empirical testing of hypotheses drawn from the model. Consequently, the opportunity to retest these implications in the present chapter further strengthens the validity of the model.

7

CENTRALIZATION

The centralization or decentralization of decision-making power in organizations has long been an important concept, and early organization theorists generally considered it one of the fundamental dimensions of organizational design. This chapter takes an information-processing perspective of centralization and its relationship to the strategic and environmental conditions facing MNCs. The purpose is to develop a two-level model that relates the degree of centralization inherent in a parent-subsidiary relationship to both company-level and subsidiary-level conditions.

PREVIOUS RESEARCH AND THEORY

Looking largely at organizations of the late nineteenth and early twentieth centuries, early theorists tended to see greater centralization as contributing to better organizational functioning and performance. Frederick Taylor (1911) viewed centralization as vertical specialization, with thinking and decisionmaking occurring near the top of the hierarchy and execution taking place at lower levels. As such, it was the natural complement to horizontal specialization and provided many of the same kinds of efficiencies. Fayol (1949) and Urwick (1947) viewed centralization as the primary mechanisms for achieving goal consistency and coordinated behavior among an organization's subunits, while Weber (1947) also saw centralization as an important contributor to impartiality and rationality in the new "bureaucracies," which he considered the most effective and efficient specie of organizational design.

Later contingency theorists have also studied and debated the relationships of centralization to a variety of organizational and environmental conditions. Many researchers have concluded that organizational size exerts an important influence on the degree of centralization in an organization and that greater size leads to more decentralization (Pugh et al. 1969; Blau and Schoenherr 1971; Hinings and Lee 1971; Child 1973; Khandwalla 1974). Hage and Aiken (1967), Lawrence and Lorsch (1967), and Galbraith (1973) have also found that environmental complexity seems to exert a strong positive influence on the extent of decentralization. Other researchers have attempted to link centralization (or more often, decentralization) directly to organizational effectiveness (Hage 1965; Price 1968; Tannenbaum 1968; Mott 1972; Child 1972; Reimann 1973; Horovitz and Thietart 1982). Empirical research by these and other researchers has generally produced contradictory results, which have been summarized in an article by Jennergren (1981). He concludes: "The winning hypothesis is Mott's, that the relationships between decentralization and effectiveness vary from one case to another, depending on situational factors. Unfortunately, these situational factors are largely unknown."

Thus, despite considerable research attention, the role that centralization plays in influencing organizational functioning and performance is not well understood. In fact, Ouchi and Harris (1974) have stated that centralization is the least understood dimension of organizational design. One possible reason for this is the apparent lack of an integrating theory that includes both the purpose or functionality of centralization in organizations and the constraints that operate on it. In addition, Mintzberg (1979) points out that there is both horizontal and vertical centralization in organizations and that the literature has frequently failed to distinguish between the two. The present study deals only with vertical centralization, which, using Mintzberg's definition, is the distribution of formal decisionmaking power along the chain of command or line of authority. In response to the lack of an integrated theory regarding centralization, the present study attempts to use information processing as a framework for describing and better understanding certain critical relationships between centralization and the strategic and environmental conditions of an organization.

AN INFORMATION-PROCESSING MODEL OF CENTRALIZATION AND ITS RELATIONSHIP TO STRATEGY AND ENVIRONMENT

As indicated in Chapter 2, Galbraith (1973) has suggested that "hierarchical referral" or vertical centralization is one of the five basic coordinating or information-processing mechanisms available to organizations. When decisionmaking is pushed up the hierarchy, a wider perspective and more comprehensive understanding of the existent goals and conditions across the various subunits of the organization can enter the decisionmaking process. Thus, centralization facilitates coordination among subunits and prevents suboptimization. While these are the information-processing capabilities provided by centralization, there are also problems or limitations associated with this approach to information processing.

A study of the literature reveals four primary disadvantages associated with the use of centralization in organizations: (1) The decisionmaking capacity of top management is quite limited and consequently subject to overload; (2) top management frequently lacks specific knowledge about conditions at the subunit level; (3) moving information up and down the hierarchy requires time and tends to delay decisionmaking; and (4) centralization can have a negative impact on the motivation of subunit managers (Galbraith 1973; Mintzberg 1979). The first three factors represent the major information-processing limitations associated with using centralization as a coordinating mechanism, while the fourth has only indirect information-processing implications.

By considering both the information-processing capabilities and limitations of centralization, one can attempt to specify under what conditions decisionmaking should be centralized and under what conditions it should be decentralized. Interdependency among subunits in an organization is one condition that has consistently been found to increase requirements for coordination and information processing (Van de Ven, Delbecq, and Koenig 1976; Tushman and Nadler 1978). If centralization is viewed as an information-processing mechanism, decisionmaking for a given subunit should be more centralized when there is a higher degree of interdependency between the subunit and the rest of the organization. In this instance, centralization provides coordination and integration across the interdependency.

Change in the strategies and environments of organizations has also been found to increase requirements for information processing between interdependent subunits (Burns and Stalker 1961; Lawrence and Lorsch 1967). Frequent strategic and environmental change at the subunit level means that information about the subunit tends to become out of date and that more information processing is required to maintain integration between the subunit and the rest of the organization. Centralizing decisionmaking for the subunit higher in the organization is one way to provide this information-processing capacity. In line with this, decisionmaking for a subunit should also tend to be more centralized when simpler information-processing mechanisms, such as the setting of standard rules and programs for the subunit (Galbraith's first information-processing mechanism), are less appropriate because of the dynamic or changing character of the subunit's strategy and environment. Thus, both interdependency and strategic and environmental change at the subunit level increase requirements for information processing between the subunit and the rest of the organization, and vertical centralization can be a suitable mechanism for providing such information processing:

> *Hypothesis 7–1.* As a subsidiary's interdependency with the rest of the organization increases, decisionmaking for the subsidiary will tend to be more centralized.

> *Hypothesis 7–2.* As the degree of change inherent in a subsidiary's strategy and environment increases, decisionmaking for the subsidiary will tend to be more centralized (provided there is interdependency between the subsidiary and the rest of the organization).

Just as conditions that increase requirements for information processing between a subunit and the rest of the organization should tend to increase the degree to which decisionmaking for the subunit is vertically centralized, conditions that challenge the limitations of centralization as an effective information-processing mechanism should encourage decentralization. Thus, conditions that threaten to overload the information-processing capacity of the organizational hierarchy or make it difficult for top management to possess adequate knowledge about conditions at the subunit level or increase the cost of delays in decisionmaking should decrease the attractiveness of vertical centralization as an effective coordinating mechanism for the organization. Complexity or heterogeneity across subunits makes centralized information processing more difficult because it threatens to overload top management with many different decisions for different subunit conditions. It also requires top management to be familiar with many different strategic and environmental conditions at the subunit level. Research has found that organizations tend to decentralize when confronted by increased strategic and environmental complexity (Lawrence and Lorsch 1967; Galbraith 1973; Mintzberg 1979).

Size of an organization has also been found to be associated with increased information-processing requirements for the center (top of the hierarchy) because it directly affects the volume of information that must be processed (Pugh et al. 1969; Blau and Schoenherr 1971). As organizational size increases, the vertical span from top management to the operating subunits also lengthens, and this tends to delay decisions that have to be centralized. Thus, both strategic and environmental complexity and increased size at the company level of analysis challenge the capability of an organization to effectively centralize decision-making for its subunits:

Hypothesis 7–3. As strategic and environmental complexity or heterogeneity at the company level increases, decisionmaking for all foreign subsidiaries in a company will be more decentralized.

Hypothesis 7–4. As the size of a company increases, decisionmaking for all foreign subsidiaries in the company will be more decentralized.

CENTRALIZATION MEASURES

The study looked at twenty-two important decisions that have to be made as a part of the management and functioning of most foreign subsidiaries. These decisions are listed below:

Marketing decisions:

1. Small changes in product prices
2. Large changes in product prices (sufficient to break or destabilize the market)
3. Small changes in product design
4. Large changes in product design (substantially altering the cost, image, and possibly end use)
5. Small changes in sales commissions or the basis on which selling agents are paid
6. Decisions regarding selling methods (whom to call on, approach to be used, and so forth)
7. Basic changes in the method of distribution (such as selling direct instead of through wholesalers)
8. Advertising and promotion decisions
9. Decisions implementing product guarantee
10. Decisions regarding how to service products

Manufacturing decisions:

11. The decision to subcontract out large portions of the manufacturing instead of expanding the subsidiary's own facilities

12. Approval of quarterly production schedules and plans
13. The decision to switch to a new manufacturing process, employing different methods and equipment, when expanding plant capacity
14. Decisions regarding routine purchasing activities
15. Decisions regarding quality control

Financial decisions:

16. The decision to significantly increase inventories in order to keep the plant full
17. Change credit terms to customers
18. Decisions involving credit checking and the extension of trade credit
19. Borrow short term from local banks
20. Decisions involving how to finance a major facilities expansion
21. Write off $100,000 of questionable inventory
22. Decisions involving what insurance to carry and whom to carry it with

The degree of centralization existent in a parent-subsidiary relationship was measured during the subsidiary-level interviews by asking the respondents which hierarchical level in the organization would have to actually approve a decision before legitimate action could be taken, even if others would later have to confirm the decision. The decisions were recorded using the levels shown on a company's organization chart. This information was later recoded into the following categories: (1) within the foreign subsidiary, (2) within the international division, worldwide product division, or geographical region headquarters, and (3) above the divisional level and within the corporate headquarters. The individual decision scores were averaged together to provide three separate scales of centralization: one for marketing decisions, a second for manufacturing decisions, and a third for financial decisions.

This type of measure is similar to that used by Pugh et al. (1968, 1969) and others. Another approach to measuring centralization has been the control graph, which attempts to measure how influence or control over a decision is distributed across the different levels of the hierarchy (Tannenbaum 1968; Heller 1971; Van de Ven and Ferry 1980). The Pugh scale would seem to be the better measure of the information-processing capacity of centralization, since it measures the highest level in the organization that has a chance to both input and receive information from the decisionmaking process. The distribution of relative influence within a decisionmaking process is probably more a measure of the political topography than it is a measure of the information-processing capacity of the process.

The decision to combine the centralization measures into three scales is partially judgmental. Some researchers who have studied centralization across the parent-subsidiary relationship in MNCs have used individual decisions rather than broader types of centralization as the unit of analysis (Picard 1977; Goehle 1980). Their results, however, are difficult to summarize and have not been used to test broader hypotheses such as those developed above. At the other extreme, Garnier (1982) constructed a "global index of autonomy" that included thirty-eight different decisions to measure centralization in MNCs. Each of the three centralization scales developed in the present study attempts to measure a relatively broad concept—the degree of centralization inherent in a set of functional activities. For example, marketing centralization embraces several different kinds of decisions: pricing, product design, distribution, and customer service. Similar breadth of scope is apparent in the manufacturing and financial scales.

When reliability tests were run for each of the scales, the Cronbach Alphas were .71 for marketing centralization, .52 for manufacturing centralization, and .67 for financial centralization. While there are no generally accepted standards for reliability tests, the results compare favorably with guidelines suggested by Van de Ven and Ferry (1980) for measuring broad constructs. Thus, the decisions that have been combined to construct the three scales seem to converge to form consistent estimators of the three types of vertical centralization.

Table 7-1 shows the means, standard deviations, and intercorrelation among the three centralization scales. The significant positive correlation among the three scales indicates there is some overall tendency toward centralization or decentralization in a parent-subsidiary relationship, even across functional areas. Yet there is still sufficient difference to consider each type of centralization individually.

TESTING THE HYPOTHESES

Seven of the eight company-level strategic and environmental conditions described in Chapter 4 are used to test Hypotheses 7–3 and 7–4. Foreign product diversity, product modification differences between

Table 7–1.   Means, Standard Deviations, and Correlation Matrix of Centralization Scales (N = 89 to 94).

	Mean	S.D.	1	2
1. Marketing centralization	1.45	.28		
2. Manufacturing centralization	1.52	.32	.49***	
3. Financial centralization	1.55	.36	.39***	.27**

** p < .01 (two-tailed test); *** p < .001

foreign subsidiaries, extent of outside ownership in foreign subsidiaries, and extent of foreign acquisitions measure aspects of the complexity of a company's strategy and environment and are used to test Hypothesis 7–3. Size of foreign operations, size of foreign manufacturing, and the number of foreign subsidiaries measure aspects of the size of the organization and its operations and are used to test Hypothesis 7–4. An additional measure of size, the number of foreign subsidiaries with manufacturing, was also included in the study. It was not included in the previous list of company-level conditions because it is highly correlated with the number of subsidiaries (R = .62). Generally, the number of foreign subsidiaries shares a slightly stronger relationship with the various features of organizational design than the number of manufacturing subsidiaries. In this chapter, however, the number of manufacturing subsidiaries shares a statistically significant relationship with one of the centralization scales, while the number of subsidiaries measure only approaches significance. Consequently, in this chapter, the number of manufacturing subsidiaries has been included as a contingency variable. Previous studies have measured either the number of manufacturing subsidiaries (Stopford and Wells 1972) or the total number of subsidiaries (Daniels, Pitts, and Tretter 1985), and, generally, no distinction has been made between the two. Conceptually, both measures represent the size of the requirement for foreign information-processing capacity, and there appears to be little reason to prefer one over the other.

Chapter 4 also describes the measurement of fourteen subsidiary-level strategic and environmental conditions, which are used to test the remaining hypotheses in this chapter. Nine of the conditions measure various aspects of the degree of interdependency a foreign subsidiary shares with the rest of the organization: marketing information dependency, sales dependency, new manufacturing information dependency, day-to-day manufacturing information dependency, new product design dependency, product design change dependency, the relative importance of a subsidiary in terms of size, intracompany purchases by a subsidiary, and intracompany sales by a subsidiary. These conditions are used to test Hypothesis 7–1. The remaining five conditions measure various aspects of the degree of change inherent in a subsidiary's strategy and environment: product change, manufacturing technology change, political environment change, competitive climate change, and supplier situation change. These conditions are used to test Hypothesis 7–2. The means, variances, and intercorrelations for all of the contingency variables (strategic and environmental conditions) are shown in Table 4–2.

Table 7–2 shows the correlations between the three centralization scales and the eight company-level and fourteen subsidiary-level strategic and environmental conditions. Figure 7–1 shows only those contingency conditions that share statistically significant correlations with the centralization scales. This figure also indicates whether or not company-level structure has a significant relationship with centralization. All of the significant correlations with company-level conditions are negative. This pattern supports both Hypotheses 7–3 and 7–4. As company-level strategic and environmental conditions become more complex and as organizational size increases, there is a consistent tendency to decentralize all three types of decisionmaking for all foreign subsidiaries in a company. It is also interesting to notice that the functional areas seem to differ in their responsiveness to this relationship, with marketing centralization the most responsive and financial centralization least responsive.

The preponderance of positive correlations between marketing and manufacturing centralization and the fourteen subsidiary-level conditions supports both Hypotheses 7–1 and 7–2. When a subsidiary is experiencing relatively high interdependency with the parent or a relatively high degree of strategic and environmental change, there is a tendency to centralize decisionmaking for the subsidiary. The mixed and even slightly greater number of negative correlations between financial centralization and the fourteen subsidiary-level conditions fails to support Hypotheses 7–1 and 7–2. Although higher levels of dependency on the parent for new product designs and intracompany purchases (the two statistically significant negative correlations) may have little direct influence on requirements for financial coordination and information processing between the subsidiary and the parent, the findings are, nonetheless, nonsupportive.

Table 7–2. Correlation between Centralization Scales and Strategic and Environmental Conditions (N = 69 to 94).

	Marketing Centralization	Manufacturing Centralization	Financial Centralization
Company-Level Conditions			
Foreign product diversity	-.42***	-.08	-.23*
Product modification differences	-.14	-.23***	.05
Extent of outside ownership	-.22**	-.10	-.31***
Extent of foreign acquisitions	-.16*	-.17*	-.06
Size of foreign operations	-.27**	-.08	-.12
Size of foreign manufacturing	-.15	-.28**	.20
Number of foreign subsidiaries	-.18	.08	.01
Number of manufacturing subsidiaries	-.29**	-.11	-.17
Subsidiary-Level Conditions			
Marketing information dependency	.21*	.24*	.10
Sales dependency	.11	.03	.19*
New manufacturing information dependency	.01	.14	-.19
Day-to-day manufacturing information dependency	.11	.15	-.06
New product design dependency	-.10	.16	-.25**
Product design change dependency	.10	.27**	0
Importance of subsidiary	.19	-.19	0
Intracompany purchases by subsidiary	.08	.14	-.24*
Intracompany sales by subsidiary	.27**	-.01	.24*
Product change	.24*	.08	.04
Manufacturing technology change	-.04	0	-.12
Political environment change	-.02	.17	-.01
Competitive climate change	.30**	.14	.07
Supplier situation change	-.06	.13	-.06

* $p < .05$ (one-tailed test); ** $p < .01$; *** $p < .001$.

Note: Correlations involving product modification differences, extent of outside ownership, and the extent of foreign acquisitions are Kendall's tau, since these variables are only assumed to be ordinal. The remainder are Pearson correlations. A two-tailed test was applied to those relationships that contradicted the hypothesized relationships.

The influence of structure on centralization was also examined, using analysis of variance among the four types of elementary structure. As shown in Figure 7–1, a statistically significant difference (at the .05 level) was only encountered for marketing centralization. Marketing decisions tend to be somewhat more centralized in functional and international division structures than in product division and geographical region structures, although the difference is not great. In general, company-level structure does not appear to be a very important factor to consider when evaluating the degree of centralization in an MNC.

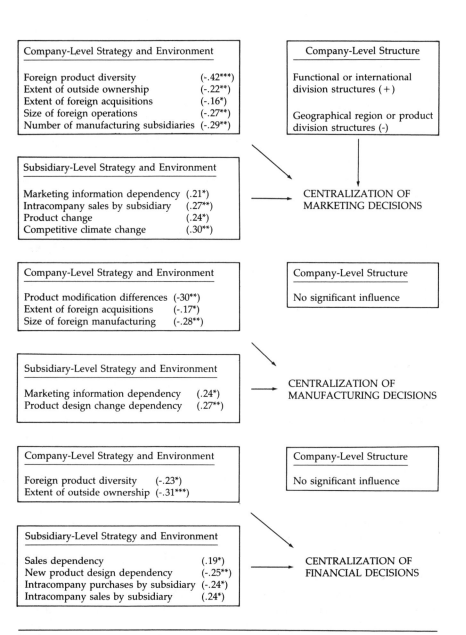

Company-Level Strategy and Environment		Company-Level Structure
Foreign product diversity	(-.42***)	Functional or international division structures (+)
Extent of outside ownership	(-.22**)	
Extent of foreign acquisitions	(-.16*)	
Size of foreign operations	(-.27**)	Geographical region or product
Number of manufacturing subsidiaries	(-.29**)	division structures (-)

Subsidiary-Level Strategy and Environment	
Marketing information dependency	(.21*)
Intracompany sales by subsidiary	(.27**)
Product change	(.24*)
Competitive climate change	(.30**)

CENTRALIZATION OF
MARKETING DECISIONS

Company-Level Strategy and Environment		Company-Level Structure
Product modification differences	(-30**)	No significant influence
Extent of foreign acquisitions	(-.17*)	
Size of foreign manufacturing	(-.28**)	

Subsidiary-Level Strategy and Environment	
Marketing information dependency	(.24*)
Product design change dependency	(.27**)

CENTRALIZATION OF
MANUFACTURING DECISIONS

Company-Level Strategy and Environment		Company-Level Structure
Foreign product diversity	(-.23*)	No significant influence
Extent of outside ownership	(-.31***)	

Subsidiary-Level Strategy and Environment	
Sales dependency	(.19*)
New product design dependency	(-.25**)
Intracompany purchases by subsidiary	(-.24*)
Intracompany sales by subsidiary	(.24*)

CENTRALIZATION OF
FINANCIAL DECISIONS

Numbers in parentheses are correlation coefficients with degree of centralization.

$* p < .05$ (one-tailed test); $** p < .01$; $*** p < .001$.

Figure 7–1.   The Determinants of Centralization.

THE INFLUENCE OF OTHER FACTORS ON CENTRALIZATION

The eight company-level and fourteen subsidiary-level conditions evaluated above were selected because they seemed to possess information-processing implications. In addition to these conditions, the study also examined the influence of a number of other factors that previous research has frequently associated with the degree of centralization in MNCs (Picard 1977; Goehle 1980; Hedlund 1981; Garnier 1982). These factors include size of company, age of company abroad, size of subsidiary, age of subsidiary, parent company nationality, and industry. Measurement of these factors is also described in Chapter 4. With the exception of the two size measures, these factors do not have any information-processing implications, and our conceptual framework would exclude them as meaningful contingency variables for a theory of centralization in organizations. The two size measures were excluded from the previous analysis because they do not as strongly or directly influence parent-subsidiary information-processing requirements as do the selected measures of organizational size. The correlations between these two size measures and the selected measures of organizational size range from -.30 to.15.

Table 7–3 shows the correlations between the three centralization scales and these other factors. Interestingly, the larger the company (in terms of total number of employees), the greater the tendency to centralize marketing decisions for foreign subsidiaries. This contrasts with the tendency to decentralize such decisions as the relative size of foreign operations and the number of foreign subsidiaries increase. The latter two measures of size are better measures of the volume of parent-foreign subsidiary information-processing requirements than is size of the total company. In addition, marketing centralization tends to be greater for larger subsidiaries than for smaller subsidiaries. It also appears that the more experience a company has abroad (the greater the age of the company abroad), the more it decentralizes all three types of decisionmaking. Financial decisionmaking also tends to be more decentralized for older subsidiaries than for newer subsidiaries.

Nationality of the parent company shares a number of significant relationships with centralization, as can be seen in Table 7–4. UK MNCs tend to decentralize marketing and manufacturing decisions, while European MNCs have the most decentralized financial decisionmaking. U.S. MNCs have a tendency to centralize both marketing and financial decisions relative to UK and European MNCs. Because nationality shares significant relationships with both centralization and a number

Table 7–3. Correlation between Centralization Scales and Other Factors ($N = 78$ to 94).

	Marketing Centralization	Manufacturing Centralization	Financial Centralization
Size of company	.25*	-.14	-.17
Age of company abroad	.21*	-.11	-.29**
Size of subsidiary	.28**	-.16	-.02
Age of subsidiary	-.01	.06	-.28**
Nationality of parent company (dummy variables):			
U.S.	.19	.07	.21*
UK	-.22*	-.25*	.14
European	-.05	.10	-.31**

* $p < .05$ (two-tailed test); ** $p < .01$.

Note: Correlations are Pearson correlations.

of the strategic and environmental conditions, the analysis so far is somewhat confounded (that is, it is unclear to what extent nationality is moderating and perhaps spuriously causing the relationships already identified between centralization and the strategic and environmental conditions). In order to address this problem, the correlations shown in Table 7–2 between centralization and the strategic and environmental conditions were rerun for each of the three nationality groups. Although the subsample sizes are smaller and the levels of significance frequently reduced, the subsample patterns are generally similar to the total sample patterns. For each of the centralization scales, however, the UK subsample showed more of a tendency to diverge from the general pattern than either the U.S. or European subsamples. More will be said about this in a later chapter. Overall, this analysis tends to support our argument that although nationality may strongly influence

Table 7–4. Centralization by Parent Country Nationality ($N = 89$ to 94).

	U.S.	UK	European	F
Marketing centralization	1.51	1.28	1.43	3.1*
Manufacturing centralization	1.54	1.31	1.56	3.0
Financial centralization	1.63	1.68	1.41	5.0**

*$p < .05$ (two-tailed test); ** $p < .01$.

strategic and environmental conditions, the important relationships between these strategic and environmental conditions and organizational design tend to be generalizable across nationality groups. The effects of industry on all of the organizational design features, including the degree of centralization, are shown in the Appendix. In this case, they are only significant for marketing centralization. Here, automobile and industrial equipment companies show the greatest degrees of centralization and chemical companies the least.

A significant degree of correlation between centralization and such familar and readily visible differences as nationality, age, and overall size of the organization cannot be denied. The more relevant question, however, when attempting to establish the value of an information-processing theory of centralization, is, To what extent can such factors explain differences in centralization that cannot otherwise be explained by factors with information-processing implications? This will be examined near the end of the next section, which first attempts to evaluate the relative influence of company-level and subsidiary-level conditions on centralization.

THE RELATIVE INFLUENCE OF COMPANY-LEVEL AND SUBSIDIARY-LEVEL CONDITIONS ON CENTRALIZATION

The generally successful testing of all four hypotheses indicates that centralization in organizations seems to be the product of two conflicting pressures or sets of fits. At the company (total organization) level, increases in strategic and environmental complexity and size pressure an organization to decentralize decisionmaking for all subsidiaries in order to buffer the hierarchy from information-processing overload. At the subsidiary (subunit) level, increases in interdependency with the parent and strategic and environmental change pressure the organization to centralize decisionmaking for the subsidiary in order to provide more coordination and information-processing capacity between the parent and the subsidiary. An interesting and relevant question is, What are the relative strengths of these two pressures or sets of fits?

In order to answer this question, a number of regression analyses were run. First, those company-level conditions that shared significant correlations with the marketing centralization scale (see Figure 7–1) were regressed on marketing centralization and the adjusted R^2 or percentage of variation in marketing centralization that could be explained by company-level conditions was noted. Next, the subsidiary-level conditions that shared significant correlations with marketing centralization were entered into the same regression model in order to determine how much additional variation in marketing centralization could be explained by subsidiary-level conditions once company-level conditions were already included in the model. In this case, the increase in adjusted R^2 or percentage of variation explained was 5.5 percent. Then the procedure was repeated, this time entering subsidiary-level conditions first, followed by company-level conditions. This second analysis was able to determine the increase in adjusted R^2 or percentage of variation explained by company-level conditions once subsidiary-level conditions were already included in the model (in this case 10.8 percent). This same set of analyses was repeated for manufacturing and financial centralization, in each case using as the independent variables those company- and subsidiary-level conditions from Figure 7–1 that shared statistically significant correlations with the respective centralization scale.

The beta weights and changes in R^2 associated with each of the six regression models are shown in Table 7–5. The two regression models constructed for financial centralization contain only those subsidiary-level conditions that share statistically significant positive correlations with financial centralization. The two conditions with statistically significant negative correlations were excluded because they cannot be considered to explain variation in centralization in the manner hypothesized.

Figure 7–2 is a pictorial representation of the contributions made by company- and subsidiary-level conditions to explain each of the three types of centralization. The information is taken from Table 7–5. The percentage of variation shown alongside the "shared" arrow can be explained by either set of variables, while the other two percentages represent the additional variation that can be explained only by the respective company- or subsidiary-level conditions.

Several important conclusions can be drawn from this analysis. Company-level conditions are stronger predictors of all three types of centralization than are subsidiary-level conditions. This implies that the degree of centralization or decentralization existent in a parent-subsidiary relationship is primarily required to fit the complexity of the firm's strategy and environment and organizational size at the company level. As complexity and size at the company level increase, there is a consistent tendency to decentralize decisionmaking. Although company-level information-processing requirements are the main consideration, there is, however, a second force at work. To the extent that an individual

Table 7–5.   Regression Analyses to Partial Out Variation to Company-Level and Subsidiary-Level Conditions.

Dependent Variable: Marketing Centralization (N = 77)

	Enter company level	Add subsidiary level	Add other factors	Enter subsidiary level	Add company level	Add other factors
Independent Variables						
Company-level						
Foreign product diversity	-.25	-.20	-.20		-.20	-.20
Extent of outside ownership	-.17	-.13	-.22		-.13	-.22
Extent of foreign acquisitions						
Size of foreign operations	-.12	-.12			-.12	
Number of manufacturing subsidiaries	-.18	-.15	-.13		-.15	-.13
Subsidiary-level						
Marketing information dependency		.20	.19	.14	.20	.19
Intracompany sales by subsidiary		.11		.21	.11	
Product change				.14		
Competitive climate change		.15	.11	.24	.15	.11
Other factors						
Size of company			.29			.29
Age of company abroad			.16			.16
Size of subsidiary						
UK parent			-.19			-.19
Adjusted R^2	.197	.252	.343	.144	.252	.343
Contribution of subsidiary-level variables		.055				
Contribution of company-level variables					.108	
Contribution of other factors			.091			.091

Notes: SPSSX stepwise regression analysis was used with a minimum entering and exiting F of 1.0 and a tolerance of .5. The three columns under each run indicate the beta weights of the three groups of independent variables that were successively entered into the model

Table 7–5. (continued)

	Dependent Variable:			Financial Centralization (N = 80)		
	Enter company level	Add subsidiary level	Add other factors	Enter subsidiary level	Add company level	Add other factors
Independent Variable						
Product modification differences	-.16					
Extent of foreign acquisitions	-.16	-.15	-.14		-.15	-.14
Size of foreign manufacturing	-.19	-.22	-.18		-.22	-.18
Subsidiary-level						
Marketing information dependency		.19	.18	.20	.19	.18
Product design change dependency		.14	.13	.24	.14	.13
Other factors						
UK parent			-.13			-.13
Adjusted R^2	.099	.130	.134	.089	.130	.134
Contribution of subsidiary-level variables		.031				
Contribution of company-level variables					.041	
Contribution of other factors			.004			.004

Note: Regression analyses for Financial Centralization are shown on the following page.

subsidiary's strategy and environment cause the subsidiary to face high levels of change and interdependency with the rest of the company, MNCs tend to centralize marketing and manufacturing decisions for the subsidiary.

In addition to partialing out the variation in centralization that can be explained by company and subsidiary-level conditions, the regression analyses reported in Table 7–5 also reveal how much additional variation can be explained by the other factors. This was accomplished by adding the other factors previously identified in Table 7–3 as having a

Table 7–5.　(continued)

	Dependent Variable: Financial Centralization (N = 80)					
	Enter company level	Add subsidiary level	Add other factors	Enter subsidiary level	Add company level	Add other factors
Independent Variables						
Company-level						
Foreign product diversity						
Extent of outside ownership	-.37	-.35	-.25		-.35	-.25
Subsidiary-level						
Sales dependency		.20	.18	.18	.20	.18
Intracompany sales by sub.		.14	.16	.23	.14	.16
Other factors						
Age of company abroad			.26			.26
Age of subsidiary						
U.S. parent						
European parent			-.17			-.17
Adjusted R^2	.127	.168	.246	.063	.168	.246
Contribution of subsidiary-level variables		.041				
Contribution of company-level variables					.105	
Contribution of other factors			.078			.078

statistically significant relationship with a centralization scale, to the regression model after company- and subsidiary-level conditions were already entered. The increases in adjusted R^2 that were observed when the appropriate other factors were entered are 9.1 percent for marketing centralization, .004 percent for manufacturing centralization, and 7.8 percent for financial centralization. Thus, for marketing and financial centralization, the size of the company, nationality of the parent company, and the age of the company abroad could still provide significant

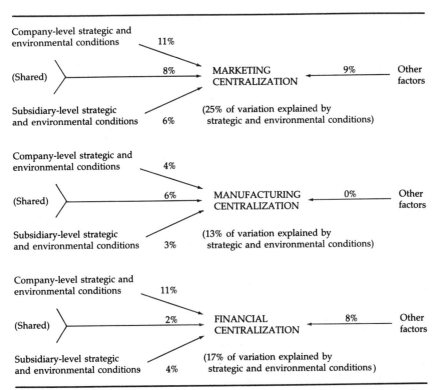

Company-level strategic and
environmental conditions   11%

(Shared)   8%   MARKETING   9%   Other
                                  CENTRALIZATION   factors

Subsidiary-level strategic   (25% of variation explained by
and environmental conditions   6%   strategic and environmental conditions)

Company-level strategic and
environmental conditions   4%

(Shared)   6%   MANUFACTURING   0%   Other
                                  CENTRALIZATION   factors

Subsidiary-level strategic   (13% of variation explained by
and environmental conditions   3%   strategic and environmental conditions)

Company-level strategic and
environmental conditions   11%

(Shared)   2%   FINANCIAL   8%   Other
                                  CENTRALIZATION   factors

Subsidiary-level strategic   (17% of variation explained by
and environmental conditions   4%   strategic and environmental conditions)

Note: The figures beside the arrows show the percentage of variation in the designated centralization measure that can be uniquely explained by company-level conditions, subsidiary-level conditions, or, alternatively, by either.

Figure 7–2. How Company- and Subsidiary-Level Conditions Explain
Centralization.

explanation beyond that already provided by those strategic and environmental conditions with information-processing implications. For manufacturing centralization, however, the other factors proved to be unimportant after the relevant strategic and environmental conditions were taken into account.

DISCUSSION

This part of the study has attempted to clarify and better understand the relationship between the degree of centralization within an organization and important characteristics of the organization's strategy and environment. While many relationships between centralization and a variety of contingency conditions have been previously studied and documented, the findings have been difficult to integrate and at times even contradictory (Gates and Egelhoff 1986).

The present study has sought to add some clarity and understanding by viewing centralization as an information-processing mechanism. By explicitly defining the capabilities and limitations of centralization as an information-processing mechanism, the functional role of centralization in complex organizations seems to emerge. Early organization theorists (Weber 1947; Fayol 1949) focused strongly on the functionality of centralization and saw it as the primary means for coordination in organizations. While recognizing its capabilities, they tended to ignore its limitations. The information-processing view of centralization is also able to integrate the limitations of centralization, that more recent research has tended to reveal. Both the functional role of centralization as an information-processing, coordinating mechanism for dealing with interdependency and change and its limitations when confronted by complexity and size tend to be supported by the sample data.

The study has also attempted to extend previous empirical efforts to explain centralization by viewing centralization as the outcome of two different sets of pressures or fits. By definition, the concept of vertical centralization transcends levels of analysis, existing as a relationship between two different levels of an organization (in this case the parent or company level and the subunit or subsidiary level). Previous studies have not really examined centralization as the joint product of two different levels of organizing (or two different levels of contingency variables). The sample data tend to support the argument that vertical centralization is an element of both company-level and subsidiary-level organizational design and in successful organizations, they tend to satisfy the critical fits at both levels.

At the company level, such elements of strategic and environmental complexity as foreign product diversity, product modification differences between subsidiaries, significant levels of outside ownership in foreign subsidiaries, and growth through foreign acquisitions create pressures to decentralize decisionmaking for all foreign subsidiaries. These pressures are based on the information-processing limitations of the firm. As each of the four types of complexity increases, it complicates information processing between the parent and its foreign subsidiaries and challenges these limitations. As product diversity and modification differences increase, both more decisions and a broader, more varied type of knowledge are required. This challenges the increasingly limited decisionmaking capacity available as decisions move up the hierarchy. Also challenged is the lack of specific knowledge about a broader and broader range of subsidiary-level conditions.

Higher levels of outside ownership and foreign acquisitions also challenge the information-processing limitations associated with centralization. Outside ownership complicates the goal structure of a subsidiary and places additional constraints on the way a subsidiary can be managed. Foreign subsidiaries that are acquired introduce new complexities into an organization because they come equipped with their own organizational cultures and management practices, which are different from those of the acquiring organization. Both types of complexity challenge the ability of higher levels of management to possess sufficient specific knowledge to deal effectively with such diverse subunit conditions. In order to avoid overloading the limited decisionmaking capacity and causing decisions to be made with insufficient knowledge about specific subunit conditions, the successful MNCs in the sample tend to decentralize decisionmaking as complexity at the company level grows.

Company-level size—or in this case, the size of the foreign part of a company—also challenges the limitations of centralization as an information-processing mechanism. As the relative size of an MNC's foreign operations, foreign manufacturing, and number of foreign subsidiaries with manufacturing increase, the volume of information processing required to support centralized decisionmaking increases. This threatens to overload the decisionmaking capacity of the hierarchy and its ability to move sufficient information up and down the hierarchy in a timely manner. Once again, the companies in the sample decentralize decisionmaking when size starts to challenge these limitations.

It is interesting to notice that the measures of organizational size are not as strongly connected to the centralization scales as are the measures of strategic and environmental complexity. There has been a lengthy debate within organization theory concerning the relative importance of size versus complexity as determinants of centralization (Pugh et al. 1969; Hall 1972; Child 1973). Actually this debate has involved internal or organizational complexity (specialization) rather than external or environmental complexity. But because there is isomorphism between strategic and environmental complexity and organizational or internal complexity (Hannan and Freeman 1977), the present study can also reflect on this debate. The information-processing perspective recognizes that both size and complexity contribute to information-processing requirements that tend to challenge the limitations of centralization as an effective information-processing mechanism. From this perspective, the debate perhaps becomes less interesting because it is really the balance between information-processing requirements and the capacity of centralization to handle these requirements that determines when decentralization will tend to occur.

At the subsidiary level, the nine measures of parent-subsidiary interdependency share fewer significant relationships with the centralization scales than do the company-level conditions. Yet the correlations with marketing and manufacturing centralization are decidedly positive, indicating a consistent tendency to centralize marketing and/or manufacturing decisions for a subsidiary when the subsidiary depends more on the parent for marketing information and product design changes, and when the subsidiary sells more of its output to other subunits of the company. As all three types of interdependency increase, information-processing requirements between the parent and the foreign subsidiary increase. It appears that the sample companies tend to deal with this increase by centralizing more of the subsidiary's decisions further up the hierarchy. This positive relationship between interdependency and centralization does not apply to financial decisions, however, where the correlations tend to be distributed more or less evenly in opposite directions and two of the four statistically significant correlations are negative. More will be said about this in a later paragraph.

The measures of strategic and environmental change at the subsidiary level also tend to be positively related to marketing and manufacturing centralization. Only product change and competitive climate change, however, share statistically significant relationships with marketing centralization. As both the subsidiary's product line and competitive climate change at a faster rate, marketing information and decisions become outdated more quickly and the need to reconcile subsidiary and parent-level information and decisions increases. To provide this increased information-processing capacity, the companies in the sample have tended to increase the centralization of marketing decisions.

The lack of significant relationships between manufacturing technology change and manufacturing centralization, and between political environment change and marketing centralization may at first appear puzzling. Certainly, technology change tends to increase requirements for information processing related to manufacturing, and change in the political environment tends to increase requirements for both marketing and manufacturing information processing. The sample data in Table 7–2 are probably not denying that these information-processing requirements exist. Instead, they are saying that the companies in the sample do not seem to be responding to variation in these requirements for information processing by altering centralization. Centralization, after all, is only one of the information-processing mechanisms available to organizations. In fact, it is a common practice in many MNCs to temporarily assign large numbers of parent company nationals to a foreign subsidiary when substantial technology transfer is required. Other firms bring local subsidiary nationals to the parent for periods of training and subsequent reassignment back to the subsidiary. Both mechanisms transfer technological information without affecting centralization. Edstrom and Galbraith (1977) have documented how MNCs use managerial transfer as a coordinating and information-processing mechanism.

Financial centralization seems to be largely unrelated to subsidiary-level change, just as it shared a mixed relationship to parent-subsidiary interdependency. There appear to be at least two explanations for this. An examination of the fourteen subsidiary-level conditions reveals that the majority should have little or no direct impact on financial information-processing requirements. Political environment change and supplier situation change might conceivably have the most direct impact on financial information-processing requirements, but neither is related to financial centralization. A second reason for the lack of meaningful relationship is that financial centralization in MNCs may be relatively high in all cases and therefore not consistently related to strategic and environmental conditions at the subsidiary level. Indeed, Vernon (1971) and other international business theorists have argued that the kinds of synergies achieved through financial centralization constitute the primary rationale for the MNC form. If this is true, the lack of meaningful relationship or fit between financial centralization and subsidiary-level conditions is not surprising.

The regression analyses reveal that while both company and subsidiary-level conditions contribute to the explanation of centralization, company-level conditions are the stronger predictors. This implies that the need for centralization in large, complex organizations (such as MNCs) to fit the constraints stemming from company-level complexity and size are most compelling. Failure to adequately centralize individual parent-subsidiary relationships in order to achieve better fit with subsidiary-level conditions will only tend to produce suboptimal performance for certain subsidiaries. However, failure to decentralize adequately to fit company-level constraints threatens the entire system or company with suboptimal performance. Thus, the study results suggest that the ability of MNCs to vary centralization from subsidiary to subsidiary to better fit local conditions and information-processing requirements is severely constrained by the ever present danger of information-processing overload at the company level. One must be careful in generalizing this conclusion to other organizations. It undoubtedly applies to the population of other large, complex organizations (for which the fifty MNCs used in the study are a representative sample). It may not apply to smaller, simpler organizations, which are not near the boundary specified by the limitations of centralization as an information-processing mechanism.

While company-level conditions are the stronger predictor of centralization, subsidiary-level conditions also seem to exert a weak but consistent influence on the degree of marketing and manufacturing centralization inherent in a parent-subsidiary relationship. Within the overall company-level pressure to decentralize, MNCs face specific subsidiary-level pressures to increase parent-subsidiary information-processing capacity. The analyses indicate that the sample MNCs manage to respond rather consistently (if not strongly) to these pressures by increasing centralization for those parent-subsidiary relationships where information-processing requirements are greatest. Thus, centralization still needs to be viewed as the product of two opposing pressures or sets of fits. In fact, the ability of organizations to respond to increased parent-subunit information-processing requirements with increased centralization might be expected to be greater in smaller, less complex organizations where the limitations of centralization as an information-processing mechanism are less binding.

Also contributing to the explanation of centralization in MNCs are other factors, which lack direct information-processing implications.

The most important were the overall size of the company, its nationality, and the age of the company abroad. For marketing centralization, these three factors could explain an additional 9 percent of the variation, in addition to the 25 percent already explained by the strategic and environmental conditions with information-processing implications. For financial centralization, it was 8 percent in addition to the 17 percent already explained, and for manufacturing centralization no additional explanation was provided by these factors. Although still significant, it is apparent that the strategic and environmental conditions with direct information-processing implications have stolen much of the potential explanation that has frequently been attributed to these other factors. The modest amount of additional variation accounted for by these other factors strengthens the argument that the information-processing perspective is an integrating and reasonably sufficient (in terms of the variation it can explain) approach to understanding the use of centralization in organizations.

In many cases, these other factors tend to be proxies for the strategic and environmental conditions with direct information-processing implications. For example, nationality is significantly related to seven of the eight company-level conditions, while age abroad is significantly related to four of the conditions. Yet explaining variation in centralization in terms of nationality and age is not very useful. As causal contingency variables for organizational design, both concepts are too broad to be conceptually meaningful. Nationality, for example, represents not only seven of the eight company-level conditions used in the study, but a variety of largely unspecified political, legal, and cultural differences. The most useful model of centralization in organizations need not necessarily contain all significant predictors of its dependent variable. Conceptual clarity of the contingency variables and their relationship to centralization is more important than simply maximizing predictive power.

In summary, it seems fair to say that the information-processing model of centralization in organizations appears to possess reasonable levels of both conceptual clarity and empirical support. Two general fits are important for the degree of centralization. The first, and most important, protects the parent from information-processing overload—in this case, from having to make too many decisions about subsidiary operations when these operations are complex and vary from one subsidiary to the next. The second fit is an attempt to selectively use greater centralization for those subsidiaries facing more environmental change and interdependency with the rest of the company to provide a higher level of coordination between them and the parent. Although firms may not consciously think about centralization in these terms or deliberately design standards of authority in this manner, the two fits uncovered by the analysis describe what a broad group of successful MNCs actually do in practice. The two fits are important because conceptually (using the information-processing perspective) they lead to effective organizational functioning—the balancing of information-processing requirements and capacities in an organization.

8

CONTROL SYSTEMS

Another important feature of MNC organizational design is the formal control system used by the parent to monitor various aspects of subsidiary performance (such as profits, sales of specific products, production quality control). The primary purpose of this chapter is to better understand what influences the level of formal performance control exercised over foreign subsidiaries and under what conditions successful MNCs tend to use more or less of this potentially important information-processing mechanism.

PREVIOUS RESEARCH AND THEORY

Headquarters control of subunit behavior and performance is a necessary integrating function in all complex organizations. Some organizational theorists, such as Williamson (1975), have even viewed the loss of control from one level of the organization to another as the limiting factor reflected in an organization's design and structure (that is, the ability to retain control as an organization grows is the factor that determines how large or complex an organization can become and still function). The importance of control as an integrating mechanism within organizations stems from the fact that it reduces uncertainty, increases predictability, and ensures that behaviors originating in separate parts of the organization are compatible and support common organizational goals. Given the complex environment facing most MNCs and the greater physical and cultural distances separating its subunits, exercising organizational control at the parent-subsidiary level is generally viewed as a much greater problem in multinational than in domestic companies (Brooke and Remmers 1970; Hawkins and Walter 1981).

There is an extensive and varied literature dealing with control systems and control processes in organizations (Hofstede 1967; Anthony, Dearden, and Vancil 1972; Giglioni and Bedeian 1974; Lorange and Scott Morton 1974; Newman 1975; Ouchi and Maguire 1975; Ouchi 1977). Although almost all empirical studies of organizational control have been in domestic organizations, there are a few exceptions. Brandt and Hulbert (1976) studied certain aspects of control exercised by U.S. MNCs over their Brazilian subsidiaries, and Youssef (1975) analyzed the use of a rather wide variety of control mechanisms in U.S. MNCs.

Formal performance control systems can be viewed as a form of cybernetic control. The general model of a cybernetic control process contains three basic elements: (1) a measuring unit that monitors some activity or output; (2) a comparing unit that evaluates and compares the measurements against some standard; and (3) an intervening unit that provides feedback, when necessary, to adjust the activity or process being controlled (Hofstede 1967). All cybernetic processes possess these three elements. Noncybernetic forms of control and influence are also important in organizations, and those that parent HQs exert over foreign subsidiaries include the centralization of decisionmaking (sometimes referred to as "direct control") and the socialization of subsidiary managers (Edstrom and Galbraith 1977). The former was dealt with in Chapter 7, and the latter will be considered in Chapter 9.

AN INFORMATION-PROCESSING MODEL OF CONTROL SYSTEMS AND THEIR RELATIONSHIP TO STRATEGY AND ENVIRONMENT

Just as centralizing decisionmaking at the parent level provides coordination and information-processing capacity between foreign subsidiaries and the parent, formal control systems represent another mechanism for parent-subsidiary information processing. When measures of subsidiary performance are sent to a parent HQ, evaluated and compared against some standard by the HQ, and either tacit or active feedback is provided to a subsidiary, some significant degree of information processing has usually taken place between the two levels of organization.

One can use an approach similar to that used for centralization in the previous chapter to define the information-processing capabilities and limitations of formal control systems. In the previous chapter, it was argued that both interdependency between a subsidiary and the rest of the company and change in the strategy and environment of a foreign subsidiary would lead to information-processing requirements between the subsidiary and the parent HQ. Increasing the degree of centralization between this subsidiary and the parent HQ is one way of satisfying these requirements for information processing. Increasing the level of cybernetic control exercised by the parent HQ over the foreign subsidiary (that is, increasing the amount and frequency of control information transmitted by the subsidiary to the parent HQ and the amount and frequency of feedback from the parent to the subsidiary) would be another way of providing the required information-processing capacity. We will ignore, for the moment, when an MNC might choose to use a formal control system as opposed to more centralization but will return to this issue later in the chapter. This line of reasoning leads to the following hypotheses, which parallel those developed and tested in the chapter on centralization:

Hypothesis 8–1. As a subsidiary's interdependency with the rest of the organization increases, the level of performance control exercised by the parent over the subsidiary will increase.

Hypothesis 8–2. As the degree of change inherent in a subsidiary's strategy and environment increases, the level of performance control exercised by the parent over the subsidiary will increase.

As was the case with centralization, company-level conditions that threaten to overload the information-processing capacity of the parent HQ (that is, conditions of complexity and size) might be expected to decrease the level of performance control a parent can reasonably exercise over its foreign subsidiaries. The risk of information-processing overload, however, is sometimes thought to be less for control systems than for centralization. The analysis of control information and feedback to the subsidiaries can frequently be handled by staff groups, and only seriously deviant or important information need be dealt with by higher levels of management. Nevertheless, one must hypothesize that there is a negative relationship between company-level complexity or size and the level of performance control a parent exercises over its foreign subsidiaries:

Hypothesis 8–3. As strategic and environmental complexity or heterogeneity at the company level increases, the level of performance control exercised by the parent over all foreign subsidiaries in a company will decrease.

Hypothesis 8–4. As the size of a company increases, the level of performance control exercised by the parent over all foreign subsidiaries in a company will decrease.

CONTROL MEASURES

The study measured the frequency with which the following sixteen important performance control items were received by the parent from each of the ninty-four foreign subsidiaries in the sample:

Marketing control:

1. Total sales revenue
2. Sales revenue by product line
3. Sales to specific accounts
4. Total selling expense
5. The components of selling expense (such as commissions, travel expense)
6. Selling expense by product or product line

Manufacturing control:

7. Total manufacturing expense
8. The components of manufacturing expense
9. The cost of specific raw materials
10. Units of output by product
11. Manufacturing variances from a standard cost system
12. Quality control data

Financial control:

13. Subsidiary total profit
14. Subsidiary profit by product line
15. Inventory levels
16. Accounts receivable turnover

These data were collected during the subsidiary-level interviews. The above list was intended to be a representative and not an inclusive list of those aspects of subsidiary performance that are typically included in formal control systems. The frequency with which a subsidiary reported such information to its parent HQ varied from daily to weekly, monthly, quarterly, annually, or not at all.

The individual control items were subsequently combined to produce three separate scales of formal control, one for marketing activities, a second for manufacturing activities, and a third for financial activities. This was done by averaging together the normalized scores of each item. Such a technique has the advantage of weighting each item in a scale equally, so that an extremely high frequency on one item will not distort the entire scale. As an example of such an extreme, one automobile company HQ was receiving sales data by auto model on a daily basis from all its subsidiaries. Reliability tests produced Cronbach Alphas of .52 for marketing control, .76 for manufacturing control, and .31 for financial control. The results for marketing and manufacturing control compare favorably with those suggested by Van de Ven and Ferry (1980) for measuring broad constructs.

The Alpha value for the financial control scale, however, is too low for this measure to be regarded as having good scale properties. The four control items that were combined to construct this measure (total subsidiary profit, profit by product line, inventory levels and turnover, and accounts receivable turnover) clearly are representative of the kinds of financial control information transmitted by foreign subsidiaries to parent HQs. Yet they do not share much linear relationship, and, consequently, they do not converge well around a single dimension of control. Despite the multidimensional character of this control scale (which, strictly speaking, should only be referred to as a measure), it tends to share the predicted relationships with the contingency variables, and it was deemed appropriate to go ahead and report on it in this chapter. As a precaution, however, the analyses were rerun using each of the four control items as a separate measure of financial control. Although the results were much weaker than for the financial control scale or composite measure, they tend to confirm the broader relationship that will be reported for financial control.

The use of these measures assumes that the level of control exercised by the parent over the foreign subsidiary is positively related to the amount of performance information received by the parent. Given that this information is usually demanded by the parent rather than being volunteered by the subsidiary, it seems reasonable to assume that such information is routinely compared against standards and that variances produce cybernetic feedback from the controlling parent HQ to the foreign subsidiary. In order to test this assumption, two-thirds of the respondents were asked which of the above items would prompt a response from the parent if it deviated from some standard such as the budget by 25 percent or more. The respondents indicated that in 81 percent of the cases such a deviation would prompt an immediate response from the parent (for example, a meeting to discuss the deviation, a request for more information from the subsidiary), strongly indicating that such information is generally used by the parent to exercise cybernetic control over the subsidiary.

Table 8–1 shows the means, standard deviations, and intercorrelation among the three control scales. The significant positive correlation among the three scales, similar to that observed for centralization, means that there is an overall tendency toward high or low control in a parent-subsidiary relationship, even across functional areas. Yet there is still sufficient difference to consider each type of control individually.

Table 8–1. Means, Standard Deviations, and Correlation among Control Scales (N = 86 to 90).

	Mean	S.D.	Marketing control	Manufacturing control
Marketing control	0	.54		
Manufacturing control	0	.67	.74***	
Financial control	0	.61	.50***	.29**

** $p <$ .01 (two-tailed test); *** $p <$ .001.

TESTING THE HYPOTHESES

Empirical testing of the four hypotheses follows the procedure used in Chapter 7. The seven company-level strategic and environmental conditions that measure complexity and size are used to test Hypotheses 8–3 and 8–4. The fourteen subsidiary-level strategic and environmental conditions that measure interdependency and change are used to test Hypotheses 8–1 and 8–2.

Table 8–2 shows the correlations between the three control scales and the seven company-level and fourteen subsidiary-level strategic and environmental conditions. Figure 8–1 shows only those contingency conditions that share statistically significant correlations with a control scale and more clearly reveals the extent to which these relationships support or contradict the four hypotheses. It is interesting to observe that all of the statistically significant correlations with elements of company-level strategy and environment are negative. The majority of the nonsignificant correlations are also negative. These results tend to support Hypotheses 8–3 and 8–4. When strategy and environment at the company level are complex, there is a consistent tendency to reduce the degree of performance control that a parent HQ exercises over its foreign subsidiaries. A similar tendency to reduce the degree of performance control exercised over foreign subsidiaries is observed as the size of a firm's foreign operations increases. It is interesting to observe that this tendency is stronger for manufacturing and financial control than for marketing control.

Table 8–2. Correlation between Control Scales and Strategic and Environmental Conditions (N = 71 to 90).

	Marketing Control	Manufacturing Control	Financial Control
Company-Level Conditions			
Foreign product diversity	-.14	-.19*	-.29**
Product modification differences	.12	.10	-.01
Extent of outside ownership	-.12	-.19**	-.23**
Extent of foreign acquisitions	-.05	-.19*	-.21*
Size of foreign operations	-.26**	-.27**	-.27**
Size of foreign manufacturing	-.10	.15	-.18
Number of foreign subsidiaries	-.10	0	-.30**
Subsidiary-Level Conditions			
Marketing information dependency	.03	.11	.07
Sales dependency	-.03	.04	.06
New manufacturing information dependency	-.12	-.11	.05
Day-to-day manufacturing information dependency	.11	.02	.17
New product design dependency	-.06	-.10	.01
Product design change dependency	-.06	.03	.07
Importance of subsidiary	.08	.17	-.07
Intracompany purchases by subsidiary	.01	-.12	-.07
Intracompany sales by subsidiary	.15	.32**	-.11
Product change	.26**	.40***	.22*
Manufacturing technology change	-.03	-.03	.18*
Political environment change	-.07	-.12	.06
Competitive climate change	.12	.09	.30**
Supplier situation change	.03	0	.19*

* p < .05 (one-tailed test); ** p < .01; *** p < .001.

Note: Correlations involving product modification differences, extent of outside ownership, and the extent of foreign acquisitions are Kendall's tau, since these variables are only assumed to be ordinal. The remainder are Pearson correlations. A two-tailed test was applied to those relationships that contradicted the hypothesized relationship.

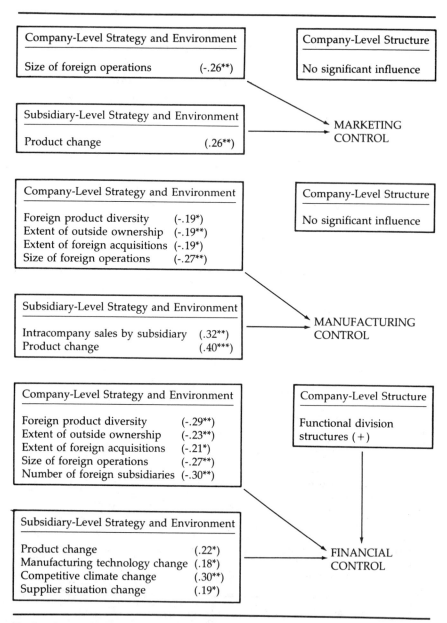

Numbers in parentheses are correlation coefficients with degree of control.
* $p < .05$ (one-tailed test); ** $p < .01$; *** $p < .001$.

Figure 8–1.   The Determinants of Control.

Figure 8–1 shows that all of the significant correlations between the three control scales and the fourteen subsidiary-level conditions are positive. This supports Hypotheses 8–1 and 8–2. When a subsidiary experiences relatively high interdependency with the rest of the company or a relatively high degree of strategic and environmental change, there is a tendency for the parent to exercise a relatively high degree of performance control over that subsidiary. As was the case with company-level conditions above, this tendency appears to be stronger for manufacturing and financial control than for marketing control.

The influence of structure on the degree of performance control was also examined, using analysis of variance among the four types of elementary structure. As indicated in Figure 8–1, a statistically significant difference (at the .001 level) was encountered for financial control. The degree of financial control exercised over foreign subsidiaries tends to be the greatest in firms with functional and international division structures and the lowest in firms with product division structures.

THE INFLUENCE OF OTHER FACTORS ON CONTROL

Following the procedure used in the previous chapter, the study also examined the influence of the six other factors on the degree of performance control exercised over foreign subsidiaries. These factors are size of company, age of company abroad, size of subsidiary, age of subsidiary, parent company nationality, and industry. Measurement of these factors is described in Chapter 4. While lacking direct information-processing implications, these factors are often thought to influence or share important relationships with various aspects of organizational design.

Table 8–3 shows the correlations between the three control scales and these other factors. Larger subsidiaries tend to experience a higher degree of manufacturing control than do smaller subsidiaries. It also appears that the more experience a company has abroad (the greater the age of the company abroad), the less financial performance control it exercises over its foreign subsidiaries. Older foreign subsidiaries also tend to receive less financial control than do newer subsidiaries. It is interesting to note that age of company abroad and age of subsidiary shared similar relationships with the degree of financial centralization.

As was also the case with centralization, nationality of the parent company shares a number of significant relationships with performance control. Table 8–4 shows that U.S. MNCs tend to exercise the highest degree of performance control across all three functional areas, while

Table 8–3. Correlation between Control Scales and Other Factors (N = 77 to 90).

	Marketing Control	Manufacturing Control	Financial Control
Size of company	.16	.17	.01
Age of company abroad	-.20	-.09	-.34**
Size of subsidiary	.16	.29**	-.10
Age of subsidiary	-.18	-.01	-.39***
Nationality of parent company (dummy variables):			
U.S.	.31**	.25*	.23*
UK	-.03	-.04	.09
European	-.30**	-.24*	-.30**

* p < .05 (two-tailed test); ** p < .01; *** p < .001.
Note: Correlations are Pearson correlations.

Table 8–4. Control by Parent Country Nationality (N = 86 to 90).

	U.S.	UK	European	F
Marketing control	.17	-.05	-.21	5.1**
Manufacturing control	.15	-.09	-.22	3.1*
Financial control	.14	.14	-.23	4.3*

* p < .05 (two-tailed test); ** p < .01.

European MNCs tend to exercise the lowest. UK MNCs generally fall somewhere in between. These findings tend to be consistent with those of two earlier studies. Examining foreign subsidiaries in Brazil, Hulbert and Brandt (1980) found that U.S. MNCs had heavier reporting requirements than either European or Japanese MNCs. In a study of control in UK, French, and German companies, Horovitz (1980) found that reported control information was more detailed and frequent in UK companies than in French or German companies. The implications of different patterns of control in U.S., UK, and European MNCs is also interesting and has been discussed elsewhere (Egelhoff 1984).

As was done in Chapter 7, the correlations shown in Table 8–2 between control and the strategic and environmental conditions were rerun for each of the three nationality groups. The subsample patterns are generally similar to the total sample pattern, although, once again, the UK subsample showed some tendency to diverge from the general pattern and the European subsample showed no tendency to increase manufacturing control as subsidiary-level interdependency and change increased.

The effects of industry on control are shown in the Appendix. They are significant only for manufacturing control, where automobile and tire companies exercise the highest degree of performance control and pharmaceutical companies the least.

THE RELATIVE INFLUENCE OF COMPANY-LEVEL AND SUBSIDIARY-LEVEL CONDITIONS ON CONTROL

The generally successful testing of all four hypotheses indicates that, like centralization, performance control in organizations seems to be the product of two conflicting pressures or sets of fits. At the company (total organization) level, increases in strategic and environmental complexity and size pressure an organization to reduce the degree of performance control the parent HQ exercises over all subsidiaries in order to buffer the hierarchy from information-processing overload. At the subsidiary (subunit) level, increases in interdependency with the parent and strategic and environmental change pressure the parent HQ to exercise greater control over a subsidiary in order to provide more coordination and information-processing capacity between the parent and the subsidiary. Once again, we are interested in evaluating the relative strengths of these two pressures or sets of fits.

Following the procedure used in the previous chapter, a number of regression analyses were run. First, the single company-level condition that shared a significant correlation with the marketing control scale (see Figure 8–1) was regressed on marketing control and the adjusted R^2 or percentage of variation in marketing control that could be explained by company-level conditions was noted. Next, the single subsidiary-level condition that shared a significant correlation with marketing control was entered into the same regression model in order to determine how much additional variation in marketing control could be explained by subsidiary-level conditions once company-level conditions were already included in the model. In this case, the increase in adjusted R^2 or percentage of variation explained was 4 percent. Then the procedure was repeated, this time entering the subsidiary-level condition first, followed by the company-level condition. This second analysis was able to determine the increase in adjusted R^2 or percentage of variation explained by company-level conditions once subsidiary-level conditions were already included in the model (in this case also 4 percent). This same set of analyses was repeated for manufacturing and financial control, in each case using as the independent variables those company and subsidiary-level conditions, from Figure 8–1, which shared statistically significant correlations with the respective control scale.

Because of its considerable length, a table similar to Table 7–5 in the previous chapter (which more fully presents the step-wise regression runs) will not be included in this and subsequent chapters. The procedure used to interpret the step-wise regression runs, however, is exactly the same as was used in Chapter 7. The reader can refer to Chapter 7 to see how the step-wise regression runs were analyzed to produce the results shown in Figure 7–2 and know that the same procedure was used to produce the results shown in Figure 8–2.

Figure 8–2 is a pictorial representation of the contributions made by company and subsidiary-level conditions to explain each of the three types of control. The information is taken from the regression runs. The percentage of variation shown alongside the "shared" arrow can be explained by either set of variables, while the other two percentages represent the additional variation that can be explained only by the respective company- or subsidiary-level conditions.

A number of important conclusions can be drawn from this analysis. The degree of performance control exercised by the parent HQ over marketing matters does not seem to be nearly as responsive to variations in strategy and environment as the degrees of control exercised over manufacturing and financial matters. Also, control over manufacturing matters appears to be much more responsive to subsidiary-level strategy and environment than to company-level strategy and environment. This is the first instance where this has occurred in our analysis.

In addition to partialing out the variation in control that can be explained by company and subsidiary-level conditions, the regression analyses reported in Figure 8–2 also reveal how much additional variation can be explained by the other factors. This was accomplished by adding the other factors previously identified in Table 8–3 as having a statistically significant relationship with a control scale, to the regression model after company and subsidiary-level conditions were already entered. The increases in adjusted R^2 that were observed when the appropriate other factors were entered are 4 percent for marketing control (contributed by nationality), 2 percent for manufacturing control (contributed by size of subsidiary and nationality), and 5 percent for financial control (contributed by age of subsidiary). Thus, the other fac-

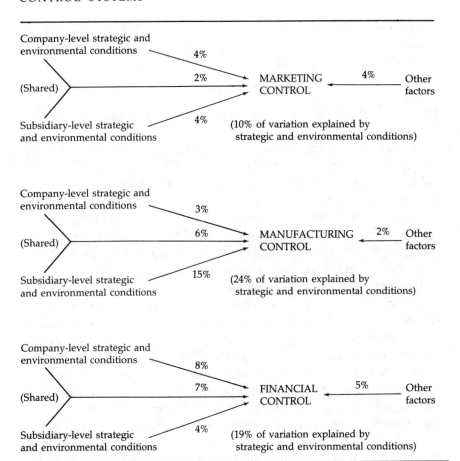

Note: The figures beside the arrows show the percentage of variation in the designated control measure that can be uniquely explained by company-level conditions, subsidiary-level conditions, or, alternatively, by either.

Figure 8–2. How Company- and Subsidiary-Level Conditions Explain Control.

tors provide only a modest amount of explanation beyond that already provided by those strategic and environmental conditions with information-processing implications.

DISCUSSION

This part of the study has attempted to better understand the relationship between the level of performance control exercised within an organization and the organization's strategy and environment. Although performance control systems have been less studied at the macro levels of organizations than centralization, their use in organizations has been just as prevalent.

As with centralization, the conceptual framework used in this chapter has viewed performance control as another information-processing mechanism. The general capabilities and limitations of performance control as an information-processing mechanism are defined as similar to those of centralization. Higher levels of parent-subsidiary interdependency and change in a subsidiary's strategy and environment should increase information-processing requirements between the two and it was hypothesized that this could be met by increasing the level of performance control the parent exercises over the subsidiary. Similarly, greater complexity and size at the company-level should threaten the parent HQ with information-processing overload if it attempts to receive, analyze, and respond to too much control information. Therefore, these conditions were hypothesized to encourage a decrease in the level of performance control exercised over foreign subsidiaries. Both the functional role of performance control as an information-processing mechanism for dealing with interdependency and change as well as its limitations when confronted by complexity and size are important design criteria, and both tend to be supported by the sample data.

Performance control frequently exists between organizational levels (such as the parent HQ and foreign subsidiary), and this chapter has explained it as the joint product of two different levels of contingency variables. There are numerous negative relationships between performance control and the company-level conditions, often overlapping the same conditions that shared significant negative relationships with centralization. As was the case with centralization, most of the subsidiary-level conditions are not strongly related to performance control. Those that are, however, all share a positive relationship.

In all but one instance, the significant relationships are with the change variables as opposed to the interdependency variables. In fact, the degree of product change in a subsidiary shares a significant positive relationship with all three types of control. Although control appears to be most responsive to subsidiary-level change, centralization was more responsive to subsidiary-level interdependency. Here eight of the ten significant relationships involved interdependency variables, and all of the relationships involving manufacturing and financial centralization were with interdependency variables. Thus, there is some suggestion that MNCs may tend to increase performance control to better monitor subsidiary-level change but increase centralization when a subsidiary shares high interdependency with the parent.

The regression analyses to partial out variation in the control variables between company-level and subsidiary-level conditions show in Figure 8–2 a more balanced situation than was the case for centralization. There, company-level conditions were the stronger predictors of centralization, while control seems to be more equally influenced by both. Manufacturing control, in fact, is largely responsive to subsidiary-level conditions, which can explain 21 percent of its variation. Thus, in the manufacturing area, control seems to provide a more variable and responsive level of information processing between parent and subsidiary than does centralization.

The fact that company-level conditions exert somewhat less influence over each of the control variables than over the corresponding centralization variable could suggest that the use of performance control is not as constrained by company-level complexity and size as is centralization. As indicated in Chapter 7, some theorists believe that control systems are less subject to information-processing overload than is centralization. Still, company-level complexity and size do share a decidedly negative relationship with control, as they do with centralization, so the difference is one of degree, not direction.

The strategic and environmental conditions explain only 10 percent of the variation in marketing control, but 25 percent of the variation in marketing centralization. Conversely, they explain 24 percent of the variation in manufacturing control but only 13 percent of the variation in manufacturing centralization. Financial control and centralization, on the other hand, exhibit more similar patterns of variation.

The residual influence of such other factors as nationality, size of company, age of company abroad, size of subsidiary, and age of subsidiary on control can also be seen in Figure 8–2. While nationality has a strong association with level of control (see Table 8–4), its influence is greatly reduced after taking into consideration the previous impacts of company- and subsidiary-level conditions on control. It still continues to explain 4 percent of the variation in marketing control, a reflection of the fact that U.S. MNCs exert more performance control over subsidiaries than European MNCs do. Age of subsidiary also remains important, and it explains 5 percent of the variation in financial control. This reflects the fact that MNCs tend to exert less financial control over older subsidiaries than they do over newer subsidiaries. With these two exceptions, the nationality, size, and age variables were not able to add any additional explanation to variation in control that was not already provided by the company and subsidiary-level strategic and environmental conditions.

Directionally, the pattern of association between company and subsidiary-level conditions and performance control parallels the pattern previously found for centralization. This is an interesting finding, since it is sometimes thought that formal controls facilitate decentralization. The implication, of course, is that there should be a negative or inverse relationship between formal controls and the degree of centralization. Table 8–5 shows that for the sample companies, the relationship is consistently positive.

Table 8–5. Correlation between Control and Centralization (N = 85 to 90).

	Marketing Control	Manufacturing Control	Financial Control
Marketing centralization	.38***	.48***	.34**
Manufacturing centralization	.04	.17	.26*
Financial centralization	.31**	.45***	.16

* $p < .05$ (two-tailed test); ** $p < .01$; *** $p < .001$.

The above suggests that at the parent-foreign subsidiary level of organization, centralization and performance control tend to be part of the same managerial system and are not alternative approaches to managing the parent-subsidiary relationship. One reason for this might be that centralizing decisionmaking at divisional and corporate levels requires that more current information about subsidiary operations exist at these levels. Formal performance control systems are probably the most economical way to transfer this information from the subsidiaries to the parent level of the organization. Thus, from an information-processing perspective, there seems to be a reason for the joint or covariation of centralization and performance control.

9

STAFFING THE FOREIGN SUBSIDIARY

Another feature of MNC organizational design that appears to be important when managing foreign operations is the staffing of the foreign subsidiary. The forerunner of today's foreign subsidiary—the eighteenth-century trading and colonizing ventures of European joint stock companies—relied heavily on the selection of suitable leaders to ensure their success. By the latter half of the nineteenth century, in the emerging European MNC, this form seems to have evolved into what Franko has called the mother-daughter relationship (1976). Here, family members or trusted employees were sent out from the parent company to manage the foreign subsidiary, generally with a great deal of local autonomy. Staffing was the primary way that an MNC influenced the operation of its foreign subsidiaries. In today's MNC, the parent-subsidiary relationship has grown in complexity to embrace many other dimensions of organizational design. Yet staffing, the original dimension for managing a foreign operation, remains important today, although perhaps for a different reason than in the past.

PREVIOUS RESEARCH AND THEORY

Research on the staffing of foreign subsidiaries is limited and provides only a partial picture of how staffing might be related to either the strategic and environmental conditions surrounding a firm or other features of its organization design. Daniels (1974) and Toyne (1980) describe a variety of characteristics of managers in the foreign subsidiaries of U.S. MNCs and contrast these with the characteristics of local managers in domestic firms of the foreign countries. Hulbert and Brandt (1980:129), in a study of foreign subsidiaries in Brazil, report that European and Japanese MNCs were much more likely to staff important subsidiary positions with parent company nationals than were U.S. MNCs:

> American companies place less emphasis on the personal or company-man approach. With a more formalized control system—emphasis on planning, frequent reporting, and personal visitation—there is less need to rely on carefully trained and loyal managers from the home office to run subsidiaries. The emphasis of American companies on "system" rather than "man" makes it much easier for them to employ local nationals.

Youssef (1975), on the other hand, found that the use of expatriates as subsidiary CEOs was positively correlated with the use of other personal and impersonal forms of control in a study of U.S. MNCs, although he only examined each firm's most recent foreign subsidiary. Indeed, based on later research, Toyne and Kuhne (1983) concluded that all MNCs tend to use expatriate managers for transferring critical technology and management skills to new foreign operations.

Employing a different methodology, the case study, Edstrom and Galbraith (1977) studied foreign staffing practices and patterns in four large European MNCs. They report that frequent transfers between parent and foreign subsidiaries help to build both an integrating company culture and a verbal information network within an MNC. This produces a new kind of control, control by socialization, which they hypothesize tends to augment rather than replace the more bureaucratic forms of control (that is, centralization and performance control). Although their study dealt with company-wide practices and patterns rather than focusing on specific parent-subsidiary relationships, the information-processing implications of their conceptual framework are a useful context for the present study. Jaeger (1983) and Baliga and Jaeger (1984) also report on the use of expatriate staffing to transfer organizational culture to foreign subsidiaries. The advantages and disadvantages associated with control by culture differ from those associated with more bureaucratic forms of control.

AN INFORMATION-PROCESSING MODEL OF SUBSIDIARY STAFFING AND ITS RELATIONSHIP TO STRATEGY AND ENVIRONMENT

Whether an MNC staffs the key management positions in a foreign subsidiary with parent company nationals or local nationals is another

feature of organizational design that has information-processing implications. These need to be viewed from two different perspectives. First,
staffing important subsidiary positions with managers from the parent
company tends to directly transfer parent company values, objectives,
and ways of doing things to the subsidiary. When decisions are made
by parent company nationals within a foreign subsidiary, they will tend
to reflect these parent company attributes more than if they were being
made by managers who are local nationals. Similarly, parent company
managers within a subsidiary are more likely to exercise the same kind
of control over behavior and performance that the parent would exercise if it possessed the same control information. Thus, to some extent,
staffing with parent company nationals leads to the same result as centralizing more decisionmaking at the parent level or increasing the level
of formal performance control exercised by the parent.

A second way that staffing adds to parent-subsidiary information-
processing capacity derives from the informal networks that expatriate
managers generally maintain with previous associates in the parent
HQ. It is often common practice to "bounce ideas" off of these people
before submitting them in a formal plan or seeking HQ approval. Similarly, HQ managers can unofficially "feel out" and even seek additional
information from confidants in foreign subsidiaries before deciding on
critical matters. This kind of information-processing tends to be recipro-
cal and flexible. Often, it can better cope with the more unstructured
types of problems than can the more formal approval and control processes. In the previous chapters, it was argued that both interdependency between a subsidiary and the rest of the company and change in
the strategy and environment of a foreign subsidiary would lead to
information-processing requirements between the subsidiary and the
parent HQ. Increasing the degree of centralization and the level of performance control exercised by the parent HQ over the subsidiary
appear to be ways of addressing these requirements. Based on the
information-processing implications of staffing discussed above, it
seems reasonable to expect that increasing the percentage of parent
company nationals in a foreign subsidiary would be another way of
addressing these information-processing requirements. This leads to
the following hypotheses:

Hypothesis 9–1. As a subsidiary's interdependency with the rest of the organization increases, the percentage of parent company nationals in the subsidiary will increase.

Hypothesis 9–2. As the degree of change inherent in a subsidiary's strategy and environment increases, the percentage of parent company nationals in the subsidiary will increase.

The above hypotheses are similar to those made for centralization and performance control. Despite this similarity, there are reasons to believe that staffing with parent nationals is not a complete substitute for centralizing decision making and control at the parent level. The difference in organizational level itself means that there will be some difference in objectives between parent and subsidiary managements, regardless who occupies the parent and subsidiary management positions. Subsidiary managers will also lack current information about other parts of the company. Thus, when decisionmaking and control for a subsidiary need to reflect parent-level concerns that are not already reflected in subsidiary-level objectives and information, staffing the subsidiary with parent nationals is likely to be a relatively weak substitute for centralized decisionmaking and control.

Next, we want to consider the impact of company-level strategic and environmental conditions on subsidiary staffing. With centralization and performance control, company-level conditions that threatened to overload the information-processing capacity of the parent HQ (that is, conditions of complexity and size) were generally found to decrease the levels of centralization and performance control a parent exercised over its foreign subsidiaries. Increasing the number of parent company nationals in foreign subsidiaries should not overload the information-processing capacity of the parent HQ, but it does increase the cost of managing a company's foreign operations. The direct cost of staffing a position in a foreign subsidiary with an expatriate is usually significantly higher than staffing it with a local national. Host country regulations frequently favor the latter as well and often require some kind of compensatory action on the part of the company (such as training assignments for local nationals in the parent company), which adds to the cost of expatriate staffing. Staffing a large number of foreign subsidiaries with parent company nationals also requires a company to develop and maintain a large cadre of senior, internationally experienced managers, which is expensive. Thus, the primary deterrent to using expatriate staffing as an information-processing mechanism seems to be economic rather than the fear of overloading the scarce information-processing capacities of the parent HQ.

This raises the question of how company-level conditions of complexity and size are likely to influence the economics of using expatriate staffing as an information-processing mechanism. The more heterogeneous or complex the international strategy and environment of an MNC, the less relevant the knowledge and skills of parent company nationals are likely to be at the local subsidiary level. Conversely, the more homogeneous a firm's international strategy and environment (especially, the more similar a firm's products are around the world and the less it has to contend with outside ownership in its foreign subsidiaries), the more useful parent company knowledge and information-processing practices should be. This line of reasoning leads to the following hypothesis:

> *Hypothesis 9–3.* As strategic and environmental complexity or heterogeneity at the company level increases, the percentage of parent company nationals in foreign subsidiaries (across the entire company) will decrease.

As the size of an MNC's foreign operations, foreign manufacturing, and the number of its foreign subsidiaries increase, the absolute cost of maintaining the expatriate group will increase, but its cost relative to foreign revenues or profits should be unaffected. This line of reasoning provides little basis for hypothesizing one way or the other any relationship between company-level size and subsidiary staffing. It could be that when the absolute size and cost of expatriate management reaches a certain level, MNCs tend to develop more cost effective alternatives, such as the extensive training of local nationals in the parent company HQ. On the other hand, really large foreign operations may cause a company to "globalize" its management, as Edstrom and Galbraith (1977) found in at least one large European MNC. In order to be consistent with the hypotheses of previous chapters, we will hypothesize a negative relationship between size and the use of parent company nationals but realize that the empirical analysis here is really exploratory:

> *Hypothesis 9–4.* As the size of a company increases, the percentage of parent company nationals in foreign subsidiaries (across the entire company) will decrease.

MEASURES OF SUBSIDIARY STAFFING

The level of parent company staffing in a foreign subsidiary was measured by first identifying, with an organization chart and the help of the respondent, the number of important management positions in a subsidiary. Generally, these were positions at the department head level and higher. Then the respondent was asked to identify which of these positions were not filled with local nationals. Third-country nationals who had previously worked elsewhere for the company were treated as parent company nationals. The percentage of important positions staffed with parent company nationals was calculated separately for marketing, manufacturing and financial positions. In addition, the study measured whether the subsidiary CEO was local national (0 percent) or parent company national (100 percent). Where the top executive position was a group of individuals composed of local as well as parent company nationals, the variable was recorded as mid-way between the two extremes (50 percent).

Table 9–1 shows the means, standard deviations, and intercorrelations among the four staffing variables. The significant positive correlation among the four variables means there is some overall tendency to staff similarly in a foreign subsidiary, across the various functional areas.

Table 9–1.   Means, Standard Deviations, and Correlation among Staffing Variables (N = 82 to 92).

	Mean	S.D.	Marketing Staffing	Manufacturing Staffing	Financial Staffing
Marketing staffing	25.6	34.3			
Manufacturing staffing	31.0	38.8	.57***		
Financial staffing	43.9	42.4	.38***	.49***	
CEO staffing	59.0	46.9	.36***	.37***	.41***

*** $p < .001$ (two-tailed test).

TESTING THE HYPOTHESES

This chapter uses the same format as the previous two chapters to test the hypotheses and analyze the relationship between subsidiary staffing and the various company and subsidiary-level strategic and environmental conditions. The seven company-level conditions that measure complexity and size are used to test Hypotheses 9–3 and 9–4. The fourteen subsidiary-level conditions that measure interdependency and change will be used to test Hypotheses 9–1 and 9–2.

Table 9–2 shows the correlations between the four staffing variables and the seven company-level and fourteen subsidiary-level strategic and environmental conditions. Figure 9–1 shows only those contingency conditions that share statistically significant correlations with a staffing variable and more clearly reveals the extent to which these relationships support or contradict the four hypotheses.

Table 9–2. Correlation between Subsidiary Staffing and Strategic and Environmental Conditions (N = 69 to 94).

	Marketing Staffing	Manufacturing Staffing	Financial Staffing	CEO Staffing
Company-Level Conditions				
Foreign product diversity	-.15	.08	-.01	-.08
Product modification differences	-.06	-.19*	-.08	-.18*
Extent of outside ownership	-.01	.10	-.03	.04
Extent of foreign acquisitions	.02	.03	-.10	-.19
Size of foreign operations	.08	.17	-.04	-.13
Size of foreign manufacturing	-.26*	-.38***	-.09	-.16
Number of foreign subsidiaries	-.20*	-.08	.03	-.02
Subsidiary-Level Conditions				
Marketing information dependency	.01	.15	.04	.11
Sales dependency	.04	.22*	.10	.06
New manufacturing information dependency	.12	.13	.26**	.35***
Day-to-day manufacturing information dependency	.04	.17	-.03	.18*
New product design dependency	.18*	.18	.19*	.28**
Product design change dependency	.23*	.23*	.16	.12
Importance of subsidiary	.01	-.22	-.19	-.19
Intracompany purchases by subsidiary	-.09	0	-.07	-.11
Intracompany sales by subsidiary	-.17	-.22	-.12	-.18
Product change	.12	.09	-.01	0
Manufacturing technology change	.08	.26**	.04	.19*
Political environment change	.27**	.28**	.18*	.29**
Competitive climate change	.21*	.06	0	.20*
Supplier situation change	.42***	.42***	.27**	.21*

* p < .05 (one-tailed test); ** p < .01; *** p < .001.

Note: Correlations involving product modification differences, extent of outside ownership, and the extent of foreign acquisitions are Kendall's tau, since these variables are only assumed to be ordinal. The remainder are Pearson correlations. A two-tailed test was applied to those relationships that contradicted the hypothesized relationship.

All of the statistically significant correlations with elements of company-level strategy and environment are negative. While these results tend to support Hypotheses 9–3 and 9–4, it is notable that the number of significant relationships between company-level conditions and staffing are fewer than for centralization and performance control (see Figures 7–1 and 8–1).

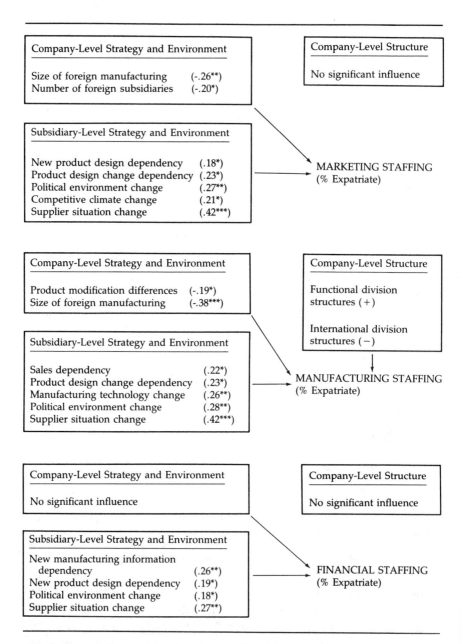

Figure 9–1. The Determinants of Subsidiary Staffing.

Figure 9–1. (continued)

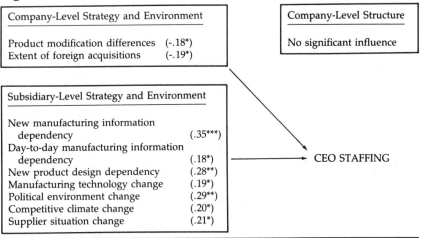

Company-Level Strategy and Environment	
Product modification differences	(-.18*)
Extent of foreign acquisitions	(-.19*)

Company-Level Structure
No significant influence

Subsidiary-Level Strategy and Environment	
New manufacturing information dependency	(.35***)
Day-to-day manufacturing information dependency	(.18*)
New product design dependency	(.28**)
Manufacturing technology change	(.19*)
Political environment change	(.29**)
Competitive climate change	(.20*)
Supplier situation change	(.21*)

CEO STAFFING

Numbers in parentheses are correlation coefficients with staffing.
* $p < .05$ (one-tailed test); ** $p < .01$; *** $p < .001$.

When product modification differences among subsidiaries are great, there is less of a tendency to staff the subsidiary CEO and manufacturing positions with expatriates than when product modification differences are low. This is consistent with the logic underlying Hypothesis 9–3. Expatriate management is most useful when the knowledge and information-processing capabilities it represents transcend local differences. When local differences dominate, the most important kinds of knowledge and information-processing capabilities are likely to lie with local national managers. Similarly, firms that grow by making foreign acquisitions are less likely to have expatriate CEOs in the foreign subsidiaries. A growth strategy involving foreign acquisitions is likely to emphasize local strengths and advantages not based on those of the parent company, and this calls for local knowledge rather than parent company knowledge. Frequently, the acquisition of competent local national management is a driving force behind such a growth strategy.

Although the overall size of an MNC's foreign operations seems to have little effect on staffing, the size of foreign manufacturing is quite negatively related to expatriate staffing. This tends to support Hypothesis 9–4, but, as was indicated earlier, we really do not have a clear logic for making this hypothesis or interpreting the empirical results. Large foreign manufacturing operations in a company may imply (1) relatively sophisticated subsidiary managements that are less dependent on the parent for information (especially manufacturing information) or (2) so

many foreign management positions (especially manufacturing management positions) that it is not feasible to staff a high percentage of
them with parent company managers. The second reason may also
explain the negative correlation between the number of foreign subsidiaries and the use of expatriate marketing managers. These findings
involving the influence of size on staffing need to be regarded as exploratory and in need of further explanation the study cannot provide.

Figure 9–1 also shows that all of the significant correlations between
the four staffing variables and the fourteen subsidiary-level conditions
are positive. This supports Hypotheses 9–1 and 9–2. Especially notable
is the influence of the change variables on staffing (manufacturing technology change, political environment change, competitive climate
change, and supplier situation change). Foreign subsidiaries that face
high rates of change in their strategies and environments clearly tend to
be staffed with higher percentages of expatriate managers than subsidiaries that face low rates of change.

Manufacturing information dependency and product design dependency also tend to be quite positively linked to expatriate staffing. Two
subsidiary-level conditions—the importance of the subsidiary (its sales
as a percentage of the company's foreign sales) and its intracompany
sales or exports—are both negatively linked to expatriate staffing.
Although none of these correlations are statistically significant, this
seeming contradiction of Hypothesis 9–1 requires some discussion.
That the largest subsidiaries in an MNC have relatively lower percentages of expatriate managers makes sense because the development of
competent local managers has usually proceeded the furthest in these
subsidiaries. Similarly, subsidiaries that manufacture and export significant volumes of product to other subsidiaries probably tend to have
relatively sophisticated local managements, or the parent would not
have decided to make the additional direct investment in the subsidiary. Although both of these conditions create important interdependencies between a subsidiary and the parent HQ, expatriate staffing may
not be the best way to coordinate this kind of interdependency or satisfy its associated information-processing requirements. If local subsidiary managements are competent, this kind of interdependency is routine, long-term, and stable. Its information-processing requirements are
also routine, and it would appear that the sample companies tend to
cope with it by increasing the centralization of marketing and financial
decisions for the subsidiary (see Table 7–2), as well as the level of performance control exercised over manufacturing operations (see Table 8–

2). Both appear to be more economical and suitable forms of information processing than expatriate staffing.

The influence of structure on subsidiary staffing was also examined, using analysis of variance among the four types of elementary structure. As indicated in Figure 9–1, a statistically significant difference was only encountered for manufacturing staffing. Here the percentage of expatriate management tends to be greatest in functional division companies and lowest in firms with an international division structure.

THE INFLUENCE OF OTHER FACTORS ON SUBSIDIARY STAFFING

Following the procedure used in the previous chapters, the study also examined the influence of the six other factors on the level of expatriate staffing in foreign subsidiaries. These factors are size of company, age of company abroad, size of subsidiary, age of subsidiary, parent company nationality, and industry. Measurement of these factors was described in Chapter 4. While lacking direct information-processing implications, these factors are often thought to influence or share important relationships with various aspects of organizational design.

Table 9–3 shows the correlations between the four staffing variables and these other factors. Only nationality shares any significant relationships with subsidiary staffing. Table 9–4 shows that European MNCs tend to have the greatest percentage of parent company nationals staffing important subsidiary positions, while UK MNCs tend to have the least. U.S. MNCs tend to fall in between, although the percentage for CEO staffing is nearly equal to that of the European MNCs. As was done in the previous chapters, the correlations shown in Table 9–2 between control and the strategic and environmental conditions were rerun for each of the three nationality groups. The subsample patterns are generally similar to the total sample pattern, although the UK subsample neither supported nor contradicted the general pattern for manufacturing staffing and the European subsample also showed less support for this pattern than the U.S. subsample.

The effects of industry on subsidiary staffing are shown in the Appendix. They are significant for marketing and manufacturing staffing, where automobile and industrial equipment companies have the highest percentage of expatriate management and electrical and telecommunications equipment and pharmaceutical companies the least. The chemical companies also tend to have a high percentage of manufacturing, but not marketing, expatriate management.

Table 9–3. Correlation between Subsidiary Staffing and Other Factors ($N = 76$ to 94).

	Marketing Staffing	Manufacturing Staffing	Financial Staffing	CEO Staffing
Size of company	.11	-.01	.05	.04
Age of company abroad	.11	-.05	-.08	.01
Size of subsidiary	.13	-.02	-.09	-.07
Age of subsidiary	.16	.03	.06	.04
Nationality of parent company (dummy variables):				
U.S.	-.17	-.19	-.03	.07
UK	-.14	-.27*	-.08	-.21*
European	.27*	.39***	.09	.08

* $p < .05$ (two-tailed test); *** $p < .001$.
Note: Correlations are Pearson correlations.

Table 9–4. Subsidiary Staffing by Parent Country Nationality ($N = 86$ to 94).

	U.S.	UK	European	F
Marketing staffing	20	14	37	3.5*
Manufacturing staffing	24	6	51	8.9***
Financial staffing	42	35	49	.5
CEO staffing	62	33	64	2.1

* $p < .05$ (two-tailed test); *** $p < .001$.

THE RELATIVE INFLUENCE OF COMPANY-LEVEL AND SUBSIDIARY-LEVEL CONDITIONS ON SUBSIDIARY STAFFING

While all four hypotheses tended to be supported, it is apparent that subsidiary-level strategic and environmental conditions have more influence on the staffing of foreign subsidiaries than do company-level conditions. The purpose of this section is to more systematically evaluate the relative strengths of these two sets of contingency variables.

Following the procedure used in the previous two chapters, a number of regression analyses were run. First, the two company-level conditions that shared a significant correlation with marketing staffing (see Figure 9–1) were regressed on marketing staffing and the adjusted R^2 or percentage of variation in marketing staffing that could be explained by company-level conditions was noted. Next, the five subsidiary-level conditions that also shared significant correlations with marketing staffing were entered into the same regression model in order to determine how much additional variation in marketing staffing could be explained by subsidiary-level conditions once company-level conditions were already included in the model. In this case, the increase in adjusted R^2 or percentage of variation explained was 19 percent. Then the procedure was repeated, this time entering the subsidiary-level conditions first, followed by the company-level conditions. This second analysis was to determine the increase in adjusted R^2 or percentage of variation in marketing staffing explained by company-level conditions once subsidiary-level conditions were already included in the model (in this case only 1 percent). This same set of analyses was repeated for manufacturing, financial, and CEO staffing, in each case using as the independent variables those company and subsidiary-level conditions, from Figure 9–1, which shared statistically significant correlations with the respective staffing variable.

Because of its considerable length, a table similar to Table 7–5 in Chapter 7 (which more fully presents the step-wise regression runs) will not be included in this chapter. The procedure used to interpret the step-wise regression runs, however, is exactly the same as was used in Chapter 7. The reader can refer back to Chapter 7 to see how the step-wise regression runs were analyzed to produce the results shown in Figure 7–2 and know that the same procedure was used to produce the results shown in Figure 9–2.

Figure 9–2 is a pictorial representation of the contributions made by company- and subsidiary-level conditions to explain each of the four types of staffing. The information is taken from the regression runs. The percentage of variation shown alongside the "shared" arrow can be explained by either set of variables, while the other two percentages represent the additional variation that can be explained only by the respective company or subsidiary-level conditions.

A number of important conclusions can be drawn from this analysis. Staffing in foreign subsidiaries seems to be largely influenced by subsidiary-level conditions. When local subsidiary strategic and environmental conditions call for more information processing between the subsidiary and the parent, there is a consistent tendency to assign more parent nationals to the subsidiary. Company-level strategic and environmental conditions apparently play a very minor role in staffing decisions. For financial and CEO staffing, company-level conditions can provide no additional explanation of staffing patterns beyond what has already been explained by subsidiary-level conditions. Only for manufacturing staffing do company-level conditions seem to have much influence on staffing patterns. And even here, most of the explanation of variation in manufacturing staffing (9 percent) overlaps or is confounded with the explanation provided by subsidiary-level conditions. Thus, unlike centralization and most areas of performance control, subsidiary staffing appears to be an information-processing mechanism that is primarily responsive to subsidiary-level conditions.

It is also worth noting that financial staffing does not appear to be nearly as responsive to variations in strategy and environment as the other three staffing areas. This is interesting, given that the standard deviation of financial staffing is reasonably high compared to the deviations of the other staffing areas (see Table 9–1). Thus, while financial staffing does vary across the subsidiaries in the sample, the strategic and environmental conditions, as well as the other factors, are not explaining very much of this variation.

In addition to partialing out the variation in subsidiary staffing that can be explained by company- and subsidiary-level conditions, the regression analyses reported in Figure 9–2 also reveal how much additional variation can be explained by the other factors. This was accomplished by adding the other factors previously identified in Table 9–3 as having a statistically significant relationship with a staffing variable, to the regression model after company- and subsidiary-level conditions were already entered. The increases in adjusted R^2 that were observed when the appropriate other factors were entered are 1 percent for marketing staffing (contributed by nationality), 4 percent for manufacturing staffing (contributed by nationality), and 0 percent for both financial and CEO staffing. Thus, the other factors provide very little explanation beyond that already provided by those strategic and environmental conditions with information-processing implications.

DISCUSSION

This chapter has attempted to understand how the staffing of an MNC's foreign subsidiaries is influenced by the organization's strategy and environment. The conceptual framework used in this chapter has viewed expatriate staffing as another parent-subsidiary information-processing mechanism. The capabilities for parent-subsidiary information processing are viewed as greater when important management positions in a foreign subsidiary are staffed with parent company nationals rather than local nationals. The reasoning is that parent company nationals will possess more of the values and knowledge of the

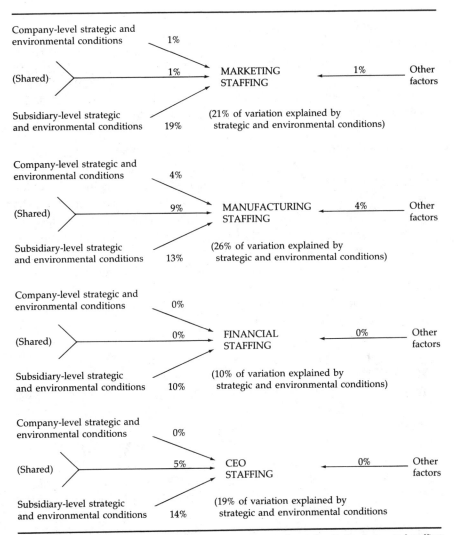

Note: The figures alongside the arrows show the percentage of variation in the designated staffing measure that can be uniquely explained by company-level conditions, subsidiary-level conditions, or, alternatively, by either.

Figure 9–2. How Company- and Subsidiary-Level Conditions Explain Subsidiary Staffing.

parent and better personal communication networks with individuals in the parent HQ than will local national managers. In companies where local national managers have spent significant periods of time at the parent HQ or as expatriate managers in other foreign subsidiaries, this reasoning and the distinction made between the information-processing capabilities of parent company nationals versus local national managers will, perhaps, tend to disappear. As Edstrom and Galbraith (1977) seem to indicate, however, such companies appear to be few in number.

Consistent with the approach used in previous chapters, this chapter has examined and sought to explain subsidiary staffing patterns as the joint product of two different levels of contingency variables. Unlike the findings of previous chapters, however, subsidiary staffing seems to be largely the product of local subsidiary strategic and environmental conditions. Company-level conditions would appear to play only a minor role in determining staffing patterns.

The level of change reflected in a subsidiary's strategy and environment seems to have a major influence on its staffing pattern (see Table 9–2). When political environment change and supplier situation change are high in a subsidiary, increasing requirements for parent-subsidiary information processing, all management areas in the subsidiary tend to be staffed with a greater percentage of parent company nationals. A higher level of manufacturing technology change leads to more parent company nationals in manufacturing and the CEO positions, while more change in the competitive climate is associated with more parent company nationals in marketing and the CEO positions. These types of change are generally associated with high levels of uncertainty and consequently should require more unstructured or nonroutine information processing between a subsidiary and the parent. Staffing would seem to be a common way of providing this kind of information-processing capacity in the sample companies.

Product change, which is the percentage increase or decrease in a subsidiary's product line over the past five years, would appear to be a different kind of change. It is usually more routine and predictable, less associated with uncertainty, and therefore should be more amenable to routine planning and control processes than the previous types of change (Argote 1982). This could be the reason why product change is so unrelated to staffing, but so significantly related to performance control and, to a lesser extent, centralization (see Tables 8–2 and 7–2). Thus, there seems to be some indication in the data that the kind of information processing provided by staffing is different from the kind provided by centralization and performance control.

Most of the variables measuring interdependency between a subsidiary and the parent are also positively correlated with staffing. New manufacturing information dependency, new product design dependency and product design change dependency are the conditions most strongly connected to the use of more parent company nationals in staffing a foreign subsidiary. Once again, these kinds of interdependency would seem to be associated with more uncertainty than some of the other conditions that do not share such strong relationships with staffing. As discussed above in "Testing the Hypotheses," the importance of a subsidiary (as measured by its percentage of a company's foreign sales) and the extent to which it imports or exports products to the rest of the company are interdependencies that usually can be coordinated with more routine and economical forms of information processing. This tends to support the suggestion made in the previous paragraph, that staffing foreign subsidiaries with parent company nationals seems to be providing a different kind of information-processing capacity than centralization or performance control.

Although the influence of company-level conditions on subsidiary staffing appears to be relatively unimportant, all of the significant correlations between these conditions and staffing are negative and support the hypotheses. The reasoning presented above in "An Information-Processing Model" was that company-level conditions of complexity and size should not constrain the use of expatriate staffing the way they constrain the use of centralization or performance control. As strategic and environmental complexity and organizational size increase, they threaten to overload the limited information-processing capacities of parent HQs that rely heavily on centralization and performance control to manage their foreign subsidiaries. A heavy use of expatriate staffing, on the other hand, does not threaten the parent HQ with information-processing overload. Instead, we have argued that there is a likely tendency for expatriate staffing to become less useful as company-level complexity increases and less economical as international operations become large. While the quantitative data cannot directly test this line of reasoning, they are at least consistent with it.

Indeed, the few company-level conditions that seem to share some relationship with subsidiary staffing are not so much limitations on the company's ability to staff subsidiary positions with parent company nationals as they are reasons why it might be less important or useful to do so. A high level of foreign manufacture instead of parent exports, more local product modification differences, and growth through foreign acquisitions tend to reduce the operating interdependencies between a parent and its foreign subsidiaries and with this the need to directly influence subsidiary decision making and control processes by staffing key positions with parent company nationals.

Centralization and, to a lesser extent, performance control systems tend to be more consistent across all parent-subsidiary relationships in a company and to vary more from one company to another. Consequently, they are largely determined or respond to constraints that exist at the company level. Naturally, these features can be altered to some extent to fit subsidiary-level conditions, but the capacity to do this is limited by the generally stronger requirement to fit the company-level constraints. Subsidiary staffing, on the other hand, faces no strong company-level constraints. Aside from economic cost and the availability of parent company managers for foreign positions, there are no real constraints at the company level. There are only a few general conditions that either favor or do not favor a high level of parent influence at the subsidiary level. Thus, subsidiary staffing appears to be the most flexible and perhaps the most useful mechanism for adapting the information-processing capacities of a specific parent-subsidiary relationship to better fit the unique strategic and environmental conditions surrounding it.

The residual influence of such other factors as nationality, size of company, age of company abroad, size of subsidiary, and age of subsidiary on staffing can also be seen in Figure 9–2. While nationality has a strong association with marketing and manufacturing staffing (see Table 9–4), its influence is greatly reduced after taking into consideration the previous impacts of company and subsidiary-level conditions on control. It still continues to explain 4 percent of the variation in manufacturing staffing, which reflects the fact that European MNCs tend to staff a greater percentage of manufacturing positions with expatriates than U.S. or UK MNCs do. The present study supports the Hulbert and Brandt (1980) conclusion that relative to European MNCs, U.S. MNCs rely more on "system" (centralization, performance control) than "man" (expatriate staffing) to manage their foreign subsidiaries. Yet it appears that such differences in organizational design tend to accompany differences in strategy and environment, which can alternatively explain much of the variation.

It is interesting that none of the measures of size and age for the subsidiary or the company have a significant relationship to the staffing variables. This may appear to contradict Youssef's (1975) findings that subsidiary size and age were important predictors of expatriate staffing in foreign subsidiaries. Yet his sample was confined to the newest subsidiary in each company, and the present study may simply be saying that his findings cannot be generalized across older subsidiaries in MNCs. Because subsidiary staffing is one of the most flexible and least formal aspects of organizational design, it is perhaps not surprising that size and age, which are frequently linked to the more formal and bureaucratic aspects of organizations, have no particular influence on it.

Chapter 8 concluded by suggesting that centralization and performance control are part of the same managerial system and that they should not be viewed as alternative approaches to managing the parent-subsidiary relationship. Chapter 9 has suggested that staffing foreign subsidiaries with parent company nationals provides a different kind of information-processing capacity than centralization or performance control, and therefore one might expect its use to be generally independent of the degree of centralization or performance control in an MNC. Table 9–5 shows that for the sample companies, subsidiary staffing is not correlated with either centralization or performance control. While some research (Doz and Prahalad 1981; Jaeger 1982) suggests that staffing foreign subsidiaries with parent company nationals could facilitate more decentralized management, the present study has found that the two are relatively independent of each other. This suggests that expatriate staffing is used more to complement the information-processing capacities provided by centralization and performance control than to replace them. This proposition is consistent with the view suggested by Edstrom and Galbraith (1977) that the assignment of expatriate managers to foreign subsidiaries can lead to a new form of control by socialization, which augments the more bureaucratic forms of control.

Table 9–5. Correlation of Subsidiary Staffing with Centralization and Control ($N = 79$ to 94).

	Marketing Staffing	Manufacturing Staffing	Financial Staffing	CEO Staffing
Marketing centralization	.16	.01	-.06	.01
Manufacturing centralization	.12	.18	-.03	.18
Financial centralization	0	-.01	.12	-.18
Marketing control	-.02	-.05	-.07	-.15
Manufacturing control	-.03	-.06	.02	-.15
Financial control	.06	.04	-.09	-.02

Note: Two-tailed test of significance.

At the beginning of this chapter, it was stated that staffing is still an important dimension of organizational design for MNCs but that its role and reason for being important has probably changed over time. Originally, staffing a foreign subsidiary with parent company nationals was probably a substitute for the centralization and performance control that a parent could not exercise over the subsidiary because of distance and poor communications. For some MNCs that have not developed elaborate planning, control, and approval systems, expatriate staffing may still be largely a substitute for a more bureaucratic form of control (some smaller U.S. and European MNCs may fall in this category). The large, successful MNCs in our sample, however, tend to already have well-developed bureaucratic systems of control. And for them, expatriate staffing seems to have evolved into a new role. Although we did not hypothesize this role, the data seem to indicate that for these companies, expatriate staffing tends to be used when subsidiary-level uncertainty is greatest to provide more nonroutine information-processing capacity between parent and subsidiary. In this role, expatriate staffing tends to augment rather than substitute for more bureaucratic forms of control.

10

PLANNING SYSTEMS

Formal business and corporate-level planning systems are generally thought to be essential for managing large organizations such as MNCs (Dymsza 1984). Yet anyone who has looked at recent planning articles or read the planning literature soon realizes that this is one of the most difficult areas in which to do empirical research. There is very little agreement about how to describe or measure one company's planning system so that it can be meaningfully compared to another company's planning system. This chapter takes an information-processing perspective of planning and its relationship to the strategic and environmental conditions facing MNCs.

PREVIOUS RESEARCH AND THEORY

The literature on business and corporate-level planning systems can be divided into three primary streams. One stream has sought to empirically relate formal planning to organizational performance (Ansoff et al. 1970; Thune and House 1970; Herold 1972; Karger and Milik 1975; Wood and La Forge 1979). Here the results have produced a mixed picture, although they generally favor the view that formal planning contributes to performance (Armstrong 1982). A second stream has concentrated on conceptually examining the limitations of formal planning and generally argues for a less formal and more incremental approach to planning (Lindblom 1959; Mintzberg 1978; Quinn 1980; Bresser and Bishop 1983). These researchers point out that formal planning tends to suppress creativity and spontaneity and instead encourages a rigidity in organizational behavior that is often dysfunctional. The third stream of research has sought to link various characteristics of formal planning processes to various characteristics of the planning situation in an attempt to develop a contingency theory of planning (McCaskey 1974; Lindsay and Rue 1980; Boulton et al. 1982; Javidan 1984; Grinyer, Al-Bazzaz, and Yasai-Ardekani 1986). While there are a number of studies which compare planning practices across countries (Kono 1976; Gotcher 1977; Gouy 1978; Capon et al. 1984), few studies have focused on planning practices within MNCs (Hulbert and Brandt 1980).

The present study falls under the contingency stream of research, but it attempts to address—with an information-processing perspective— some of the key issues raised by the first two research streams. At the present time, the contingency approach to understanding formal planning systems is still in a more formative stage than it is for structure, centralization, or control. What aspects of planning systems to measure and what kind of contingency variables are most important are still very open questions.

AN INFORMATION-PROCESSING MODEL OF PLANNING AND ITS RELATIONSHIP TO STRATEGY AND ENVIRONMENT

Galbraith (1973) includes planning and goal setting as one of the five basic types of information-processing mechanisms available to organizations (see Chapter 2). Yet he seems to view the plans or goals that result from a planning process as the primary information-processing implications of planning. Within established plans or goals, subunits can perform interdependent subtasks, confident that they will be properly coordinated or integrated. This is the traditional view of how planning coordinates and integrates. Differing somewhat from Galbraith's approach, the present study focuses more on the information-processing implications of the planning process itself, rather than on the goals or plans it produces.

As indicated above, selecting the actual planning variables to be measured represented a major problem. Previous research has measured a variety of different aspects of planning, but to date, no real convergence about what is meaningful or important has emerged. Hulbert and Brandt (1980) present one of the most complete descriptions of planning processes in foreign subsidiaries. In addition to this description, the present study used a number of preliminary interviews with executives in several MNCs to discover how managers described the short- and long-range planning processes in their companies and to ascertain which characteristics would be measurable. As a result, a number of planning characteristics were selected because (1) they seemed to measure the information-processing capacities of a planning system or planning process and (2) they appeared measurable in structured interviews.

Despite these precautions, a number of the characteristics could not be described by the respondents during the interviews, and in other cases it became apparent that the questions were not producing a consistent measure of the intended concepts. In the end, the study produced a relatively modest number of usable planning variables. Two sets of planning variables were selected for presentation in this chapter because they appear to best illustrate the information-processing implications of planning processes. Six variables measured the degree to which three critical steps in both the short-and long-range planning processes were centralized or decentralized. All MNCs in the sample had both a formal short-range plan and a formal long-range plan. The short-range plan generally went out one year (that is, an annual plan), although in a few cases it also included a second year in less detail. The planning horizon for the long-range plan varied from three to ten years, but for 70 percent of the sample companies it was five years. The three steps for which degree of centralization was measured were the setting of planning bases, the development of planning alternatives, and the choosing among alternatives.

A second set of three variables was used to measure different aspects of the intensity of parent-subsidiary communications during the short-range or annual planning process: (1) the intensity of communications during the building of the plan, (2) whether face-to-face meetings were used to review the plan, and (3) the extent to which new issues tended to be raised during the review of the plan. These variables differ from those used in previous studies, but all seem to have predictable information-processing implications and should therefore contribute to an information-processing perspective of planning in MNCs. The remainder of this section discusses these implications and attempts to draw testable hypotheses from them. Measurement of the variables is described in the following section.

Whether key decisions in the foreign subsidiaries' planning processes are centralized at either the divisional HQ or parent HQ levels or left with the foreign subsidiaries influences the level of information-processing capacity a planning process provides for integrating subsidiary strategies and activities at either the divisional or total company levels. Centralizing planning decisions should be an effective information-processing mechanism between the parent and its foreign subsidiaries for the same reasons that centralizing operating decisions is effective (see Chapter 7). Guth (1976) has pointed out that strategic change or strategic decisionmaking tends to be "disjointed incrementalism" if there is significant decentralization or fragmentation of decisionmaking in organizations. When a parent HQ is involved in setting the planning bases for foreign subsidiaries, developing planning alternatives, and choosing among the possible alternatives, there is an opportunity to input parent-level knowledge and values into the planning of subsidiary-level strategy. When such centralization occurs, there is likely to be more integration among individual subsidiary strategies and more congruence between them and parent-level strategies.

The limitations of planning centralization as an effective information-processing and integrating mechanism across the parent-subsidiary relationship are also similar to those described for the centralization of operating decisions in Chapter 7. As the complexity of an organization's strategy and environment and the size of an organization increase, centralization tends to overload the limited information-processing capacities of the divisional and parent HQs. This leads to the following hypotheses:

Hypothesis 10–1. As strategic and environmental complexity or heterogeneity at the company level increases, planning decisionmaking for all foreign subsidiaries in a company will be more decentralized.

Hypothesis 10–2. As the size of a company increases, planning decisionmaking for all foreign subsidiaries in the company will be more decentralized.

The second set of planning characteristics measured in the study describes the intensity of parent-subsidiary communications during the short-range or annual planning process. Unlike the previous characteristics, which were measured for each company, these characteristics were measured for each of the ninty-four parent-subsidiary relationships in the sample. Therefore, these characteristics need to be conceptually linked to both company-level and subsidiary-level strategy and environment.

When interdependency between a subsidiary and the parent is great and there is considerable change in the strategic and environmental conditions facing a subsidiary, information-processing requirements between the subsidiary and the parent will be relatively high. The previous chapters have found that MNCs tend to address this requirement with increased centralization, more performance control, and higher levels of expatriate staffing. Another potentially important information-processing mechanism might be the annual planning process. By (1) increasing the intensity of parent-subsidiary communications during the building of the plan, (2) using face-to-face meetings between parent and subsidiary management when the plan is reviewed, and (3) raising many new issues during the review process, an MNC can increase the information-processing capacity provided by the annual planning process and better cope with the increased requirements stemming from greater interdependency and change. This line of reasoning leads to the following hypotheses:

> *Hypothesis 10–3.* As a subsidiary's interdependency with the rest of the organization increases, the three intensity variables (that is, the intensity of parent-subsidiary communications during the building of the annual plan, the use of face-to-face meetings when the plan is reviewed, and the raising of new issues during the review) will tend to increase.

> *Hypothesis 10–4.* As the degree of change inherent in a subsidiary's strategy and environment increases, the three intensity variables will tend to increase.

Just as conditions that increase requirements for information processing between a subunit and the rest of the organization should tend to increase parent-subsidiary communications during the annual planning process, conditions that threaten to overload the information-processing capacity of the parent should decrease the attractiveness of using the annual planning process as an information-processing mechanism. HQ management and staff can quickly become overloaded if they engage in intense communication and face-to-face reviews with too many foreign subsidiaries and attempt to discuss too many different issues and problems. When international strategies and environments of firms are relatively simple or homogeneous, there is less danger of overloading the information-processing capacities of the HQ than when international strategies and environments are complex.

Similarly, when foreign operations are relatively small, communications with any given subsidiary can be more intense, fewer review meetings are required, and there should be more time to raise new issues. In other words, decreased size should reduce the danger of overloading the information-processing capacity of the HQ. Thus, in addition to subsidiary-level interdependency and change, company-level complexity and size can potentially influence and constrain the level of parent-subsidiary communications that can occur during the planning process:

> *Hypothesis 10–5.* As strategic and environmental complexity at the company level increase, the three intensity variables will tend to decrease.

> *Hypothesis 10–6.* As the size of a company increases, the three intensity variables will tend to decrease.

PLANNING MEASURES

The degree to which planning decisions are centralized was measured at the company level as a generalization across all parent-subsidiary relationships in a company. The decision to measure these six centralization variables as company-level phenomena was made after preliminary interviews with a number of executives in several MNCs indicated that these relationships tended not to vary much from one parent-subsidiary relationship to another and that generalization across all such relationships in a company appeared reasonable. As will be discussed later, this still appears a reasonable assumption, but it is admittedly a weakness of the study that it remains an assumption rather than an empirically supported fact. The reason that these variables were not measured at the subsidiary level was time constraints during the interviews. Following the pretest, the subsidiary-level interview instrument had to be shortened in order to stay within the requested time period, and this was one area where it appeared reasonable to move questions from the subsidiary-level interview to the company-level interview.

The degree to which planning decisions are centralized was measured by asking the company-level respondent to describe the short-range or annual planning process for foreign subsidiaries and then to specify how and at what level (1) planning bases were set, (2) planning alternatives were developed and analyzed, and (3) choice among alternatives took place. The same question was then repeated for the long-range planning process. Answers were subsequently coded using the following five-point scale to measure hierarchical level: (1) subsidiary, (2) jointly by subsidiary and divisional HQ (international division, geographical region, or product division HQ), (3) divisional HQ, (4) jointly by divisional HQ and parent HQ (or, for firms with worldwide functional division structures, jointly by subsidiary and parent HQ), and (5) parent HQ.

Table 10–1 shows the means, standard deviations, and intercorrelation among all nine planning variables, including the six planning centralization variables. An examination of the means reveals that long-range planning decisions are generally more centralized (are made further up the hierarchy) than are short-range planning decisions. The patterns within the short- and long-range planning processes, however, are similar. Developing alternatives is the most decentralized part of the planning process, and it is generally done either at the subsidiary level or shared by the subsidiary and divisional HQs' managements. Setting the planning bases is the most centralized part of the planning process, and it generally involves the divisional and sometimes the parent HQ managements. Choosing among alternatives generally lies between the two extremes.

Table 10–1. Means, Standard Deviations, and Correlation among Planning Variables.

	Mean	S.D.	1	2	3	4	5	6	7	8
Company-Level Variables (N = 42 to 45)										
Short-range planning process:										
1. Setting planning bases	2.0	.9								
2. Developing alternatives	1.3	.8	.64***							
3. Choosing among alternatives	1.7	1.0	.79***	.66***						
Long-range planning process:										
4. Setting planning bases	2.7	1.0	.57***	.44**	.54***					
5. Developing alternatives	1.8	1.0	.61***	.66***	.63***	.68***				
6. Choosing among alternatives	2.5	1.1	.56***	.53***	.74***	.66***	.71***			
Subsidiary-Level Variables (N = 93 to 94)										
Short range planning intensity:										
7. Intensity of communications	2.7	1.1	-.05	.11	.15	0	.16	.17		
8. Face-to-face meetings	.8	.4	.14	.13	.21	-.11	-.03	-.06	.16	
9. Extent new issues raised	2.9	1.5	-.10	-.09	-.03	-.13	-.05	-.15	.35***	.32**

*** p < .001 (two-tailed test); ** p < .01.

The strong positive correlations among the planning centralization variables mean that if one of the three types of planning decisions is centralized in a company (such as setting planning bases), the other two types of planning decisions (developing alternatives and choosing among alternatives) will also be relatively centralized. The strong positive correlations between the short-range and long-range planning centralization variables mean that this relationship tends to be true even across the short-range and long-range planning processes.

In addition to the above planning variables measured at the company level, the study also measured three short-range planning variables for each of the ninty-four parent-subsidiary relationships in the sample (that is, subsidiary-level variables). These are described below:

1. *Intensity of communications.* The extent to which the subsidiary communicates with the divisional or parent HQ while building the short-range plan. Measured with the following scale:

   1. Not at all,
   2. Only with regard to the original planning bases,
   3. Generally ask the parent for more information while building the plan,
   4. Tend to present problems and alternatives to the parent for discussion and/or advice while building the plan,
   5. We almost build the plan together.

2. *Face-to-face meetings.* Whether or not there are face-to-face meetings between parent and subsidiary managements to discuss the short range plan when it is submitted (no = 0, yes = 1).

3. *New issues raised.* The extent to which the review raises new issues that result in further exchanges of information between the parent and the subsidiary. Measured on a five-point scale varying from "hardly ever" to "almost always."

The first variable measures the intensity of parent-subsidiary communications while the annual plan is being built. The five levels of communications intensity were established during the pretest of the structured interview instrument in several companies and were found to adequately represent the range of possibilities for communications between HQ and subsidiary managements. The two other variables measured aspects of the parent's review process (whether or not the review included face-to-face meetings between parent and subsidiary managements, and the extent to which new issues were raised by the review).

Table 10–1 shows the means, standard deviations, and intercorrelation among the three short-range planning intensity variables. The positive correlations among the three variables indicate that if a parent-subsidiary relationship is characterized by high information processing in one of these aspects of planning, there is some tendency for it to be characterized by high information processing in the other aspects as well. Face-to-face meetings between parent and subsidiary managements during the review process are only marginally related to the intensity of parent-subsidiary communications during the annual plan building process. They are, however, more strongly associated with the raising of new issues during the review. Interestingly, the extent of parent-subsidiary communications during the building process is also strongly and positively related to the raising of new issues during the review.

Table 10–1 also shows the correlation between the planning centralization variables and the short-range planning intensity variables. While none of the correlations are statistically significant, the pattern is interesting. The more centralized the development of planning alternatives and the choosing among alternatives are in a company, the greater the intensity of parent-subsidiary communications during the building of the short range plan. This makes sense. Face-to-face review meetings between parent and subsidiary managements are more prevalent when short-range planning decisions are centralized than when they are decentralized. Finally, the centralization of planning decisions appears to be negatively, although weakly, linked to the extent to which new issues are raised during the short-range planning review process. One must be careful not to read too much into these weak correlations, but the patterns and their consistency do suggest some interesting hypotheses for future research—hypotheses that could further an information-processing perspective of planning systems.

TESTING THE HYPOTHESES FOR PLANNING CENTRALIZATION

This section tests Hypotheses 10–1 and 10–2, which deal with planning centralization. The chapter subsequently tests the remaining four hypotheses, which deal with short range planning intensity. The seven company-level conditions that measure complexity and size will be used to test Hypotheses 10–1 and 10–2. Table 10–2 shows the correlations between the six planning centralization variables and the seven company-level strategic and environmental conditions. All of the statistically significant correlations are negative, which tends to support Hypotheses 10–1 and 10–2. As foreign product diversity, product modification differences between foreign subsidiaries, the extent of foreign acquisitions, the size of foreign manufacturing, and the number of foreign subsidiaries increase, there is a noticeable tendency to decentralize the key decisions of the short range planning process. This pattern is similar, although weaker, than the one previously observed between the centralization of operating decisions and strategic and environmental complexity and size. In this case, decentralization buffers or protects the divisional and parent HQs from information-processing overload as strategic and environmental complexity and size increase.

Table 10–2. Correlation between Planning Centralization and Company-Level Strategic and Environmental Conditions ($N = 34$ to 45).

	Short-Range Planning Centralization			Long-Range Planning Centralization		
	Bases Setting	Alternative Development	Alternative Choosing	Bases Setting	Alternative Development	Alternative Choosing
Foreign product diversity	-.30*	-.24	-.38**	.01	-.03	-.10
Product modification differences	-.15	-.25*	-.24*	-.17	-.21	-.22*
Extent of outside ownership	-.02	-.12	-.11	.06	.10	-.08
Extent of foreign acquisitions	.01	-.28*	-.21	-.14	0	-.22*
Size of foreign operations	.07	-.03	-.07	.09	.23	0
Size of foreign manufacturing	-.24	-.20	-.23	-.21	-.22	-.14
Number of foreign subsidiaries	-.43**	-.26	-.23	-.24	-.07	.02

** $p < .01$ (one-tailed test); * $p < .05$.

Note: Correlations involving product modification differences, extent of outside ownership, and the extent of foreign acquisitions are Kendall's tau, since these variables are only assumed to be ordinal. The remainder are Pearson correlations. A two-tailed test was applied to those relationships that contradicted the hypothesized relationship.

The above pattern is just barely observable for long-range planning, where most of the correlations tend to be negative, but very few are statistically significant. Thus, the level of long-range planning centralization appears to be less influenced by company-level strategic and environmental conditions than the level of short-range planning centralization, despite the fact that both levels of centralization tend to be highly correlated.

Company-level structure is significantly related to planning centralization, but this is primarily a function of the way that centralization has been measured in functional division companies. Lacking any intervening international division, product division or geographical region HQ, all shared or joint decisionmaking tends to directly involve the parent

HQ, which leads to considerable centralization. Except for the greater degree of planning centralization associated with functional division companies, there is virtually no significant difference between firms with other structures.

THE INFLUENCE OF OTHER FACTORS ON PLANNING CENTRALIZATION

Because planning centralization was measured at the company level, the study examines only the influence of the four other factors that were also measured at the company level. These factors are size of company, age of company abroad, nationality, and industry. Measurement of these factors was described in Chapter 4.

Table 10–3 shows the correlations between the six planning centralization variables and these other factors. Only age of company abroad shares a significant relationship with planning centralization. The longer that a company has been abroad, the more decentralized the decisionmaking in its planning processes. Neither size, measured in terms of number of employees, nor nationality has a significant influence on planning centralization. Industry also reveals no significant relationship with planning centralization at the .05 level, although there is a consistent tendency for industrial equipment firms to have the highest levels of centralization. Because the differences are not significant, the usual tables showing analysis of variance for nationality and industry have been omitted.

Table 10–3. Correlation between Planning Centralization and Other Factors (N = 42 to 45).

	Short-Range Planning Centralization			Long-Range Planning Centralization		
	Bases Settings	Alternative Development	Alternative Choosing	Bases Setting	Alternative Development	Alternative Choosing
Size of company	-.12	-.02	-.14	-.21	-.11	-.12
Age of company abroad	-.35*	-.14	-.31*	-.29*	-.12	-.08
Nationality of parent company (dummy variables):						
U.S.	.02	.20	.12	.06	-.02	.13
UK	-.07	-.14	-.12	-.04	-.08	-.02
European	.02	-.11	-.04	-.03	.07	-.12

* $p < .05$ (two-tailed test).

Note: Correlations are Pearson correlations.

TESTING THE HYPOTHESES FOR SHORT-RANGE
PLANNING INTENSITY

This section uses the same format as the previous chapters to test the hypotheses and analyze the relationship between short-range planning intensity and the various company- and subsidiary-level strategic and environmental conditions. The seven company-level conditions that measure complexity and size will be used to test Hypotheses 10–5 and 10–6. The fourteen subsidiary-level conditions that measure interdependency and change are used to test Hypotheses 10–3 and 10–4.

Table 10–4 shows the correlations between the three planning intensity variables and the seven company-level and fourteen subsidiary-level strategic and environmental conditions. Figure 10–1 shows only those contingency conditions that share statistically significant correlations with a planning variable and more clearly indicates the extent to which these relationships support or contradict the four hypotheses.

There is only partial support for Hypotheses 10–5 and 10–6. Company-level complexity appears to be unrelated to the intensity of parent-subsidiary communications during the building of the annual plan, despite the fact that all four correlations with the complexity variables are negative. Among the size variables, only size of foreign operations shares a statistically significant negative correlation with the intensity of communications, which tends to support Hypothesis 10–6.

The use of face-to-face review meetings between parent and subsidiary managements shares significant negative correlations with both foreign product diversity and the size of foreign operations, and a nearly significant negative correlation with the extent of outside ownership. This tends to support both Hypotheses 10–5 and 10–6. The nearly significant positive correlation with product modification differences, however, tends to contradict the notion of a negative relationship between company-level complexity and the use of face-to-face meetings.

As Figure 10–1 indicates, the company-level conditions share an equal number of significant positive and negative relationships with the extent to which new issues are raised during the review process. The extent of outside ownership and the size of foreign operations share negative correlations with new issue raising, which tend to support Hypotheses 10–5 and 10–6. Product modification differences and the number of foreign subsidiaries, on the other hand, share positive correlations with new issue raising, and this tends to contradict both hypotheses. Clearly, the company-level conditions of complexity and size are not constraining the raising of new issues during the parent-subsidiary review process as hypothesized. More is said about this in the discussion section.

Table 10–4. Correlation between Short-Range Planning Intensity Variables and Strategic and Environmental Conditions (N = 72 to 94).

	Intensity of Communications	Face-to-face Meetings	Extent New Issues Raised
Company-level conditions			
Foreign product diversity	-.03	-.39***	-.07
Product modification differences	-.03	.17	.26**
Extent of outside ownership	-.05	-.15	-.15*
Extent of foreign acquisitions	-.04	-.09	.06
Size of foreign operations	-.22*	-.30**	-.22*
Size of foreign manufacturing	-.09	.09	.10
Number of foreign subsidiaries	.16	-.12	.29**
Subsidiary-level conditions			
Marketing information dependency	.31***	-.01	.16
Sales dependency	.30**	.12	.03
New manufacturing information dependency	-.05	-.12	.02
Day-to-day manufacturing information dependency	.21*	-.01	.27**
New product design dependency	.05	-.14	-.06
Product design change dependency	.12	-.18	-.09
Importance of subsidiary	-.03	.26**	-.05
Intracompany purchases by subsidiary	.11	-.16	-.25*
Intracompany sales by subsidiary	.17	-.04	.09
Product change	.22*	.04	.17
Manufacturing technology change	.06	-.04	.16
Political environment change	.01	-.10	.03
Competitive climate change	.09	.21*	.15
Supplier situation change	.10	-.11	.02

* $p < .05$ (one-tailed test); ** $p < .01$; *** $p < .001$.

Note: Correlations involving product modification differences, extent of outside ownership, and the extent of foreign acquisitions are Kendall's tau, since these variables are only assumed to be ordinal. The remainder are Pearson correlations. A two-tailed test was applied to those relationships that contradicted the hypothesized relationship.

Figure 10–1 shows that the statistically significant correlations between the subsidiary-level conditions and the intensity of communications and use of face-to-face meetings are all positive. This tends to support Hypotheses 10–3 and 10–4, although the large number of non-significant negative correlations associated with face-to-face meetings-

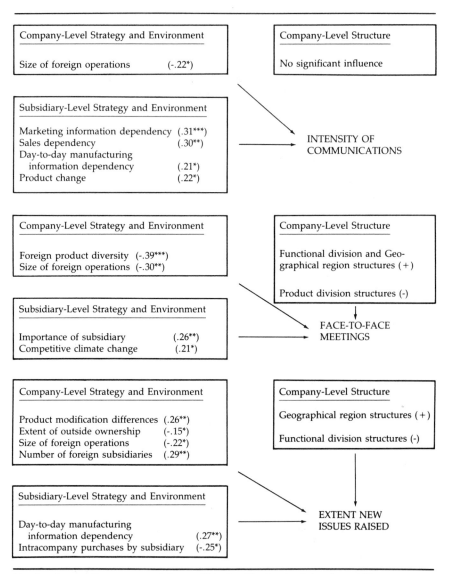

Numbers in parentheses are correlation coefficients with planning intensity variables.

· * $p < .05$ (one-tailed test); ** $p < .01$; *** $p < .001$.

Figure 10–1.   The Determinants of Short-Range Planning Intensity.

(see Table 10–4) is disturbing. The relationship between new issue rais-ing and subsidiary-level conditions is mixed, just as it was for company-level conditions. Day-to-day manufacturing information dependency is positively correlated with the raising of new issues, but intracompany purchases is negatively correlated.

Thus, the hypotheses appear to be generally supported for the first two planning intensity variables, the intensity of parent-subsidiary communications during the building of the annual plan and face-to-face review meetings between parent and subsidiary managements. The hypotheses, however, are clearly not supported by the third variable, the extent to which new issues are raised by the review process. This requires that one rethink the relationship between this planning charac-teristic and the strategic and environmental conditions, which is done in the discussion section.

The influence of structure on planning intensity was also examined, using analysis of variance among the four types of elementary struc-ture. As indicated in Figure 10–1, statistically significant differences were encountered for face-to-face meetings and the extent to which new issues are raised. MNCs with functional division or geographical region structures always used face-to-face review meetings for the sub-sidiaries in the sample, while MNCs with worldwide product division structures only used them for 48 percent of the sample subsidiaries. Functional division MNC's tend to have relatively few foreign subsidi-aries, and geographical region structures place a HQ close to most sub-sidiaries. Both characteristics facilitate face-to-face meetings between parent and subsidiary managements.

Interestingly, the extent to which new issues are raised during the review process is greatest in MNCs with the geographical region struc-ture and lowest in MNCs with the functional division structure. Despite the use of face-to-face review meetings in the latter, the relatively sim-ple and homogeneous strategies and environments associated with functional division structures apparently leads to less raising of new issues during the review process.

THE INFLUENCE OF OTHER FACTORS ON
SHORT-RANGE PLANNING INTENSITY

Following the procedure used in the previous chapters, the study also examined the influence of the six other factors on the three planning intensity variables. These factors are size of company, age of company abroad, size of subsidiary, age of subsidiary, parent company nationality, and industry. Measurement of these factors is described in Chapter 4. While lacking direct information-processing implications, these factors are often thought to influence or share important relationships with various aspects of organizational design.

Table 10–5 shows the correlations between the three planning intensity variables and these other factors. Age of company abroad is significantly and negatively correlated with planning intensity, just as it was with planning centralization. This suggests that the longer that a company has been abroad, the less intense is parent-subsidiary information processing during the annual planning process. A similar, but weaker pattern is also apparent for age of subsidiary. The results are, of course, confounded, due to the high correlation between age of company abroad and age of subsidiary in the sample data (R = .71). The regression analyses in the next section indicate that age of company abroad tends to have the stronger influence.

Table 10–5. Correlation between Short-Range Planning Intensity and Other Factors (N = 82 to 94).

	Intensity of Communications	Face-to-face Meetings	Extent New Issues Raised
Size of company	0	-.05	.24*
Age of company abroad	-.22*	-.34***	-.16
Size of subsidiary	0	.13	.16
Age of subsidiary	-.22*	-.17	-.17
Nationality of parent company (dummy variables):			
U.S.	.10	.31**	.29**
UK	-.12	.03	0
European	-.02	-.34***	-.29**

* p ‹ .05 (two-tailed test); ** p ‹ .01; *** p ‹ .001.

Note: Correlations are Pearson correlations.

The significant positive correlation between size of company, measured in terms of total employees, and the raising of new issues during the review process is also interesting. The previous section noted that the number of foreign subsidiaries was also positively correlated with the raising of new issues. This suggests that large MNC's with many foreign subsidiaries are using the annual planning process to raise new issues, despite the information-processing burden that this must place on headquarters' managements.

Table 10–6 shows that there is no significant difference between nationality groups for the intensity of communications during the building of the annual plan. There are, however, significant differences in the use of face-to-face review meetings and the extent to which new issues are raised. The review process included face-to-face meetings between parent and subsidiary managements for 94 percent of the U.S. parent-subsidiary relationships, but only 64 percent of the European parent-subsidiary relationships. U.S. MNCs also appear to raise more new issues during the review process than do European MNCs. UK MNCs tend to fall between the two extremes.

Table 10–6. Short-Range Planning Intensity by Parent Country Nationality (N = 93 to 94).

	U.S.	UK	European	F
Intensity of communications	2.8	2.3	2.6	.9
Face-to-face meetings	.94	.84	.64	6.1**
Extent new issues raised	3.4	2.9	2.3	4.8**

** $p < .01$ (two-tailed test).

As was done in the previous chapters, the correlations shown in Table 10–4 between planning intensity and the strategic and environmental conditions were rerun for each of the three nationality groups. While previous chapters generally revealed similar patterns across nationality groups, there are some significant differences for the planning intensity variables:

1. The influence of size of foreign operations and number of foreign subsidiaries is different for U.S. and European MNCs. The negative correlations between size of foreign operations and the three planning intensity variables (see Table 10–4) are entirely due to the European MNCs (and, for the intensity of communications during the building of the annual plan, the UK MNCs). Size of foreign operations tends to be unrelated to the planning intensity variables for U.S. MNCs and is even somewhat positively related to the raising of new issues ($R = .11$). The number of foreign subsidiaries is also negatively related to all three planning intensity variables for European MNC's and positively related to all three variables for U.S. MNCs. Thus, European MNCs tend to support the hypothesized negative relationship between the size variables and planning intensity, while U.S. MNCs tend to contradict it with either neutral or positive relationships. Or stated another way, size constrains the use of the annual planning process as an information-processing mechanism in European MNCs but not in U.S. MNCs.

2. The significant negative relationship between foreign product diversity and the use of face-to-face meetings is solely due to European and UK MNCs, while the relationship actually tends to be positive for U.S. MNCs ($R = .15$). Thus, once again, European MNCs tend to support the hypothesized fit, while U.S. MNCs tend to contradict it.
3. The positive correlation between product modification differences and the extent to which new issues are raised is similar and significant for both the U.S. and European subsamples, indicating that this kind of company-level complexity apparently encourages the raising of new issues for both subsamples.
4. The relationships between the planning intensity variables and the subsidiary-level conditions tend to be more similar across the nationality subsamples. All of the statistically significant positive relationships tend to be supported by the three subsamples. The single significant negative correlation, between intracompany purchases by a subsidiary and the extent to which new issues are raised during the review of the subsidiary's annual plan, is found only in the European subsample.

The effects of industry on the planning intensity variables are shown in the Appendix. They are significant only for the use of face-to-face meetings. Here, the chemical industry makes noticeably less use of face-to-face meetings to review the annual plan than other industries. Although not statistically significant, this industry is also at the low end of the other two short range planning intensity variables. Because the chemical industry is characterized by high capital intensity and relatively long planning horizons for both products and markets, parent-subsidiary information-processing during the annual planning process may be less important or problematic than in other industries.

THE RELATIVE INFLUENCE OF COMPANY-LEVEL AND SUBSIDIARY-LEVEL CONDITIONS ON SHORT-RANGE PLANNING INTENSITY

The purpose of this section is to more systematically evaluate the relative strengths of company-level and subsidiary-level contingency conditions on planning intensity and to determine whether the significant other factors still have any influence on planning intensity, once the influence of the strategic and environmental conditions has been controlled for. Following the procedure used in previous chapters, a number of regression analyses were run. First, the single company-level condition that shared a significant correlation with intensity of communications (see Figure 10–1) was regressed on intensity of communications and the adjusted R^2 or percentage of variation in intensity of communications that could be explained by company-level conditions was noted. Next, the four subsidiary-level conditions that also shared significant correlations with intensity of communications were entered into the same regression model in order to determine how much additional variation in intensity of communications could be explained by subsidiary-level conditions once company-level conditions were already included in the model. In this case, the increase in adjusted R^2 or percentage of variation explained was 4 percent. Then the procedure was repeated, this time entering the subsidiary-level conditions first, followed by the company-level conditions. This second analysis was to determine the increase in adjusted R^2 or percentage of variation in intensity of communications explained by company-level conditions once subsidiary-level conditions were already included in the model (in this case 16 percent). This same set of analyses was repeated for face-to-face meetings and extent to which new issues are raised, in each case using as the independent variables those company and subsidiary-level conditions, from Figure 10–1, which shared statistically significant correlations with the respective planning variable.

Because of its considerable length, a table similar to Table 7–5 in Chapter 7 (which more fully presents the step-wise regression runs) is not included in this chapter. The procedure used to interpret the step-wise regression runs, however, is exactly the same as was used in Chapter 7. The reader can refer back to that chapter to see how the step-wise regression runs were analyzed to produce the results shown in Figure 7–2 and know that the same procedure was used to produce the results shown in Figure 10–2.

Figure 10–2 is a pictorial representation of the contributions made by company- and subsidiary-level conditions to explain each of the three planning intensity variables. The information is taken from the regression runs. The percentage of variation shown alongside the "shared" arrow can be explained by either set of variables, while the other two percentages represent the additional variation that can be explained only by the respective company- or subsidiary-level conditions.

A number of important conclusions can be drawn from this analysis. It is largely subsidiary-level conditions that explain the intensity of parent-subsidiary communications during the building of the annual plan. This implies that altering such communications is a flexible information-processing mechanism, which companies can vary from one parent-subsidiary relationship to another in order to fit varying subsidiary-level conditions.

The use of face-to-face review meetings, on the other hand, is more constrained by company-level conditions. High levels of foreign prod-

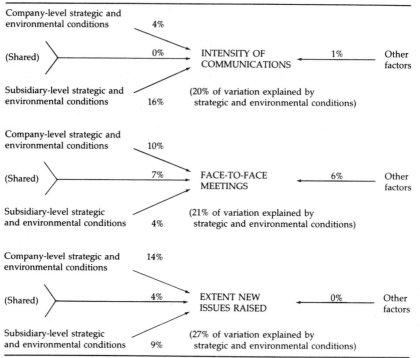

Note: The figures beside the arrows show the percentage of variation in the designated planning measure that can be uniquely explained by company-level conditions, subsidiary-level conditions, or, alternately, by either.

Figure 10–2. How Company- and Subsidiary-Level Conditions Explain Short-Range Planning Intensity.

uct diversity and large foreign operations tend to reduce the likelihood of face-to-face review meetings between parent and subsidiary managements, although this is only true in European (and for foreign product diversity, UK) MNCs. As discussed in the previous section, U.S. MNCs tend to share a weak positive relationship with the company-level conditions, while European and, in some instances, UK MNCs tend to share a much stronger negative relationship. All nationality groups tend to share relatively weak relationships with the subsidiary-level conditions. Thus, the most significant influence on face-to-face meetings tends to be the company-level constraints of complexity and size operating on European MNCs.

Company-level conditions are also the strongest predictors of the extent to which the planning review process raises new issues. The relationships, however, vary considerably across the nationality groups and are frequently not as hypothesized. Product modification differences encourage the raising of new issues for both U.S. and European MNCs, as do a large number of subsidiaries for U.S. MNCs. These are the primary contributors at the company-level to explaining the raising of new issues, and they tend to contradict the hypothesized influence of company-level complexity and size on the raising of new issues. Two subsidiary-level conditions also contribute in a significant way to explaining the raising of new issues. Day-to-day manufacturing information dependency encourages the raising of new issues across all nationality groups. This relationship is the primary contributor at the subsidiary level, and it tends to support the hypothesized fit. Intracompany purchases by a subsidiary, however, discourage the raising of new issues in European MNCs. Although this relationship contributes less to the explanation of new issue raising, it nevertheless contradicts the hypothesized relationship.

In previous chapters, attempts to use regression analysis to partial out company- and subsidiary-level explanations of some organizational feature have generally produced a straightforward and simple picture. Such has not been the case with face-to-face meetings and the raising of new issues. In both cases, there have been significant differences between nationality groups, and, especially for the latter case, the influence of the individual contingency variables have tended to go in opposite directions instead of the single hypothesized direction. Thus, aggregating across these separate contributions is perhaps less appropriate here than it has been in previous chapters.

In addition to partialing out the variation in the planning intensity variables that can be explained by company- and subsidiary–level conditions, the regression analyses reported in Figure 10–2 also reveal how much additional variation can be explained by the other factors. This was accomplished by adding the other factors previously identified in Table 10–6 as having a statistically significant relationship with a planning variable, to the regression model after company- and subsidiary-level conditions were already entered. The increases in adjusted R^2 that were observed when the appropriate other factors were entered are 1 percent for intensity of communications (contributed by nationality), 6 percent for face-to-face meetings (contributed by age of company abroad and nationality), and 0 percent for the extent to which new issues are raised. Thus, except for face-to-face meetings, the other factors provide very little explanation beyond that already provided by those strategic and environmental conditions with information-processing implications.

DISCUSSION

This chapter has sought to understand how business planning systems in MNCs are influenced by the strategy and environment of the organization. As discussed in the introduction of this chapter, contingency models of planning systems are still in a more formative stage of development than most of the previous features of organizational design. The present study has viewed planning systems and processes as another form of parent-subsidiary information processing. As a result, the study has focused on several characteristics of planning systems that appear to have strong information-processing implications, even though previous planning studies have not measured these characteristics.

The first set of planning variables measured the degrees to which key decisions in the short- and long-range planning processes are centralized in an MNC. The second set of planning variables measured the intensity of parent-subsidiary communications during the short-range planning process. Based on the information-processing implications of the planning variables and an organization's strategic and environmental conditions, a priori hypotheses linking the two were developed and subsequently tested. Because the two sets of planning variables represent different kinds of information-processing implications, they are dealt with separately in this section.

Planning Centralization Variables

The six planning centralization variables were measured at the company level and were therefore only related to company-level contingency conditions. Following the logic used to relate operating centralization to company-level strategic and environmental conditions, a negative relationship was hypothesized between planning centralization and the company-level measures of complexity and size.

The hypotheses were clearly supported for short-range planning centralization, although the relationship is not as strong as it was for operating centralization in Chapter 7. As company-level strategy and environment becomes more complex and the relevant size measures increase, all threatening to overload the information-processing capacities of the planning hierarchy, there is a consistent tendency to make short-range planning decisions at lower levels. The centralization of long-range planning decisions, however, does not appear to be so significantly influenced by such constraints, although there is a tendency for the relationships to go in the hypothesized direction.

Both short- and long-range planning centralization are greatest in MNCs with worldwide functional division structures. Age of company abroad is the only other factor that shares a significant relationship with planning centralization. The greater the international experience of a company, the more decentralized the decisionmaking in its planning processes tends to be.

Following the practice of previous chapters, this section also examines the relationship between planning centralization and the other features of organizational design, in an attempt to provide some integration across the various organizational elements. Table 10–7 shows the correlation found between the planning centralization variables and the other features of organizational design. It is necessary to remember that the planning centralization variables were measured at the company level as generalizations across all parent-subsidiary relationships in a company. Although operating centralization and control were measured as subsidiary-level variables, subsequent analysis found that both are significantly influenced by company-level strategic and environmental conditions and consequently tend to be somewhat similar for most parent-subsidiary relationships within a company. This provides a rationale for examining how the levels of operating centralization and control might be related to the level of planning centralization because to a significant degree both exist as company-level phenomena.

The large number of significant positive correlations between the degree of planning centralization and the degrees of operating centralization and control suggest that somehow the level at which planning decisions are made is related to the level at which the host of operating decisions for foreign subsidiaries are made and the extent to which operating data are reported back to the parent. This relationship is, once again, stronger for the short-range planning process than for the long range planning process. Whether subsidiary management positions are staffed with parent nationals or local nationals seems to have no influence on the level at which planning decisions are made, just as it was previously found to have no influence over the degree of operating centralization or level of performance control exerted over a foreign subsidiary. Since planning centralization was measured at the company level and subsidiary staffing is largely a subsidiary-level phenomenon (see Chapter 9), the lack of any relationship is not surprising.

Table 10–7. Correlation of Planning Variables with Centralization, Control,

	Short-Range Planning Centralization		
	Bases Setting	Alternative Development	Alternative Choosing
Marketing centralization	.31**	.39***	.32**
Manufacturing centralization	.27*	.29**	.33**
Financial centralization	-.02	.13	.03
Marketing control	.21	.24*	.24*
Manufacturing control	.12	.20	.26*
Financial control	.45***	.36***	.50***
Marketing staffing	.12	.19	.10
Manufacturing staffing	.16	.19	.10
Financial staffing	.02	.19	.10
Subsidiary CEO staffing	.10	.16	.18

$*\ p < .05$ (two-tailed test); $**\ p < .01$; $***\ p < .001$.

Note: Correlations are Pearson correlations.

While the degree to which planning decisions can be centralized needs to fit the strategic and environmental complexity of a company (Hypothesis 10–1) and the size of its operations (Hypothesis 10–2), it might also be influenced by the degree to which the parent centralizes and exercises control over the day-to-day operating affairs of its foreign subsidiaries. It is important to notice that the relationships expressed by Hypotheses 10–1 and 10–2 have information-processing implications and represent important information-processing fits. If they are violated, one would expect information-processing overload and breakdown to occur, hindering organizational functioning and performance.

The second set of relationships, between planning centralization and the operating decisionmaking and control structures of a company, has no such information-processing implications, and it is most probable that this is a direct causal relationship rather than an information-processing fit. MNCs (and all organizations) undoubtedly evolve operating systems such as levels of operating authority and degrees of operating control before they develop annual and long-range planning processes. If such is the case, it is quite possible that the degree of operating centralization and control has causally influenced the degree of planning centralization. Such influence and relationship is, of course, not captured by the information-processing model being developed.

and Staffing (N = 71 to 94).

Long-Range Planning Centralization			Short-Range Planning Intensity		
Bases Setting	Alternative Development	Alternative Choosing	Intensity of Communications	Face-to-face Meetings	Extent new Issues Raised
0	.16	.22*	.18	.30**	.24*
.15	.17	.33**	.18	.14	.04
.03	.05	.12	.26**	.21*	.28**
.15	.20	.24*	.32**	.15	.37***
.10	.09	.29*	.44***	.19	.32**
.33**	.33**	.33**	.19	.31**	.18
.04	.04	-.07	-.01	0	.07
.23	.16	.08	.06	-.29**	-.11
.16	.14	.16	.07	-.11	.04
.17	.16	.20	-.03	.01	-.03

Figure 10–3 shows the different kinds of influence—fit and causation—suggested by the preceding analysis and discussion. Arrows 1, 2, and 3 indicate important information-processing fit relationships. Each is supposed to support effective organizational functioning and performance by protecting the organization from information-processing overload and concentrating information-processing capacity where requirements are greatest. The companies in the sample tend to possess these relationships or fits to a significant degree. Arrows 4 and 5 do not appear to be critical information-processing fit relationships, despite the fact that the companies in the sample also tend to possess these relationships to a significant degree. From an information-processing perspective, there is no reason that the degrees of centralization found in the operating and planning activities of a company need to be similar (except as they may both be required to fit common strategic and environmental conditions). Yet the degrees of centralization associated with operating decisions and short- and long-range planning decisions appear to be more closely related than can be explained by their mutual association with a third set of variables, the strategic and environmental conditions. In fact, when the planning variables were regressed on both the strategic and environmental conditions and the degrees of operating centralization and performance control, it was found that the latter

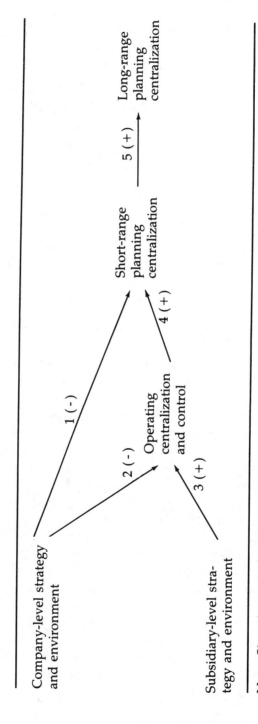

Note: Signs in parentheses indicate direction of relationship.

Figure 10–3. A Map of Influence and Causation.

variables contributed in a significant way to planning centralization, even after the strategic and environmental conditions were controlled for. Since there is a developmental sequence to these separate processes, it would appear that most sample companies have allowed the earlier process to influence the degree of centralization or decentralization associated with the latter process.

Although the study does not contain the kind of data needed to directly address this issue, the relationships found in the data are consistent with this interpretation. Figure 10-3 presents a rather complex contingency model of planning centralization. It contains two different kinds of relationships—information-processing fit and direct causation. The central argument of this book, of course, deals with the former.

Planning Intensity Variables

Consistent with the approach used in previous chapters, this chapter has examined and sought to explain the three short-range planning intensity variables as the joint product of two different levels of contingency variables. The conceptual framework has viewed the intensity of parent-subsidiary communications during the building of the annual plan, the use of face-to-face review meetings between parent and subsidiary managements, and the degree to which new issues are raised during such reviews as measures of the information-processing capacities of a short-range planning process. It was hypothesized that all three mechanisms would be encouraged by subsidiary-level conditions of interdependency and change (Hypotheses 10-3 and 10-4), but constrained by company-level conditions of complexity and size (Hypotheses 10-5 and 10-6).

The findings tend to show less support and more contradiction with the hypothesized relationships than in previous chapters. Interpretation of the findings is further complicated by the fact that a number of important relationships differ between U.S. and European MNCs (a result that has not appeared in previous chapters). Most of this difference involves the company-level conditions rather than the subsidiary-level conditions.

European MNCs tend to follow the hypothesized negative relationship between company-level complexity and size and the three planning intensity variables. That is, a high degree of foreign product diversity and large foreign operations tend to constrain the intensity of parent-subsidiary communications during the short range planning process. In U.S. MNCs, on the other hand, such conditions tend not to constrain parent-subsidiary information processing and might even encourage it. Interestingly, a higher level of product modification difference among subsidiaries tends to encourage the raising of more new issues during the planning review process for all three nationality groups. One possible explanation for this seeming inconsistency may be that while complexity and diversity at the company level have consistently acted to reduce the intensity of routine information processing between subsidiaries and the parent, they may at the same time encourage a higher level of nonroutine information processing between a parent and its subsidiaries (that is, the raising and resolving of new issues).

If a similar line of reasoning were used to explain the apparent difference between contingency relationships in U.S. and European MNCs, one might hypothesize that the short-range planning processes in U.S. and European MNCs tend to involve different kinds of information processing. The planning process in U.S. MNCs might contain a greater element of nonroutine information processing (as reflected in more face-to-face review meetings and more new issue raising), while the planning process in European MNCs might contain a greater element of routine information processing (as reflected in fewer face-to-face review meetings and less new issue raising).

Once again, the present study cannot directly address this issue, since it did not directly measure the level of routine versus nonroutine information processing in a planning process. During the interviews, however, a number of European managers expressed the belief that formal planning systems were not as developed or elaborate in European MNCs as in U.S. MNCs. This suggests that there might be some systematic difference between planning processes in U.S. and European firms and that this difference might involve different kinds of information processing.

In the United States, business schools and consulting firms have played major roles in disseminating planning knowledge and skills, but such influence has had much less effect on European firms. Thus, it is perhaps not surprising to find that planning practices differ more between U.S. and European MNCs than structure, centralization, control, or staffing. To be sure, these features of organizational design vary significantly across the nationality groups in the sample, but generally they share similar relationships with the strategic and environmental conditions surrounding firms. Thus, from an information-processing perspective, U.S. and European MNCs tend to use these features of organizational design in similar ways. It would appear that this is less true for business planning systems.

Business planning in most large U.S. MNCs has apparently evolved beyond providing the more routine forms of information required for sales and profit forecasts, cash flow projections, and operating control standards. While it still provides this kind of information, the short-range planning process in U.S. MNCs appears to also provide a good deal of nonroutine information processing between parent and foreign subsidiary. This kind of information processing is associated with more face-to-face meetings and new issue raising. It would also appear to be uninfluenced by the traditional constraints of company-level complexity and size. While this relationship has not been reported on in the litera-ture, Daft and Macintosh (1981) point out that richer, more equivocal forms of information processing differ considerably from clear, une-quivocal forms of information processing in organizations, and each tends to fit a different task situation. Thus, it is possible that the initially confusing and contradictory contingency relationships discovered for the planning intensity variables may be explained by differences in the type of information processing that goes on in a planning system.

If planning practices in European MNC's evolve toward those in U.S. MNCs, one would predict that the associated contingency relationships will also become more similar to those in U.S. firms. This would reflect an increase in the nonroutine information-processing capacity of a plan-ning process. Yet one can question whether such an evolution is required in European MNCs, despite the general admiration expressed by most of the European managers who mentioned U.S. planning prac-tices. If formal planning systems in European MNCs are not providing a high level of nonroutine information-processing capacity between for-eign subsidiaries and the parent HQ, how is such information process-ing currently provided? Reflecting back on the previous chapter, the answer might well be subsidiary staffing. Chapter 9 found that Euro-pean MNCs tend to use significantly higher levels of expatriate staffing in their foreign subsidiaries than U.S. MNCs. It also found support for the notion that expatriate staffing increases the capacity for nonroutine information processing between a foreign subsidiary and the parent HQ, and, like the planning intensity variables, staffing was not subject to the usual constraints company-level complexity and size place on routine parent-subsidiary information processing. Thus, the fact that European MNCs tend to staff critical positions in foreign subsidiaries with parent company nationals could possibly compensate for lower levels of nonroutine information-processing capacity in their planning processes.

The attempt to partial out the influences of company and subsidiary-level conditions on the planning intensity variables, shown in Figure 10–2, reveals that the level of parent-subsidiary communications during the building of the short-range plan is a flexible information-processing mechanism, capable of varying to fit subsidiary-level conditions. This pattern is similar for U.S. and European MNCs, but stronger in the former. Similar analyses for face-to-face meetings and the raising of new issues, however, are not as meaningful, given the significant nationality differences discussed above. Face-to-face meetings are almost always used in U.S. MNCs and hence tend not to vary with the strategic and environmental conditions. In European MNCs however, they tend to be equally influenced by company- and subsidiary-level conditions and fit the hypothesized relationships.

Aside from the important influence of nationality on the planning intensity variables, age of the company abroad tends to be negatively related to both planning centralization and the intensity of parent-subsidiary communications during the planning process. Older subsidiaries also tend to be involved in less intense parent-subsidiary communications during planning.

This chapter differs considerably from the preceding chapters. Although it initially follows the customary format of deducing hypotheses and testing them, the primary thrust of the chapter steps out of the usual hypotheses testing mode into a more exploratory mode. The result is less a well-defined contingency model than some new ideas about the role of planning systems in large, complex organizations, like MNCs. Planning systems are information processing mechanisms, and the present study provides some evidence that in successful organizations they tend to fit certain strategic and environmental conditions. Such fit, however, is weaker and apparently more complex than for other features of organizational design. Part of the problem may be that formal planning systems are still quite new, compared to other features of organizational design, and appear to function somewhat differently in U.S. and European MNCs. Future research needs to put more emphasis on measuring what kinds of information processing are going on within a planning process and use this to distinguish between planning processes.

Formal business planning systems are quite complex, as information-processing mechanisms go. There is some suggestion that they contain different kinds of information processing, that are subject to different contingency relationships. This might be even more apparent if parent-subsidiary planning intensity during the long range planning process were studied. If information-processing requirements become more complex in MNCs as a result of more global strategies (Hout, Porter, and Rudden 1982), one might well expect planning systems to provide much of the required capacity.

11

THE SEARCH FOR GENERAL PATTERNS OF ORGANIZATIONAL DESIGN AND GENERAL PATTERNS OF STRATEGY

The previous chapters have dealt separately with the various elements of organizational design: organizational structure, the centralization of decision making, performance control, subsidiary staffing, and planning systems. Yet all of these elements exist simultaneously in an MNC, and there is likely to be some interaction among them. We already know, for example, that when a firm centralizes operating decisions, there is also a tendency to increase the amount of control information being reported to the parent. What other relationships exist among the various features of organizational design? Can these relationships be grouped to form broader or more general dimensions of organizational design that underlie the specific features already studied? Also, do these relationships and broad patterns vary by nationality or structure of the company? These are the questions that the next section of this chapter addresses.

The third section addresses similar questions for the strategy and environment side of the model. Are there any broad patterns or general dimensions underlying the numerous specific elements of strategy and environment used in the study? Are these patterns influenced by the nationality or structure of the parent company?

The previous chapters have used simple correlation analysis between variables representing different features of organizational design to develop some sense of how one feature might be related to another. This chapter uses factor analysis to provide a more complete and simultaneous picture of these relationships. Most of the research studies referenced in this book have looked at individual features of organization design and limited sets of strategy variables. The breadth of the present study in terms of organizational design features and strategy variables provides a unique opportunity to explore the dimensionality of both in a sample of complex organizations.

The type of factor analysis used for all of the subsequent analyses is R-factor analysis, employing principle factoring with varimax rotation (form PA2 in the SPSSX statistical package). A large number of factor analyses were run under varying conditions to explore and understand patterns in the data. This chapter attempts to present the best interpretation of the data, in terms of parsimony and understandability. The number of factors specified to be extracted was equal to the number with eigenvalues of one or greater reduced, where possible, by the elimination of factors with no identifiable meaning. Such factors were eliminated only when the reduction did not significantly alter the factor structure of the remaining factors with identifiable meaning. Because previous chapters have not specified any particular relationships among the features of organizational design or among the elements of strategy and environment, these analyses need to be viewed as exploratory research.

PATTERNS OF ORGANIZATIONAL DESIGN

The search for patterns among the various features of organizational design involved ten separate searches. The first search considered all of the companies in the sample, the next three searches dealt with U.S., UK, and European MNCs separately, and the final six searches separated the sample by type of structure.

Table 11–1 shows the three broad factors of organizational design that tend to emerge when all of the companies in the sample are considered together. The three measures of short-range planning centralization and the three measures of long-range planning centralization seem to be the primary elements of the first factor, which has been called "planning centralization." The three measures of operating centralization, the three measures of control, and the three measures of short-range planning intensity all tend to co-vary and appear to be elements of a second broad factor, which has been called "operating centralization and control and short range planning intensity." Finally, the four staffing measures seem to be the primary elements of a third broad factor,

Table 11–1. Broad Factors of Organizational Design—All MNCs.

	Broad Factors of Organizational Design		
	Planning Centralization	Operating Centralization and Control and Short-Range Planning Intensity	Staffing
Operating centralization			
Marketing centralization	.23	.61	.07
Manufacturing centralization	.28	.29	.17
Financial centralization	.01	.55	.02
Performance control			
Marketing control	.21	.68	-.12
Manufacturing control	.15	.77	-.08
Financial control	.45	.42	-.05
Subsidiary staffing			
Marketing staffing	.01	.08	.69
Manufacturing staffing	.12	-.06	.78
Financial staffing	.07	-.01	.61
CEO staffing	.16	-.12	.52
Short-range planning intensity			
Intensity of communications	.05	.48	.05
Face-to-face meetings	.04	.39	-.14
Extent new issues raised	-.17	.54	.01
Short-range planning centralization			
Bases setting	.80	.07	.05
Alternative development	.71	.19	.20
Alternative choosing	.86	.19	.07
Long-range planning centralization			
Bases setting	.75	-.08	.11
Alternative development	.81	.02	.09
Alternative choosing	.81	.10	.04
Percentage of common variance explained by each factor	54	28	18
Eigenvalue	4.8	2.5	1.6

which has been called "staffing." Also contributing to the first factor are marketing and manufacturing centralization and marketing and financial control, all primary elements of the second factor. Although this reflects the positive correlation that exists between operating centralization and control and planning centralization, the factor analysis indicates that one should still view these as separate factors.

The ordering of the factors or percentage of common variance explained by each factor should not be interpreted as indicating the importance of a given set of design features. Concepts measured by a greater number of variables and concepts with a high degree of covariance (such as short-range planning centralization and long-range planning centralization) will naturally tend to load on the first factor and account for a relatively high percentage of the common variance. This reflects the measurement process and not the relative importance of these features in organizations.

Thus, the nineteen individual measures of operating centralization, control, subsidiary staffing, short-range planning intensity, and planning centralization seem to be elements of three broader, underlying factors of organizational design. This is a very useful finding. It indicates that in successful companies there tend to be some internal consistencies among individual design features, and this simplifies the way one needs to think about organizational design.

Broad Factors of Organizational Design by Nationality

In order to examine the robustness of the general pattern discovered above, the factor analysis was rerun, separating the sample first by nationality and then by structure. Due to space and cost considerations, it is not feasible to include separate tables for each of these factor analyses. Instead, a summary table (Table 11–2) describes the broad factors that emerged from each analysis.[1]

The pattern for *U.S. MNCs* is similar to that for the total sample, in that the same three broad factors can be identified. There is, however, a more significant overlap or correlation between operating centralization and control and planning centralization, with the operating centralization variables tending to load more equally on the first and second factors. While still apparent, the relationship between short-range planning intensity and operating centralization and control is not as clear or strong as in the total sample. This is consistent with the suggestion in the previous chapter that planning processes in U.S. MNCs may be providing more nonroutine information processing than in European

Table 11-2. Broad Factors of Organizational Design by Nationality and Structure.

	Broad Factors or Dimensions of Organizing			
All MNCs	Planning centralization	Operating centralization and control and short range planning intensity	Staffing	
U.S. MNCs	Planning centralization	Operating centralization and control and short range planning intensity	Staffing	
UK MNCs	Operating centralization and control, short range planning intensity, and short range planning centralization	Longe-range planning centralization	Staffing	
European MNCs	Planning centralization	Control and short range planning intensity	Staffing	Operating centralization
Functional Division MNC's	Operating centralization and control and planning centralization	Staffing		
International Division MNC's	?	?	?	
Geographical Region MNC's	Operating centralization and control and short range planning intensity	Long-range planning centralization	Staffing	
Product Division MNC's	Control and short range planning intensity	Planning centralization	Operating centralization	Staffing
Matrix MNCs	Control, short range planning intensity, and short-range planning centralization	Long range planning centralization	Staffing	
Mixed MNC's	Operating centralization and short range planning intensity	Staffing		

firms, where the intensity of short range planning tends to be more closely associated with such routine information-processing mechanisms as operating centralization and control.

Only two factors seem to be identifiable in UK MNCs. Operating centralization and marketing and manufacturing control belong to the first factor. The only design features loading in a meaningful and consistent way on the second factor are the measures of long range planning centralization. It is interesting to note that the four staffing variables, which tend to share strong positive correlations in U.S. and European MNCs, are not consistently or significantly intercorrelated in the UK MNCs. The usual positive correlation between operating centralization and short- and long-range planning centralization is also lacking in UK MNCs, where the pattern tends to be mixed. Long-range planning centralization, in fact, appears as a separate factor.

The analysis of the UK companies in the sample seems to be more confusing and less successful than it is for the U.S. and European MNCs. One possible reason is that the UK sample is much smaller than either the U.S. or European samples (six companies and twelve parent-subsidiary relationships), and this means that just a few companies can significantly distort the results. Yet it is probable that even with a larger sample, one would find that the organizing pattern in UK MNCs is significantly different in a number of respects from that in U.S. and European MNCs. The small sample, however, means that one should be less confident that the study has accurately identified and described these differences.

Four broad factors of organizing appear to be used in *European MNCs*. The first factor, "planning centralization," is similar to that found in both the total and U.S. samples. The second factor identified in the total and U.S. samples, however, subdivides into two separate factors for European MNCs. Operating centralization is not so significantly correlated with performance control in European MNCs as it is in U.S. and UK firms. As a result, operating centralization tends to emerge as a separate broad factor from control and short-range planning intensity. In European MNCs, marketing and manufacturing centralization are strongly correlated, but financial centralization is uncorrelated with either and consequently is not part of the operating centralization factor. The remaining factor, staffing, is also similar to that found for the total sample and for U.S. MNCs.

Thus, the factor analyses identify a number of broad organizing factors or general dimensions that seem to underlie the nineteen specific design features measured in the study. Organizations do not independently vary nineteen different design characteristics but instead appear to vary their configuration using from two to four general design dimensions. Each dimension implies or contains a number of specific and related organizational design features. U.S. and European MNCs seem to possess the same general dimensions, except that European MNCs tend to break out operating centralization as a fourth dimension. Also, the four European dimensions appear to be more independent of each other with less overlap than is found among the three U.S. dimensions. This indicates that there may be more tendency in U.S. firms to increase or decrease information-processing capacity along all dimensions at the same time. As already discussed, the results for the UK MNCs are the most puzzling. All of the design features except staffing and long-range planning centralization appear to vary along a single dimension. Only long-range planning centralization belongs to a separate dimension. Staffing does not appear to possess any underlying pattern. One interpretation might suggest that this two-dimensional design is a relatively simple scheme for organizing that should be most suitable for implementing relatively simple international strategies. This, however, must be taken as a very tentative suggestion, and further study is required before any conclusion should be drawn.

Broad Factors of Organizational Design by Structure

Table 11–2 also shows the broad factors that emerge when firms with each of the six different types of macro organization structure are considered separately. Two broad factors or design dimensions appear in *functional division MNCs*. The first factor contains operating centralization and control and planning centralization. The second factor emphasizes staffing. While this pattern differs from the general or total sample pattern, it is still consistent with the general pattern. For functional division companies, the operating and planning centralization factors have simply been combined into one. In a sense, the pattern found in functional division MNCs can be viewed as a simplified (two-dimensional) version of the general pattern. It is also interesting to notice that manufacturing centralization and control, which do not load on the first factor, are quite independent of marketing and financial centralization and control. The higher degree of functional separation in functional division MNCs facilitates this kind of independence.

International division MNCs differ significantly from the general pattern. In fact, it is difficult to identify or name the factors that emerge when these companies are analyzed. Only the first factor can be partially identified. Marketing and manufacturing control and a few of the planning centralization variables seem to load primarily on the first factor. The other design features load without any meaningful pattern on the three significant factors. The high level of overlap or factorial complexity (where a variable loads significantly on more than one factor) means that the factor analysis is not adding much clarity to the situation. Broad common factors or dimensions of organizing are not evident across the firms in the sample with international division structures.

Geographical region MNCs appear to fit the general pattern with only minor exceptions. Short-range planning centralization loads on all three factors but tends to be more closely linked with the first factor (operating centralization and control and short-range planning intensity) than the second (long-range planning centralization).

Product division MNCs also appear to fit the general pattern, except that operating centralization tends to be broken out as a fourth significant factor of organizing. This four dimensional pattern of organization is the same as that previously found for European MNCs. There is, of course, considerable overlap between the two samples at this point, since eight of the twelve product division MNCs are European.

The various types of *matrix structure MNCs* have all been grouped into one category for purposes of this analysis. As Table 11–2 shows, firms with matrix structures differ in some ways from the general pattern but still share many similarities with it. Operating centralization does not load in any meaningful way on a single factor, and, consequently, one cannot generalize about how it is used in matrix companies. Two of the short-range planning centralization variables are more associated with control and short-range planning intensity than with long-range planning centralization. This suggests that in matrix companies short-range planning may be more operational than strategic, and its primary purpose may be to support the control process. The sharper than usual separation between short-and long-range planning is in some ways consistent with the dual focus of a matrix structure. This is especially true when one of the dimensions of the matrix is primarily used for day-to-day tactical or operational information processing and the other dimension is largely concerned with long-range planning and strategic decision making. The third broad factor identified in matrix MNCs is staffing.

The various types of *mixed structure MNCs* have also been grouped into one category for purposes of the analysis. This time only two broad factors seem to emerge. The first factor consists largely of operating centralization and short-range planning intensity, while the second factor is principally staffing. To this extent, the design pattern for mixed structure MNCs is consistent with the general pattern. It is interesting to notice that planning centralization does not emerge as a separate factor but seems to load on both of the two factors already identified. The control variables also fail to load consistently on a given factor. Thus, one is unable to generalize about how these features are used in firms with mixed structures.

For a number of organizational design features, there is considerable overlap between the two factors, and the resultant design pattern for mixed structure firms is not very clear. Part of this may be due to the very nature of mixed structure companies, where two different structures are used for different sets of foreign subsidiaries. It is quite possible that some design features vary significantly from one set of subsidiaries to the other, even within the same company. Given this potential complication, it is interesting to observe that the patterns that do seem to emerge most clearly tend to conform to the general pattern.

Discussion of Patterns of Design

This concludes the search for patterns of organizational design among the fifty companies in the sample. The general pattern identified in Table 11–1 seems to hold, with some adaptation and variation, for most of the companies in the sample. The number of identifiable factors or general dimensions of organizing varies from two to four. Staffing always appears as a separate dimension. In a way, this is not surprising. In Chapter 9, it was observed that staffing was almost completely determined by subsidiary-level strategic and environmental conditions, while the other design features tend to have significant company-level associations. Thus, staffing decisions seem to be made independent of the other design decisions. Except in functional division and mixed structure companies, planning centralization also appears to be a separate dimension of organizing, although it is not as independent of the other dimensions as staffing. Finally, there seems to be a sort of operating dimension, consisting of operating centralization, control, and short-range planning intensity. In most companies, there is more overlap between the operating and planning dimensions than there is with staffing. When one of these dimensions tends to be relatively high in information-processing capacity, there is some tendency for the other dimension to be relatively high also.

While the three-dimensional pattern described above is apparent in most of the sample companies, nationality and company structure also produce a number of different variations on the general pattern. In European MNCs, operating centralization is split off as a kind of second independent operating dimension. In UK and matrix MNCs, short-range planning centralization appears to be more an element of the operating than the long-range planning dimension. In functional division MNCs the operating and planning dimensions are even combined and appear as a single dimension (that is, planning does not exist as an independent dimension but is essentially another facet of the operating dimension).

Thus, UK MNCs and functional division MNCs appear to have the simplest organizational patterns. While different, they both tend to be two-dimensional. UK MNCs tend to use an operating/short-range planning dimension and a long-range planning dimension. Functional division MNCs tend to use a combined operating/planning dimension and a staffing dimension. While simplified patterns of organizing are undoubtedly easier to manage, they may lack the greater flexibility a three-dimensional design provides for responding to more complex or multidimensional strategies.

Certainly, firms with international division structures are the most confusing. No broad factors or general dimensions of organizing appear that can be identified or meaningfully understood. Instead, the individual features of organizational design tend to group in ways that defy the general pattern and rationale that has evolved from our study of the other firms. One possible explanation for this is that the international division structure is a transitional structure that firms pass through as they move from domestic rationality to global rationality. Because different features of the organizational design change at different rates, the usual patterns or associations between them tend not to exist.

In all cases, one must caution that these divergences from the general pattern and their potential meaning are very tentative. The sample size for these findings is too small to be conclusive, and they should be taken as hypotheses for future research. The general pattern, however, seems to be well supported, both in the total sample (where the sample size is adequate) and in the subsequent subsample analyses.

PATTERNS OF STRATEGY AND ENVIRONMENT

The purpose of this section is to discover what patterns, if any, exist among the twenty-two elements of strategy and environment employed in the study. Eight elements are characteristics of company-level strategy and environment, while fourteen deal with subsidiary-level conditions. The search process is similar to that used in the previous section.

The first search considers all of the companies in the sample, the next three searches deal with U.S., UK, and European MNCs separately, and the final six searches separate the sample by type of structure.

In the previous section, the dimensionality of organizational design (two to four meaningful dimensions) became reasonably apparent after the first few factor analysis searches. The previous chapters, in fact, suggested some notion of the number of independent dimensions which might exist. The dimensionality of the twenty-two strategic and environmental conditions, however, is much more uncertain. Factorial complexity is noticeably greater, and it is more difficult to meaningfully identify factors. When all of the statistically significant factors in each of the searches were examined, it was impossible to meaningfully identify any of the factors beyond the first four. Consequently, all of the searches were run for four factors, except in two cases where three factors seemed to best represent the data.

Table 11–3 shows the four broad factors that tend to emerge when all of the companies in the sample are considered together. The first factor is primarily composed of two company-level measures (product modification differences among foreign subsidiaries and the size of foreign manufacturing) and four measures of interdependency between a subsidiary and the parent (dependency on the parent for new manufacturing information, new product designs, product design changes, and intracompany imports by the subsidiary).

In previous chapters it has been customary to speak of foreign manufacturing as a size measure rather than a complexity measure. In this chapter, we will conclude that it is more a measure of the complexity of a firm's international strategy and environment than a measure of the size of its international domain (as otherwise measured by the relative size of a firm's foreign operations or the number of foreign subsidiaries). The fact that foreign manufacturing varies closely with product modification differences ($R = .38$) means that it generally supports and is a part of the local adaptation strategy of an MNC. The kind of strategic and environmental complexity represented by these two variables can be referred to as "local adaptation complexity," and it differs from the kind of complexity represented by foreign product diversity, the extent of outside ownership, and the extent of foreign acquisitions. The latter three tend to group together in the third factor to represent a second kind of strategic and environmental complexity.

The first factor describes a relationship or pattern between the complexity of a company's international strategy and the degree of subsidiary-parent dependency inherent in the individual strategies of its foreign subsidiaries. It states that the two tend to vary in opposite directions. Lower company-level complexity (fewer product modifica-

Table 11–3. Broad Factors of Strategy and Environment—All MNCs.

	Broad Factors of Strategy and Environment			
	Company-Level Complexity and Subsidiary-Level Dependency	Subsidiary-Level Change and Dependency	Company-Level Complexity	?
Company-Level Conditions				
Foreign product diversity	-.06	.01	.52	.36
Product modification differences	-.73	-.13	.09	-.10
Extent of outside ownership	.05	.05	.66	-.10
Extent of foreign acquisitions	-.23	-.03	.69	-.15
Product change	.25	-.07	.25	.18
Size of foreign operations	.13	-.08	.47	-.06
Size of foreign manufacturing	-.69	-.23	-.17	.06
Number of foreign subsidiaries	-.23	-.05	0	.51
Subsidiary-Level Conditions				
Marketing information dependency	.12	.32	-.07	.10
Sales dependency	.07	.15	.01	.01
New manufacturing information dependency	.39	.15	-.07	.66
Day-to-day manufacturing information dependency	.27	.45	.17	.08
New product design dependency	.52	.21	-.02	.66
Product design change dependency	.57	.22	-.12	.17
Importance of subsidiary	-.14	-.15	.17	0
Intracompany purchases by subsidiary	.68	-.32	-.17	-.50
Intracompany sales by subsidiary	-.12	-.09	-.33	-.24
Product change	-.10	.31	-.18	-.23
Manufacturing technology change	-.08	.64	-.06	.12
Political environment change	-.01	.46	0	.10
Competitive climate change	-.03	.45	-.23	-.20
Supplier situation change	-.11	.57	.17	.01
Percentage of common variance explained by each factor	43	23	18	16
Eigenvalue	3.5	1.9	1.5	1.3

tion differences between subsidiaries and less foreign manufacturing) is associated with subsidiary-level strategies that reflect greater dependency on the parent. Similarly, greater company-level complexity is associated with reduced subsidiary dependency on the parent.

The above is a most interesting finding. First, it suggests some influence of company-level strategy on subsidiary-level strategy, and, second, the relationship or pattern possesses important information-processing implications. As company-level complexity increases (that is, as there are more product modification differences between foreign subsidiaries and more foreign manufacturing), the level of information-processing requirements placed on the parent HQ also increases. This threatens to overload the information-processing capacities of the parent HQ. The MNCs in the sample, however, appear to meet this challenge by reducing, under conditions of high company-level complexity, the degree to which individual subsidiaries are dependent on the parent. This pattern produces a more implementable company-level strategy because it places more reasonable information-processing requirements on the parent HQ.

The second factor consists largely of the five change variables and two of the interdependency variables, with the other information interdependency variables also tending to load positively on the factor. This factor reveals that for most of the parent-subsidiary relationships in the sample there is a strong positive relationship among the five measures of subsidiary-level change. High change in one area (that is, product line, manufacturing technology, political environment, competitive climate, supplier situation) is usually associated with high change in the other areas as well. The factor also shows that a high level of change is generally associated with greater dependency on the parent for information.

The third factor consists primarily of four company-level conditions: foreign product diversity, outside ownership in foreign subsidiaries, growth through foreign acquisitions, and size of foreign operations. Among the companies in the sample, these four elements tend to vary together. This factor or dimension seems to be another measure of the complexity of a company's international strategy. At one extreme, the firms in the sample appear to have a high percentage of their sales abroad, a high level of foreign product diversity, a relatively high degree of outside ownership in foreign subsidiaries, and use foreign acquisitions to spur growth. This is a complex international strategy. At the other extreme, the firms in the sample have a small percentage of their sales abroad and low foreign product diversity and avoid outside ownership and foreign acquisitions. This is a much simpler international strategy to implement than the former. It is easier to coordinate domestic and foreign operations because there are fewer products and technologies and there is more similarity in the operating environments. Also, it is less critical that a high level of integration between domestic and foreign operations is achieved because foreign operations are a smaller percentage of the total company.

It is interesting to notice that this dimension of strategic complexity does not include product modification differences and the size of foreign manufacturing. As already discussed, these two elements seem to be part of a different dimension of company-level complexity, which we have referred to as local adaptation complexity. It is this local adaptation complexity that seems to influence the degree of parent-subsidiary interdependency found in subsidiary-level strategies. The second dimension of company-level complexity, on the other hand, seems to be unrelated to subsidiary-level strategy. The fourth factor, although statistically significant, does not seem to possess an identifiable or meaningful pattern.

Broad Factors of Strategy by Nationality

As in the preceding section, separate tables for each analysis are not included. Instead, Table 11–4 summarizes the broad factors that emerged from each analysis.

The pattern for *U.S. MNCs* tends to support the general pattern. The first factor shows the negative relationship found in the total sample between the complexity of a company's international strategy and the degree of parent-subsidiary interdependency inherent in the strategies of its foreign subsidiaries. The second factor partially reflects the second dimension of company-level complexity (consisting of foreign product diversity and outside ownership). The third factor also reflects a dimension from the general pattern. It shows that the various measures of change at the subsidiary level are positively correlated and that change is also positively related to greater information dependency on the parent. Only two variables load heavily on the fourth factor, which exhibits no identifiable pattern.

Only one factor can be identified in *UK MNCs*. It is the same negative relationship between company-level complexity and subsidiary dependency on the parent that has been seen in both the overall and U.S. samples. Here, however, variables from both of the dimensions of company-level complexity load on the same factor, and size of

Table 11-4. Broad Factors of Strategy and Environment by Nationality and Structure.

	Broad Factors of Strategy and Environment			
All MNCs	Company-level complexity and subsidiary-level dependency	Subsidiary-level change and dependency	Company-level complexity	?
U.S. MNCs	Company-level complexity and subsidiary-level dependency	Company-level complexity	Sub-level change and dependency	?
UK MNCs	Company-level complexity and sub-level dependency	?	?	
European MNCs	Company-level size, complexity, and change	Sub size and dependency	Company-level complexity and size	Sub-level change
Functional division MNCs	?	Sub-level change and dependency	?	?
International division MNCs	Subsidiary-level change and dependency	?	?	
Geographical region MNCs	?	?	?	?
Product division MNCs	?	?	Company-level complexity and subsidiary-level dependency	Subsidiary-level change and dependency
Matrix MNCs	Company-level complexity and subsidiary-level dependency	Company-level complexity and size	?	?
Mixed MNCs	?	Company-level complexity and subsidiary-level dependency	Subsidiary-level change and dependency	?

foreign manufacturing loads on a different factor. Neither of the other two factors reveal any meaningful patterns among the strategic and environmental conditions. Once again, the small size (twelve parent-subsidiary relationships) makes it difficult for any but the strongest patterns to emerge in the analysis.

For the *European MNCs*, the first and third factors appear to represent the two different dimensions of company-level complexity. It is interesting to notice that both types of complexity are positively related to the size of international operations. Product change also loads heavily on the first factor. Unlike the previous samples, neither type of complexity in European MNCs appears to have a significant influence on the level of subsidiary dependency on the parent, although most of the subsidiary-level loadings are negative.

The second factor reveals a new relationship that did not appear in the general pattern. It states that relatively small subsidiaries are much more dependent on the parent for new manufacturing information and new product designs than are larger subsidiaries. This relationship is somewhat observable in the U.S. and UK samples, but in both it is confounded with other relationships and does not emerge as a separate factor. The fourth factor represents subsidiary-level change, which is positively related to day-to-day manufacturing dependency. Otherwise, change does not seem to be associated with more dependency on the parent, as it was in the overall and U.S. samples.

Thus, when the total sample is split by nationality, there is some support for the general pattern but not as strong as the support found earlier for the general pattern of organizational design. The U.S. and European subsamples indicate that the complexity of company-level strategy needs to be measured along more than one dimension (two tended to emerge in the study). The negative relationship found in the overall sample between the first type of company-level complexity (the one based on product modification differences) and the dependency of subsidiaries on the parent is supported by the U.S. and UK subsamples but not by the European subsample. This relationship helps to keep MNC strategies from creating information-processing requirements that threaten to overload the parent HQ. For some reason, this buffering tendency is not apparent in the strategies of European MNCs.

Another relationship that appeared in the overall sample is a positive relationship among the subsidiary-level change variables. This also appeared in the U.S. and European subsamples but not in the UK subsample. The level of change inherent in a foreign subsidiary's strategy and environment tends to be unrelated to characteristics of company-level strategy. Subsidiary-level change, however, tends to be positively related to dependency on the parent for information.

Broad Factors of Strategy by Structure

Table 11–4 also shows the broad factors that emerge when firms with each of the six different types of macro organization structure are considered separately. Once again, the purpose of this analysis is to see whether the patterns or relationships underlying subsidiary- and company-level strategy vary by structure or whether there is some consistency across structural types. The small size of the subsamples precludes a thorough analysis of this issue, but one can get some idea of how robust the general patterns are through an examination of the subsamples.

The analysis of *functional division MNCs* is difficult to interpret. The broad factors that make up the general pattern of strategy in the sample are not very apparent in the functional division MNCs. The second broad factor, which shows a strong relationship between subsidiary-level change and dependency on the parent, is mildly apparent in functional division companies. The impact of company-level complexity on parent-subsidiary interdependency is not apparent in the analysis, and the relationship between size of foreign manufacturing and the other elements of company and subsidiary-level strategy seems to be different. The irregularity with which many of the strategy elements load on the four factors makes it difficult to identify meaningful strategic patterns.

The factors that emerge from an analysis of *international division MNCs* are also not very supportive of the general pattern. The first factor shows a strong correlation among many of the elements of subsidiary-level interdependency and change. It also reveals interdependency to be greater for smaller subsidiaries. Although the second factor shows the usual positive correlations between product modification differences and the size of foreign manufacturing, it does not otherwise support any of the general patterns. Like the first factor, the third also shows a weak link between subsidiary-level change and dependency. Overall, however, the general strategic patterns are not very apparent in the international division companies of the sample.

The factors associated with *geographical region MNCs* are also difficult to interpret because many of the variables tend to load highly on more than one factor. None of the relationships contained in the general pattern can be clearly seen in the factors, and the analysis does not help to identify any other meaningful patterns of strategic relationships.

Two of the general strategic relationships can be identified in *product division MNCs*. The third factor shows the negative relationship between company-level complexity (product modification differences and size of foreign manufacturing) and subsidiary dependency on the parent. The fourth factor also reflects a positive relationship among several of the change variables and marketing information and day-to-day manufacturing information dependency. Although these patterns are discernible, the heavy overlap between factors (variables loading heavily on more than one factor) makes it difficult to draw conclusions about the overall pattern of strategy in these companies.

The first two factors in *matrix structure MNCs* show a weak negative relationship between both forms of company-level complexity and subsidiary-level dependency. The first factor also indicates that relatively large subsidiaries tend to be less dependent on the parent than do small subsidiaries. Once again, the heavy overlap and confounding of relationships leaves one with a rather unclear picture of strategy in these companies.

The last analysis shown in Table 11–4 deals with *mixed structure MNCs*. The second factor largely measures the degree of subsidiary dependency on the parent and indicates that it tends to be negatively related to company-level complexity (especially product modification differences). The third factor shows a positive relationship between some measures of subsidiary-level change and dependency on the parent. Overlap and confounding of relationships are again a problem.

Discussion of Patterns of Strategy

While the total sample analysis revealed several meaningful patterns among the twenty-two strategy variables, there is a less enlightening picture of strategy at the subsample level of analysis. Only the national subsamples (U.S., UK, and European MNCs) provide meaningful support for the general strategy patterns found in the full sample. For the structure subsamples (functional division, international division MNCs), clear strategy patterns either supporting or contradicting the general patterns tend not to emerge. Because the full and larger subsample analyses produce much more interpretable and meaningful pictures of strategy patterns, it is probable that the absence of similar patterns in the smaller subsample analyses is primarily due to inadequate sample size.

As already pointed out, the patterns that do emerge in the total sample provide meaningful but limited insight into the nature of strategy in successful MNCs (and probably complex organizations in general). One finding is that there seem to be two different types of complexity inherent in company-level strategies. The first type of complexity measures the extent to which products (and probably business practices) are locally adapted to different markets and environments. This was operationally measured in the study by the extent of product modification differences between foreign subsidiaries. It is also closely related to a significant level of foreign manufacturing. Local adaptation is difficult when the finished products are imported from the parent. Local adaptation complexity is low when a company can treat the world as a single, largely undifferentiated market for its products.

The second type of company-level complexity revealed in the study is product diversity, not in the sense of local adaptation, but in the number of different product markets the company is attempting to compete in on a global basis (such as pharmaceuticals or cosmetics). Among the sample companies, foreign product diversity is frequently associated with relatively large foreign operations, outside ownership in foreign subsidiaries, and growth through foreign acquisitions. We are not saying that these are the only types of company-level complexity one needs to consider, but they are the two that emerged in the present study.

A second strategic pattern that emerges in the study shows the impact of company-level complexity on parent-subsidiary interdependency. When local adaptation complexity is high in a company, there is a definite tendency for subsidiaries to be less dependent on the parent for new manufacturing information, new product designs, changes to existing designs, and product exports. This buffers the parent HQ from information-processing overload and leaves the company with a strategy that can be implemented. The type of complexity associated with product diversity, on the other hand, does not generally share a consistent relationship with parent-subsidiary interdependency.

The third strategy pattern that emerges from the analyses shows a strong positive correlation among the various types of change reflected in a foreign subsidiary's strategy and environment. Thus, change in the product line, manufacturing technology, political environment, competitive climate, and supplier situation all tend to vary together. And when change is high, there tends to be greater dependency on the parent for information (especially for marketing information and day-to-day manufacturing information).

Figure 11–1 attempts to pictorially show the three strategy relationships discussed above. The degree of subsidiary dependency on the parent reflected in a subsidiary's strategy is dually affected by both the degree of change inherent in the subsidiary's strategy and environment

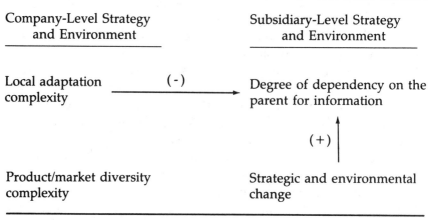

Figure 11–1. Patterns of Strategy Emerging from the Total Sample Analysis.

and the local adaptation complexity inherent in the parent company's strategy. The second type of complexity found in parent company strategies relates to product/market diversity and appears to be independent of the other strategic constructs which have emerged.

SUMMARY AND CONCLUSIONS

Previous chapters have sought to understand how MNC's organize to fit or implement their strategies by carefully analyzing the relationships between specific features of organizational design and specific elements of strategy and environment. Guided by an information-processing perspective, our ability to understand and predict such strategy-organizational design relationships appears to be reasonably good.

In the present chapter, we have sought to explore the structures of MNC strategy and MNC organizational design. More specifically, we have attempted through the use of factor analysis to uncover and identify any general patterns or dimensions that might underlie the specific features of organizational design and elements of strategy that have appeared in the study.

When all of the variables measuring the various features of organizational design are factor analyzed, three broad factors or general dimensions of organizational design seem to emerge:

1. Planning centralization (the extent to which critical decisions in the short- and long-range planning processes are centralized) emerged as one broad factor or general dimension of organizational design

in MNCs. It varies from decentralizing to the subsidiary level the making of critical decisions in the planning processes (associated with low parent-subsidiary information-processing capacity) to centralizing such decision making at the parent level (associated with high information-processing capacity).

2. Operating centralization and control and short-range planning intensity all tend to vary in the same direction at the same time. These features seem to constitute a kind of operating dimension in an organization's design that can vary from low parental influence in the operating decisions of a subsidiary (associated with low parent-subsidiary information-processing capacity) to high parental influence (associated with high information-processing capacity).

3. All four staffing variables also tend to co-vary, and they constitute a third independent dimension along which an organization's design can be measured. This dimension varies from a low percentage of parent company nationals in a foreign subsidiary (associated with low parent-subsidiary information-processing capacity) to a high percentage of parent company nationals (associated with high information-processing capacity).

Although the three general dimensions described above appear when the total sample is factor analyzed, a number of different variations on the general pattern appear when the sample is split into subgroups by nationality and company structure:

1. In European MNCs, operating centralization splits off from control and short-range planning intensity to form a second operating dimension. Thus, there tend to be four major dimensions of organizing in European MNCs.

2. In UK MNCs, short-range planning centralization is more related to the operating dimension than the long-range planning dimension. Also, staffing does not appear as a separate dimension, so UK MNCs tend to have two dimensions of organizational design.

3. In functional division MNCs, the operating and planning dimensions are combined and appear as a single dimension. This also leaves functional division MNCs with two-dimensional organizational designs.

4. International division MNCs presented the most confusing picture. No broad factors or general dimensions of organizational

design appeared that could be identified or meaningfully understood. It was suggested that this loss of the general pattern may be due to the fact that the international division structure is frequently a transitional structure that firms pass through as they move from domestic rationality to global rationality.

One must be aware that these divergences from the general pattern and their potential meaning are very tentative. The sample size for the subgroups is too small to be conclusive. The general pattern, however, seems to be well supported.

The search for general patterns that might underlie the various elements of strategy and environment produced several interesting findings:

1. There seem to be two different types of complexity inherent in company-level strategies. The first type is characterized by the extent of product modification differences between foreign subsidiaries. It is also closely related to a significant level of foreign manufacturing. This first type of complexity measures the extent to which products (and probably business practices) are locally adapted to different markets and environments. It ranges from low local adaptation (when a company can treat the world as a single, largely undifferentiated market, which simplifies parent-subsidiary information processing) to high local adaptation (which complicates parent-subsidiary information processing).

2. The second type of complexity inherent in company-level strategies can be characterized by foreign product diversity. Foreign product diversity is generally associated with relatively large foreign operations, outside ownership in foreign subsidiaries, and growth through foreign acquisitions. This dimension of complexity varies from low product diversity (which reduces requirements for parent-subsidiary information processing) to high product diversity (which increases requirements for information processing).

3. A third dimension that seems to run through the strategies of the sample companies is change at the subsidiary level. Thus, change in a subsidiary's product line, manufacturing technology, political environment, competitive climate, and supplier situation all tend to vary together. Usually when change is high, there also tends to be greater dependency on the parent (especially for marketing information and day-to-day manufacturing information). This dimension varies from low change (which reduces requirements for parent-subsidiary informa-

tion processing) to high change (which increases requirements for information processing).

4. In addition to the three dimensions of strategy discussed above, the factor analysis also revealed another strategic pattern that shows the impact of company-level complexity (local adaptation complexity) on parent-subsidiary interdependency. When local adaptation complexity is high in a company, there is a definite tendency for subsidiaries to be less dependent on the parent for new manufacturing information, new product designs, changes to existing designs, and product exports. Thus, when company-level strategy is complex (which complicates and increases requirements for parent-subsidiary information processing), there is a tendency in the subsidiary-level strategies to reduce the level of subsidiary dependency on the parent (which reduces requirements for information processing). This buffering tendency protects the parent HQ from information-processing overload and leaves the company with a strategy that is easier to implement. We consider this to be a new and important fit, not between strategy and organizational design, but between different levels of strategy within a company. The successful MNCs in the sample appear to possess this fit.

While the total sample analysis has revealed a number of meaningful patterns underlying the elements of strategy and environment, we have a more confusing and less enlightening picture when the same analyses are made for the national and structural subgroups. Because the full sample analysis produced a much more interpretable and meaningful picture of the patterns underlying strategy, it is probable that the absence of similar patterns in the subgroup analyses is primarily due to inadequate sample size.

Before concluding this chapter, there is a final point worth making. Despite shortcomings in sample size, it is clear that the strategy patterns apparent in the sample of successful MNC's are weaker and not as consistent across firms as are the organizational design patterns. This suggests the not unlikely proposition that there is more variety among the strategies and environments of MNCs than there is among the organizational designs of MNCs.

NOTES

1. For those who are interested, tables similar to Table 11–1, which show the factor loadings and eigenvalues for each analysis, are available from the author.

12

CONCLUSION

This final chapter attempts to pull together the many fit relationships that have been developed in the preceding chapters, so that a more comprehensive model of the strategy-organizational design relationship emerges. Because each of the preceding chapters has already presented its own set of conclusions, the purpose here is to integrate the separate portions of the model and discuss the general issues that underlie the study as a whole. In addition to describing the model, this chapter returns to two important issues introduced near the beginning of the book: (1) the outlook for an information-processing perspective of strategy and organizational design and (2) dealing with fit and performance in organizational research.

The first, of course, is the conceptual framework that the present study has attempted to operationalize in order to model and study strategy and organizational design in complex organizations (MNCs). The second issue is perceived by some as the Achilles' Heel of this and many other research studies that have attempted to further a contingency theory of organizational design. Although both issues were discussed at length in Chapters 2 to 4, it seems appropriate to reconsider them after the reader has been through the empirical study. Two final sections round out the conclusion of this book: one discusses how the model developed in this book can be used by managers of MNC's and other large organizations; the other presents some concluding thoughts on organizations and fit.

COMPLETING THE TWO-LEVEL MODEL OF STRATEGY
AND ORGANIZATIONAL DESIGN

This section begins by reconsidering the initial model of strategy and organizational design first presented in Chapter 3 (see Figure 3–1). This model set forth the idea that good fit between strategy and organizational design must exist at both the company level and the subsidiary level in successful MNCs. It hypothesized that three types of fit are important and need to be considered when MNCs organize to implement their strategies or cope with their environments. The skeleton model presented in Figure 3–1 has been redrawn in Figure 12–1 to reflect the more specific fits and relationships that the preceding chapters have developed. As can be seen, the overall structure of the model remains basically the same. The three types of fit hypothesized to exist between strategy and organizational design were found to exist in the sample of successful MNCs.

In addition, an interesting relationship between company and subsidiary-level strategy appeared, which was not previously hypothesized. This has been included in Figure 12–1 as Type Four Fit. In each case, the preceding data analysis has more specifically identified and described the general strategy-organizational design relationships expressed by the preliminary model in Figure 3–1.

Type One Fit

The three different types of fit between strategy and organizational design work to provide overall congruence between information-processing requirements and capacities at both the company and subsidiary levels. Type One Fit is based on the different information-processing capacities of the various types of macro organizational structure available to an MNC (Table 5–2 describes the information-processing capacities of the four elementary structures). The specific criteria for Type One Fit were developed in Chapter 5 and are presented again in Table 12–1.

The criteria indicate that the successful companies in the sample match structure and strategy by selecting the most efficient or low-cost structure that satisfies the information-processing requirements inherent in the strategy. Strategies with relatively simple, undifferentiated product lines and markets can be most efficiently implemented with a worldwide functional division structure. Similarly, strategies involving relatively small foreign operations can most economically be imple-

Table 12-1. Type One Fit: Important Fits between Company-Level Strategy and Environment and Type of Organizational Structure.

Company-Level Strategy and Environment	Type of Organization Structure			
	Functional Divisions	International Division	Geographical Regions	Product Divisions
Foreign product diversity	Low foreign product diversity		High foreign product diversity	
Product modification differences	Low product modification differences between subsidiaries			
Product change				High rate of product change
Size of foreign operations		Relatively small foreign operations	Relatively large foreign operations	Relatively large foreign operations
Size of foreign manufacturing			High level of foreign manufacturing	
Number of foreign subsidiaries	Few foreign subsidiaries	Low to moderate number of foreign subsidairies	Large number of foreign subsidiaries	Large number of foreign subsidiaries
Extent of outside ownership	Low level of outside ownership in foreign subsidiaries			
Extent of foreign acquisitions	Few foreign acquisitions			

Figure 12–1. Two-Level Model of Strategy and Organizational Design in MNCs.

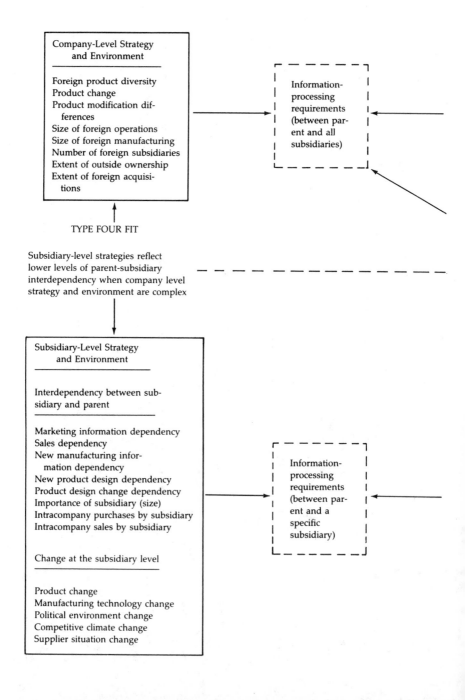

TYPE ONE FIT

The selection of macro-organization
structure matches information processing capabilities with the information processing requirements
inherent in company-level strategy.
The basic response is to select the
most efficient or low-cost structure
that satisfies the information processing requirements. (see Table
12–1 for details of this fit.)

Information-
processing
capacities
(between par-
ent and all
subsidiaries)

Company-Level
Organizational Design

Type of structure

TYPE THREE FIT

Operating and planning centralization,
marketing, and financial control, the use of
face-to-face meetings and the raising
of new issues during short-range
planning primarily respond to company-
level information processing requirements. The basic response is to
buffer the parent HQs from information processing overload when company
level strategy and environment are
complex. (see Table 12–3 for details
of this fit.)

Company Level

Subsidiary Level

TYPE TWO FIT

Staffing of all functional areas,
manufacturing control, and intensity of communications during short range
planning primarily respond to subsidiary level information processing
requirements. The basic response is
to concentrate information processing capacity where information processing requirements are highest.
(See Table 12–1 for details of
this fit.)

Information-
processing
capacities
(between par-
ent and a
specific
subsidiary)

Parent-Subsidiary Level
of Organizational Design

Degree of centralization
Level of control
Staffing of foreign subsidiary
Planning system characteristics

Effectiveness is a
function of the quality
of three types of fit.

mented with an international division structure. These are matches based on fitting low-cost structures to strategies with relatively constrained information-processing requirements. It is apparent from Table 12–1 that all of the key fits for these structures constrain or reduce the requirements for parent-subsidiary information-processing.

The geographical region and worldwide product division structures are high cost structures with several regional or product HQs, each managing a portion of the firm's foreign operations. Here the match is based on ensuring that the strategy justifies this high cost. It is apparent from Table 12–1 that all of the key fits for these structures insure relatively large and/or complex parent-subsidiary information-processing requirements.

In addition to the specific fits identified for the four types of elementary structure, Chapter 6 also presented some conceptual and empirical support for when to use matrix and mixed structures. Generally, higher-cost matrix structures should be used only when company-level strategy and environment present conditions that overlap or combine the fit criteria of two of the elementary structures. Such conditions require the simultaneous information-processing capacities of two of the elementary structures, and this is exactly what a matrix structure provides.

Type Two Fit

Type Two Fit focuses on the strategies and environments of individual subsidiaries and those organizational design features that can vary from one parent-subsidiary relationship to the next. The goal behind Type Two Fit is to match parent-subsidiary information-processing capacity to the level of parent-subsidiary interdependency and the degree of strategic and environmental change inherent in each subsidiary's strategy. Because requirements for information processing will vary from one subsidiary to the next and because providing too much information-processing capacity is uneconomical, there is a need for those organizational design features that facilitate Type Two Fit to vary in response to changing subsidiary-level conditions.

The preceding analysis has revealed that subsidiary staffing is the design feature that is most responsive to local subsidiary conditions. As change and interdependency with the parent increase, there is a strong tendency to assign more parent company nationals to key positions. Manufacturing control and the intensity of parent-subsidiary communications during short-range planning also vary largely with the information-processing requirements inherent in subsidiary-level strategy.

While the other features of organizational design, such as operating centralization and marketing and financial control, also vary in response to subsidiary-level conditions, their flexibility to respond to such conditions seems to be more limited. In most MNCs, altering staffing and the intensity of communications during planning appear to be the primary ways of varying information-processing capacities across subsidiaries. Both tend to be independent of each other (that is, they belong to two different broad factors or dimensions of organizing).

Table 12–2 shows the statistically significant fits found in the study between design and subsidiary-level strategy. It is important to notice that all design features—those with high subsidiary-level adaptability such as staffing, and those with limited adaptability such as operating centralization—show a consistent relationship with subsidiary-level strategy. They vary in such a way as to provide more information-processing capacity when a subsidiary's strategy calls for more dependency on the parent and/or more change. And they provide less information-processing capacity when the opposite is the case. Unlike Type One Fit, where a firm's choice of structure precludes other choices, Type Two Fit is really the sum of a number of other, more specific, fits. This suggests that there might be some flexibility as to which features or information-processing mechanisms are used. For example, if local host government policies preclude more staffing with parent company nationals, information-processing capacity might also be increased by raising the intensity of parent-subsidiary communications during the planning process.

Type Three Fit

Type Three Fit focuses on the same subsidiary-level design features as Type Two Fit but relates them to the information-processing requirements of company-level strategy and environment. This fit basically recognizes that in complex organizations, such as MNCs, company-level conditions impose an additional constraint on the parent-subunit relationship. The present study has found that operating centralization, planning centralization, marketing and financial control, the use of face-to-face planning meetings, and the extent to which new issues are raised during short-range planning are more strongly influenced by company-level than by subsidiary-level strategy and environment.[1] The implication is that these are the design features that most heavily tax or threaten to overload the information-processing capacities of the parent HQ.

Table 12-2. Type Two Fit: Important Fits between Subsidiary-Level Strategy and Environment and Subsidiary-Level Organizational Design.

Subsidiary-Level Strategy and Environment	Operating Centralization	Control	Staffing	Short-Range Planning Intensity
High subsidiary dependency on parent	Centralize (marketing, manufacturing)	Increase control (manufacturing)	More parent company nationals (all areas)	More communications and new issue raising
Low subsidiary dependency on parent	Decentralize (marketing, manufacturing)	Decrease control (manufacturing)	Fewer parent company nationals (all areas)	Less communications and new issue raising
High degree of change in strategy and environment	Centralize (marketing)	Increase control (all areas)	More parent company nationals (all areas)	More communications and face-to-face planning meetings
Low degree of change in strategy and environment	Decentralize (marketing)	Decrease control (all areas)	Fewer parent company nationals (all areas)	Less communications and fewer face-to-face planning meetings

Table 12–3 shows the statistically significant fits found in the study between subsidiary-level design and company-level strategy and environment. As was the case with Type Two Fit, there is a very consistent pattern. As company-level strategy and environment become more complex and/or foreign operations become larger, there is a consistent tendency to reduce the level of parent-subsidiary information-processing across all subsidiaries in a company. This buffers or protects the parent HQ from information-processing overload. The only exception to this is the raising of new issues during the short-range planning process. When company-level conditions are more complex, it appears that more new issues are likely to be raised during the parent's review of its subsidiaries' short range plans.

Thus, Type Three Fit is basically an economizing or buffering tendency used to cope with complexity and large size. It is important because the information-processing resources of an organization are finite and, in large, successful companies, probably more constraining on organizational performance than are its financial resources. This buffering tendency appears to be consistent with Weick's (1976) argument that at times a looser coupling between organizational elements can enhance the survival and adaptive qualities of an organization. Type Two Fit, on the other hand, attempts to distribute information-processing capacity in a way that will do the most good (that is, successfully implement the most subsidiary-level strategies). It does this by selectively concentrating information-processing capacity where requirements are high and reducing the available information-processing capacity where requirements are low.

Type Four Fit

In addition to the three types of fit between strategy and organizational design, the study also found a buffering tendency operating between the company and subsidiary levels of strategy. Interestingly, this pattern was not found in the European subsample. When company-level strategy is complex (and, more specifically, when local adaptation complexity is high), there is a tendency for subsidiary-level strategies to specify lower levels of parent-subsidiary interdependency. Because both complexity and interdependency increase information-processing requirements between the parent and its subsidiaries, this tendency reduces the risk of overloading the information-processing capacities of the parent HQ and produces a more implementable strategy. This tendency is shown in Figure 12–1 as Type Four Fit.

Table 12-3. Type Three Fit: Important Fits between Company-Level Strategy and Environment and Subsidiary-Level Organizational Design.

Company-Level Strategy and Environment	Operating Centralization	Control	Staffing	Short Range Planning Intensity	Planning Centralization
Complex strategy and environment	Decentralize (all areas)	Decrease control (all areas)	Fewer parent company nationals (manufacturing)	Fewer face-to-face planning meetings, more new issue raising	Decentralize short range planning decisions
Simple strategy and environment	Centralize (all areas)	Increase control (all areas)	More parent company nationals (manufacturing)	More face-to-face planning meetings, less new issue raising	Centralize short range planning decisions
Relatively large foreign operations	Decentralize (marketing)	Decrease control (all areas)	—	Less communications, fewer face-to-face planning meetings	—
Relatively small foreign operations	Centralize (marketing)	Increase control (all areas)	—	More communications, more face-to-face planning meetings	—

Except in case studies, the relationship between different levels of strategy in an organization has not been empirically studied. Consequently, there is little formal theoretical or conceptual understanding of the critical relationships between levels of strategy in a firm. It is quite possible that the present finding has uncovered one of these critical relationships, since it seems to be both useful (by producing more implementable strategies) and clearly reflected in the U.S. subsample of successful companies. If, indeed, it is an important relationship, it once again stresses the criticality of protecting the hierarchy in complex organizations from information-processing overload.

The study also found some relationship between company-level structure (such as worldwide functional divisions) and the various features of subsidiary-level organizational design. Overall, however, this relationship was weak and not very meaningful. The only pattern to emerge from this analysis was that functional division companies tend to use more centralization, performance control, and staffing with parent company nationals than do companies with other structures. But even this is true only for certain functional areas. Our conclusion is that this is not as important a relationship as the other fit relationships already discussed. For this reason, the model shown in Figure 12–1 does not show any required fit between company-level structure and the features of subsidiary-level organizational design.

Finally, the model needs to be considered in light of Hypothesis 3–1, which states that other factors, such as nationality, industry, size of company, age of company abroad, size of subsidiary, and age of subsidiary will have no significant influence on the organizational design of an MNC, once the influence of those strategic and environmental conditions with information-processing implications has been taken into account. Overall, this hypothesis tends to be true. These other factors, which have appeared as important contingency variables in many research studies, explain only small amounts of the variation in organizational design once the influence of the strategic and environmental conditions has been taken into account. Although parent country nationality, in particular, strongly influences a number of the strategic and environmental conditions surrounding MNC's, its influence on organizational design can be explained largely in terms of these conditions. It is also interesting to notice that, in general, nationality does not strongly moderate the relationships found between the various organizational design features and the strategic and environmental conditions. The strongest exception to this conclusion seems to lie in the planning area, where it was suggested that the planning processes in U.S. and

European MNCs may differ significantly in the type of information processing each provides. In general, however, the strategy-organizational design
relationships contained in the model tend to hold across the nationality
groups represented in the sample. Thus, the study findings tend to support
a culture-free perspective of organizational structure and design (Birnbaum
and Wong 1985).

The consistency with which the information-processing approach
was able to predict and describe the wide variety of relationships (fits)
measured in the study is impressive. If there is a reason for doubt or
concern, it probably lies with the strength of the relationships revealed
in the study. In most of the chapters, the elements of strategy were able
to explain 15 to 25 percent of the variation of some feature of organizational design. There are two primary reasons why the strengths of the
relationships are not greater. First, measurement of the macro level
strategy and organizational design concepts is a major problem. The
available operational measures tend to only tap small portions of the
concepts contained in the model. If one could measure concepts more
completely (such as change inherent in a subsidiary's strategy or the
level of parent control exercised over a subsidiary's marketing activities), one could probably account for a higher percentage of the variation.

Second, the relationships or fits contained in the model are by nature
not as tightly connected as those found in the physical sciences. There
does not have to be anything close to a one-to-one relationship between
strategy and organizational design for the concepts and their relationships to have value. The assumption that strategy and organizational
design share some nice monotonic and even linear relationship when
good fit is present, is probably unwarranted. This is a convenience of
the modeling technique that, undoubtedly, overstates the orderliness of
the phenomenon itself. Given these two drawbacks, it is probably more
meaningful to use the consistency of the relationships as a measure of
the power of the model than the percentage of variation explained. If
consistency rather than strength is the criterion, then the model seems
to be an accurate depicter of the strategy-organizational design relationship in successful MNCs.

EVALUATING THE INFORMATION-PROCESSING
PERSPECTIVE OF ORGANIZATIONAL DESIGN

Aside from contributing to what is known about organizational design
in MNCs, a primary purpose of this book has been to consider and, if

possible, extend conceptual theory about macro organizational design in complex organizations. Because this attempt has used an information-processing perspective to model the relationship between strategy and organizational design, it seems appropriate to evaluate the advantages and problems associated with this conceptual framework. In order to do this, it is necessary to reconsider some of the issues and problems discussed in the early chapters of the book.

As identified in Chapter 1, one of the primary problems facing structuralcontingency theory is that "the various operational contingency models . . . have not integrated well into grander, more abstract notions about organizations." The preceding chapters of this book have attempted to demonstrate that the information-processing perspective can encompass and explain earlier models and empirical results that have previously been associated with structure, centralization, and control. The same perspective also has been used to provide some new understanding of matrix structures, subsidiary staffing, and planning processes. Such integration across a wide variety of specific strategy-organizational design fits is possible because the notion of fitting information-processing requirements and capacities is sufficiently general and abstract.

A number of theorists have criticized contingency theory for being "oriented more to designing than to understanding organizations" (Aldrich 1979:57). Mintzberg (1979:12) states that "Most of the contemporary literature fails to relate the description of structure with that of the functioning of the organization," and Daft and Weick (1984) point out that research has produced very little understanding about how different organizational configurations influence the ability of an organization to interpret its environment. Information-processing models hold promise for addressing these criticisms because they are implicitly process models. A great deal about how organizations coordinate and process information has been described in the preceding chapters and in the references to other information-processing studies. All of this is implicitly a part of the information-processing framework and model, even if the explicit variables used by the model (and measured in the study) tend to be structural.

It is the ability of information-processing models to provide a process model kind of understanding that makes this approach particularly attractive for modeling macro organizational design. Other approaches to modeling macro design tend to be purely structural and lack a link to the functioning of the organization. In the present study, the information-processing model and conceptual framework have been used to generate the testable hypotheses of the study. This links the specific findings back to (1) some general conceptual framework and (2) some understanding about how form or design might influence organizational behavior (information processing) and what types of organizational behavior (information processing) are required to successfully cope with specific strategic and environmental conditions. Such linkages represent a constructive response to the above criticisms.

Although generality and abstraction are needed to support higher levels of theory, there is little merit in building theory about a weak concept (that is, a concept weakly linked to organizational performance). Because organizational performance is the dependent variable that structural contingency theory attempts to maximize, subject to a variety of constraints, the concept of information processing must be strongly linked to it. Otherwise, there is no assurance that good information-processing fit will be associated with good organizational performance. The study has assumed that information processing between organizational subunits is an important aspect of organizational functioning, which contributes significantly to performance. This assumption is supported by the work of earlier theorists such as Barnard (1938) and Katz and Kahn (1966), who identified the importance of information processing in any broad theory of organizations. While they did not, in the strict sense of the word, empirically link information processing to performance, they strongly implied that for large, complex organizations, such a linkage exists.

The consistency with which the sample companies act to avoid information-processing overload (by reducing the level of parent-subsidiary information processing), when confronted with high levels of company-level complexity and size, suggests that the danger of information-processing overload in these organizations is a very real and important problem. Similarly, the consistency with which these same firms increase information processing between the parent HQ and a specific subsidiary when the subsidiary faces higher levels of change or interdependency with the parent suggests that such information processing is also important. The fact that information-processing capacities appear to vary in successful organizations in relation to information-processing requirements tends to support the view suggested by Barnard and Katz and Kahn, that information processing is important in complex organizations and significantly linked to performance. It is important to realize, however, that while there is some support for the above view and no significant evidence against it, the linkage between information processing fit and organizational performance remains largely an assumption.

Operationally, information processing is being used differently in the present study than in previous studies, which have constructed information-processing models of more micro level subjects (usually coordination at the work group level). For example, Van de Ven, Delbecq, and Koenig (1976) measured information processing at the work-flow level in a state employment agency in terms of the extent to which policies and procedures, work plans, personal coordination, and meetings existed. Tushman (1978) measured information processing at the project group level in a research laboratory in terms of the number of oral, work-related communications made by members of the group. These more direct measures of information processing are operationally more feasible when the subject of study is at the micro level rather than the macro level of organizations.

In order to apply an information-processing approach to macro level subjects such as the strategy-organizational design relationship, information processing has been utilized as an abstract intervening concept, useful for positing conceptual relationships between elements of strategy and characteristics of structure. Conceptually, the role played by information processing is the same in both the micro and macro level models (that is, information-processing capacities need to fit information-processing requirements in order for there to be effective organizational functioning). In the macro level model, however, information processing is not directly measured. Instead, the assumed relationships between information processing and elements of strategy and structure are indirectly tested when the hypotheses drawn from the macro information-processing model are empirically tested. Because direct measurement and testing are preferable to indirect measurement and testing, there is a natural tendency to feel more comfortable with the information-processing approach in micro level than in macro level studies. Yet this is largely a characteristic of micro and macro level studies in general and has little to do with the validity of extending the information-processing approach to the examination of macro level issues.

Strictly speaking, micro level studies have not directly measured information processing either. For as Daft and Macintosh (1981: 210) point out, it is virtually impossible to measure the amount of information which has been conveyed, " because information does not have tangible properties." Instead, micro level studies have tended to measure such aspects of information processing as the frequency and mode of communication between work groups and assume that this is related to the amount of information processed.

The real question, however, is not whether the information-processing approach can be extended to the macro level while retaining all of the operational characteristics it possesses at the micro level. Or stated somewhat differently, the relevant comparison when assessing the value of a model is not between micro and macro level models that are linked by a common conceptual framework (but clearly address different problems and issues), but between a model and other models of differing conceptual frameworks that tend to address the same problems and issues. Viewed within this context, the information-processing model of strategy and organizational design seems to provide an improved way of understanding and conceptualizing this complex relationship.

The model is more explicit in its identification of critical variables and relationships than the loose, descriptive models of strategy and organizational design that are contained in most case studies. In fact, it has generally been impossible to aggregate these case studies into a more general model of strategy and organizational design. Although previous survey studies of strategy and organizational design have served to identify a number of recurrent relationships, their lack of an underlying conceptual framework limits extending the empirical findings to either (1) new variants of strategy and organizational design or (2) a more fundamental understanding of why these relationships are important to organizational performance. By modeling a common and important part of organizational functioning (information processing), the present study has used a different approach to attack an old, but increasingly complex, problem. While additional research that more directly links types of strategy and organizational design to characteristics of information processing is required, the ability of the information-processing perspective and model to address many of the limitations inherent in current structural contingency models argues for its further application and development.

In Chapter 4 it was suggested that for the information-processing perspective to advance, what is needed is a more precise translation of the measured strategy and design variables into the abstract information-processing concepts that are so useful for general theory building. This will be easier to accomplish if one first identifies the dimensions of information processing that are important to the type and level of organization being modeled and then constructs decision rules for mapping the measured strategy and design variables onto these dimensions.

The present study followed the above suggestion rather explicitly in Chapters 5 and 6, where four explicit dimensions of information processing were used to relate strategy and structure. In subsequent chapters, however, the nature or type of information processing provided by centralization, control, staffing, and planning is generally unspecified, although at times implied by the nature of the contingency relationships. For example, the contingency relationships associated with staffing and planning imply that these mechanisms may possess more nonroutine information-processing capacity than centralization or control. Future research which attempts to apply an information-processing perspective to macro level organizational design should strive to use a more multidimensional model of the information-processing capacities of these mechanisms.

For example, distinguishing between routine and nonroutine information processing when hypothesizing and measuring planning relationships would probably provide a more complete understanding of the various forms of information processing provided by planning and the rather complex set of contingency relationships that seem to be associated with it. A number of general dimensions of information processing have been identified in more micro level studies, that generally focus on the task as the unit of analysis. Randolph and Finch (1977) measured and analyzed the direction and frequency of information processing. Daft (1981) and Daft and MacIntosch (1981) measured and established the importance of information ambiguity. O'Reilly (1982) has measured and studied the quality and accessibility of information. These and other dimensions of information processing can probably be used to construct more multidimensional models for relating strategy and environment to macro level organization design.

Although the existing measures of these concepts may not be feasible in more macro level research studies, ways can undoubtedly be found to measure both strategy and organizational design along these dimensions. For example, the degree of ambiguity inherent in a subsidiary's strategy might be measured in terms of how analyzable or unanalyzable management perceives a number of different problem solving situations (such as predicting the market's acceptance of a new product or anticipating competitors' reactions). On the other hand, the capacity of a planning process for coping with information-processing ambiguity might be measured in terms of the levels of personal communication or face-to-face interaction associated with the process and the extent to which it tends to raise new issues.

Defining information-processing requirements and capacities is laborious, and at times the researcher may have to employ measures that are qualitative rather than quantitative in nature. Yet this kind of explicit model building is an improvement over the lack of conceptual framework and the implicitness of fit relationships in many contingency studies. Although the present study frequently lacks the more elaborate, multidimensional perspective of information processing just described, it, nevertheless, demonstrates that an information-processing perspective can be used to rather consistently and meaningfully relate strategies and environmental conditions to features of macro organizational design.

While at points the information-processing framework approaches a "master conceptual scheme" (Merton 1957) or metaparadigm (Kuhn 1970), the present study has largely developed a theory of the middle range—a theory "intermediate to the minor working hypotheses evolved in abundance during the day-to-day routines of research, and the all-inclusive speculations comprising a master conceptual scheme. . . " (Merton 1957: 5).

It is when information-processing concepts function as a general physics within the population ecology perspective for linking organizational design to strategy and environment (see the second paragraph of Chapter 2 for Aldrich's comments about the need for such a physics) that the information-processing framework approaches being a master conceptual scheme or metaparadigm. It is important to notice that at the metaparadigm level the primary concept of information-processing fit and performance in organizations is very simple and abstract. This concept is the notion that fit between information-processing requirements and capacities enhances performance, while misfit detracts from it. This conceptual linkage of fit and performance exists at the metaparadigm level because it is thought to hold across many levels of analysis (individual, group, organization).

The information-processing studies discussed in Chapter 2 have generally attempted to develop middle-range theory at the group level of analysis (Van de Ven, Delbecq, and Koenig 1976; Tushman 1978). The present study has attempted to develop theory at the organization level of analysis. At the present time, the degree of integration and generalization across these middle range theories is weak, and there is little in the way of a metaparadigm regarding information processing in organizations.

THE RELATIONSHIP OF FIT TO PERFORMANCE

The conceptual issues surrounding fit were discussed at the end of Chapter 3. Organizational performance and the difficulties associated with measuring it were discussed in Chapter 4. The purpose of this section is to summarize how both subjects were handled in the present study and discuss how they should be incorporated into future research designs.

The present study has used an interaction approach to model fit between strategy, organizational design, and organizational performance. This approach states that organizational design and strategy interact to influence performance and that such interaction can be described as a series of pair-wise fits. A systems model of fit would capture the simultaneous interaction of the numerous elements of strategy with the numerous features of organizational design and relate overall fit to performance. Only in Chapters 5 and 6, where multiple discriminant analysis was used to simultaneously test sets of strategy-structure fits, does the present study employ a systems approach. Otherwise, the measures and relationships are not specified at a level that supports the kind of interval scale comparisons and aggregations which are necessary for a true systems model.

It is important to notice that most of the fits included in the model of Figure 12–1 are directional or scalar in nature rather than precise or interval scale. As company-level complexity increases, there should be some tendency to decentralize decisionmaking but to what level is not specified. Also, it is not very clear how substitutable one form of information processing is for another (such as planning for staffing). Some way of integrating across these different measures is necessary before one can proceed to a systems level of modeling. It is likely that measurement along more specific dimensions of information processing, as discussed in the previous section, will facilitate the move toward more of a systems model.

Where it is difficult to measure organizational fit with a systems model, it also will be difficult to link organizational fit to organizational performance. In situations such as the present study, where there are numerous strategy-organizational design fits, no single measure of organizational performance seems suitable. The overall notion of fit in contingency theory is relatively simple, but at the operational level, there are numerous fits that share complex interdependencies. This is what makes the subject so difficult for researchers and managers alike. It is unlikely there is any single operational fit that contributes in a consistently strong way to some broad measure of organizational performance (such as profitability or return on investment). We assume that overall fit relates strongly to overall performance but cannot measure fit or its relationship to performance at this level.

As already discussed in Chapter 4, structural contingency theory has had a difficult time showing a consistent relationship between organizational fit and organizational performance. Critics of macro organizational contingency research have increasingly required fit to show some positive relationship with a performance measure for the work to be considered a contribution to the field. A frequent recommendation has been to use multiple performance measures (such as profitability, return on investment, or sales growth) to overcome some of the criticism of a single performance measure.

Despite this trend, the empirically demonstrated link between macro organizational fit and various goal-oriented performance measures (Zammuto 1982) has been weak and unconvincing. Our criticism of this research is that there is frequently no convincing logic or rationale linking some particular type of organizational fit to the specific goal-oriented performance measures employed. This is different from the usual criticism directed at a lack of statistical significance.

It is interesting to notice that the ability of more micro organizational studies, usually conducted at the task level, to find a significant relationship between some design fit and some performance measure is seemingly much greater than it has been for macro organizational studies. Generally the logic or rationale linking design fit to the performance measure is also more convincing, which probably accounts for the higher incidence of statistical support. It is simply easier, and more appropriate, to link design fit at the micro organizational level to specific performance measures (such as supervisory rankings of team performance) than it is at the macro organizational level, where performance measures tend to be less influenced by any specific organizational design fit.

As a result of the difficulties associated with using goal-oriented performance measures to evaluate the quality of macro organizational fit, the present study has used a different approach to demonstrate a link between organizational design fit (as defined and measured in the study) and performance. The information-processing perspective plays a crucial role in this research design.

The study begins by making the initial assumption that some reasonable level of fit between information-processing requirements and information-processing capacities must exist for large, complex organizations to survive and grow (both are generally considered basic aspects of organizational performance). Based on this assumption, a number of functional information-processing fits are hypothesized between the features of a firm's organizational design and elements of its strategy and environment. When these hypotheses are empirically tested with a sample of successful MNCs, the evidence tends to support the fit hypotheses. In addition to testing the logic of the hypotheses, this also provides a weak test of the initial assumption about the link between performance and information-processing fit in large, complex organizations.

In order to challenge the present model, critics must

1. Find significant numbers of companies that possess the fits described in the model that fail (that is, evidence that such fit is unrelated to performance), or
2. Find significant numbers of companies that lack such fits that survive and grow (that is, further evidence that such fit is unrelated to performance).

While the present study tends to support the fit hypotheses, it does not test the consequences of misfit. Instead, the thrust of the study has been to more elaborately and completely define the dimensions of fit across a variety of organizational design features and elements of strategy at two levels of analysis.

There are some critics who would prefer to hold up further elaboration and extension of structural contingency theory until the link between fit and performance and misfit and poor performance has been more strongly demonstrated. Instead, we think there is a need for two different kinds of contingency research. The one to further explore and define the linkage between fit and performance; the second to further explore and define functional fits between the features of organizational design and strategy and environment. The two kinds of research are different in purpose and design, but complementary in contributing to the development of stronger structural contingency theory.

Donaldson's (1984) study of the influence of structural fit and misfit on organizational performance is a good example of the first type of research. It indicates that differences between fit and misfit must be examined longitudinally over relatively long time periods in order to observe the effects on performance. Given their focus and primary concern, such studies will tend to use relatively simple models of strategy and organizational design. This stream of research should also be concerned with attempting to resolve the current impasse over how to measure or represent organizational performance in macro organizational theory.

The present study clearly identifies itself with the second type of research. This stream of research needs to primarily concern itself with finding better ways to represent and understand strategy-organizational design fit and improving the operational measurement of both of these phenomena. The present study has especially attempted to contribute to the former by utilizing an information-processing perspective to develop a two-level model of fit. Although organizational performance must also be represented in such studies, we have argued that a weaker approach (such as that used in the present study) is adequate. This will allow research studies that seek to more fully define and understand the nature of organizational fit to go ahead. Given the incomplete manner in which performance is represented in such studies, however, researchers must be careful to use a strong conceptual framework to hypothesize fit.

Too often research and criticism has failed to distinguish between these two different types of research, and this has added to the confusion and disillusionment surrounding contingency theory. Because it is not generally feasible to address both sets of problems and issues in the same empirical study, the criteria used to design and evaluate the studies should differ. In the interest of constructive criticism, those who would cast stones should at least be sure they are casting them at the appropriate target.

PRACTICAL APPLICATIONS FOR MANAGERS OF MNCs AND OTHER LARGE ORGANIZATIONS

While this book has primarily addressed itself to the concerns of researchers and theorists, the model of strategy and organizational design developed here has important implications for those who seek to understand and manage large, complex organizations.

Guidelines for Good Fit

The study has identified four general types of fit that need to exist between the strategy and environment of an MNC and its organizational design. Within these general fits, the large number of specific fits that have been found to exist in successful MNCs provide useful guide-lines that can be used *to evaluate the effectiveness of existing features of an organization's design.* For example, if one subsidiary is facing a high rate of change in its competitive climate and supplier situation, while a second subsidiary faces very stable conditions for both of these, a company can check whether it is adequately varying the information-processing capacities provided between the parent and both subsidiaries. The level of staffing with parent company nationals and the intensity of parent-subsidiary communications during the planning process should proba-bly be greater for the first subsidiary than for the second.

The guidelines can also be used *to evaluate potential changes to an organ-ization's design,* in order to determine the likely impact of such changes on strategy implementation. An interesting example might serve to illustrate this. About a year after the data collection, one of the sample companies changed its structure to another structure that clearly vio-lated some of the key fits called for in Table 12–1. We understand that difficulties ensued, and a year later the structure was changed once again. Because the new structure seems to fit the key strategic and environmental conditions of the company, one would predict that it will facilitate implementing the company's strategy. While the first change could easily be explained in terms of the political pressures existing inside the company, sooner or later good fit needs to be restored if a firm is to survive and prosper in a competitive environ-ment. Because sooner is better than later, knowledge of the specific fits can probably save some of the trial-and-error and lead to a higher rate of success when making organizational changes. Such knowledge might also help to de-politicize organizational decisions in a firm, by providing some kind of objective frame of reference that can be used when debating such decisions.

A third way in which the specific fits or guidelines can be used is *to evaluate potential changes in the strategy and environment of an MNC.* Other research studies report that most often key strategic and environmental conditions change without complementary changes in organizational design. Only after strategy implementation has been seriously impaired and performance is suffering are the necessary organizational changes made. If extensive trial-and-error are required, the company can even fail before good fit is restored. Undoubtedly, one of the best ways to improve strategy implementation is to critically evaluate the firm's capacities to implement a strategy at the time it is formulated. The guidelines emerging from the study help one to do this. For example, the shift toward a variety of global strategies (Ghoshal 1987) can be evaluated in terms of the design changes required to fit such changes. Sometimes it may be necessary to abandon a proposed strategy because the chances of implementing it successfully are deemed to be small.

What Managers Need to Monitor

In addition to identifying specific fits between elements of strategy and organizational design, the study highlights the kinds of things managers in MNCs need to focus on and monitor. Recently, there has been increasing interest in environmental scanning (Keegan 1974). Dynamic and competitive environments need to be carefully monitored. Yet the environments of most MNCs are so broad that no management can look at everything. Selectivity is required. The present study identifies the kinds of things environmental scanning activities need to pick up if they are to support organizing for strategy implementation. Various measures of environmental change, complexity, and the size or scope of the company's interface with the environment seem to be most critical.

Similarly, managers need to monitor various aspects of organizational design. In many organizations there is frequent change, and with this goes change in the information-processing capacities being provided. This book has covered a number of the most important information-processing mechanisms and indicated how their information-processing capacities might be estimated.

Developing a Personal Model of Strategy Implementation

Perhaps the most useful output of the study is a conceptual framework and perspective for looking at the problem of strategy implementation. The information-processing model (the notion of balancing information-processing requirements and capacities, and the importance of considering four different types of fit in MNCs) tends to be supported by the study. We believe this is a perspective that can significantly help managers deal with problems involving strategy and organizational design. For this to happen, however, a manager needs to further develop and personalize the general model to address his or her own problems. The manager needs to decide which are the critical elements of the firm's strategy and environment, what type of information processing is needed to deal with them, and which features of organizational design are providing this information-processing capacity. With this kind of picture, a manager can assess and even project the impact that changes in (1) strategy and environment and (2) organizational design are going to have on the adequacy of information processing within the company.

Managers at the subsidiary level will tend to focus on the strategies and environments of specific foreign subsidiaries. They have the primary responsibility for Type Two Fit. In addition, they also will need some familiarity with the general strategic and environmental conditions of the overall company, so that they can also appreciate and take Type Three and Type Four Fit into consideration. Managers at the parent HQ level will primarily need to understand company-level strategy and environment. They have primary responsibility for Type One, Type Three, and Type Four Fit. As a result of these differences in responsibility, managers at different levels of the organization will tend to fill in different parts of the model with greater detail.

Based on the managers we met during the study, we would have to conclude that most managers have a rather poor understanding of macro organizational design and fit. While the individual manager frequently has considerable insight into some particular aspect of the parent-subsidiary relationship, it is seldom integrated at the macro level with other aspects of the relationship. Most of the explicit understanding of organizational design and fit seems to be specific, rather than general or abstract. As a result, the real understanding of fit at the parent-subsidiary level tends to be dispersed across many people. In fact, much of a company's understanding of design and fit seems to be implicit in the institutionalized practices and ways of thinking in a company. Usually, managers cannot link these practices and ways of thinking back to some more general rationale of fit or notion of contingency theory. In other words, no single person has a very complete picture or explicit understanding of strategy-organizational design fit in large organizations. There are simply too many variables and interdependencies, and managers lack the general, abstract models that are needed to integrate across all of this complexity.

As an analogy, we think most managers understand organizational design and fit the way a good mechanic understands an engine. Such understanding is specific and largely based on experience. It works well as long as the engine and the conditions it must operate under are relatively stable. When substantial change is encountered, however, the more general and abstract understanding of a design engineer (that is, one familiar with mechanical and materials engineering) is usually required to redesign the engine. While all firms appreciate the value associated with the general and abstract models of mechanical and materials engineering, few firms seem to appreciate the value associated with a more general and abstract understanding of organization theory.

We think that the conceptual framework and model developed in the present study provides the kind of general and abstract understanding of organization theory that managers can begin to apply. Although the understanding is much weaker than the understanding associated with mechanical and materials engineering, this is not the relevant comparison. While the onus to develop better theory rests more on the organizational researcher than the manager, nothing extends and refines theory quicker than the attempt to apply it.

SOME CONCLUDING THOUGHTS ON RESEARCH AND ORGANIZATIONS

Recently it has become fashionable to study organizing rather than organizational design—the dynamic rather than the static character of organizations. This movement can be aptly characterized by Wicker's (1980:714) description of Weick's view about organizations: "For Weick, the noun organization is a myth by which organizations are seen as substantial, rigid, solid, static. Reality is better captured by the verb organizing, with its imagery of movement, patterning, timing, sequences, interactions, and loose linkages." There is of course merit to this view, and considerable research on the process of organizing has occurred since the *Social Psychology of Organizations* (Weick 1979) was first published.

Yet the static side of organizations is also reality, even if it is less apparent beneath the flux of dynamic "interactions and loose linkages." Moreover, the static relationships uncovered by structural contingency research are not just the reality of a moment, unique and fleeting, but pattern which exists for most organizations at most points in time— pattern that transcends the dynamic flux that also characterizes organizations. The one is no less reality than the other. There is a strong need to understand both the relatively static as well as the relatively dynamic properties of organizations.

It is important to recognize that organizations do not have our model in front of them as they make the various decisions that result in fits or misfits between strategy and the various features of organizational design. Indeed, such decisionmaking is diffused across many levels and areas of the organization. Yet among the successful MNCs, there is a consistent tendency toward fit and away from misfit, as these are defined in the model. This strongly suggests that such fits are probably necessary, but not sufficient conditions for success.

Given the size and complexity of information-processing requirements in large MNCs and the very real limitations on information-processing capacities, it is something of a wonder that such organizations exist and succeed in implementing their strategies. We think the study has uncovered at least a faint outline or picture of the magical balance and fit that seems to exist in successful MNCs. Like balance and fit in nature, no one could ever plan precisely how such a complex system should work. Instead, organizational research tries in a very humble way to understand what broad factors seem to underlie good balance or good fit, in the belief that such knowledge will help organizations to move in this direction.

NOTES

1. It should be remembered that planning centralization was measured as a company-level variable. Consequently, the lack of any significant relationship between planning centralization and subsidiary-level conditions was assumed rather than empirically tested by the study.

APPENDIX

Centralization, Control, Staffing, and Short-Range Planning Intensity by Industry ($N = 86$ to 94).

	Auto	Electrical and Telephone Equipment	Industrial Equipment	Chemical	Pharmaceutical	Consumer Packaged Goods	Tires	Others	F
Marketing centralization	1.73	1.35	1.63	1.29	1.38	1.36	1.46	1.55	5.0***
Manufacturing centralization	1.65	1.43	1.74	1.54	1.45	1.44	1.52	1.53	1.2
Financial centralization	1.42	1.58	1.83	1.40	1.58	1.51	1.65	1.65	1.6
Marketing control	.08	.24	.32	-.06	-.14	-.26	.15	-.33	2.0
Manufacturing control	.37	0	.08	-.17	-.28	-.23	.60	-.25	2.5*
Financial control	.24	.04	.39	-.28	-.33	-.08	.18	.09	2.0
Marketing staffing	46	9	56	29	12	23	12	16	3.1**
Manufacturing staffing	46	18	55	58	0	18	41	28	3.9***
Financial staffing	52	44	64	42	38	34	67	14	1.3
CEO staffing	70	55	75	70	60	45	65	35	.8
Short-range planning:									
Intensity of communications	2.5	2.8	2.7	2.5	2.6	2.4	3.2	3.5	1.1
Face-to-face meetings	1.00	.87	.75	.43	.84	.88	.75	1.00	3.1**
Extent new issues raised	2.8	4.0	2.8	2.2	2.6	2.9	2.3	3.5	1.9

* $p < .05$ (two-tailed test); ** $p < .01$; *** $p < .001$.

BIBLIOGRAPHY

Aguilar, F.J. 1967. *Scanning the Business Environment.* New York: MacMillan.

Albaum, G. 1964. "Horizontal Information Flow: An Exploratory Study." *Academy of Management Journal* 7, no. 1, 21–33.

Aldrich, H.E. 1979. *Organizations and Environments.* Englewood Cliffs, NJ: Prentice-Hall.

Aldrich, H.E., and J. Pfeffer. 1976. "Environments of Organizations." *Annual Review of Sociology* 82, 929–964.

Ansoff, H.I. 1965. *Corporate Strategy, an Analytic Approach to Business Policy for Growth and Expansion.* New York: McGraw-Hill.

Ansoff, H.I., J. Avner, R.C. Brandenburg, F.E. Portner, and R. Radosevich. 1970. "Does Planning Pay? The Effect of Planning on Success of Acquisitions in American Firms." *Long Range Planning* 3, no. 2: 2–7.

Anthony, R.N., J. Dearden, and R.F. Vancil. 1972. *Management Control Systems.* Homewood, IL: Irwin.

Argote, L. 1982. "Input Uncertainty and Organizational Coordination in Hospital Emergency Units." *Administrative Science Quarterly* 27, no. 3: 420–434.

Armstrong, J.S. 1982. "The Value of Formal Planning for Strategic Decisions: Review of Empirical Research." *Strategic Management Journal* 3: 197–211.

Astley, W.G., and A.H. Van de Ven. 1983. "Central Perspectives and Debates in Organization Theory." *Administrative Science Quarterly* 28, no. 2: 245–273.

Baliga, B.R., and A.M. Jaeger. 1984. "Multinational Corporations: Control Systems and Delegation Issues." *Journal of International Business Studies,* Fall: 25–40.

Barnard, C.I. 1938. *The Functions of the Executive.* Cambridge, MA: Harvard University Press.

Bartlett, C.A. 1979. "Multinational Structural Evolution: The Changing Decision Environment in International Divisions." Doctoral dissertation, Harvard Business School.

————. 1983. "MNC's: Get off the Reorganization Merry-go-round." *Harvard Business Review* 61, no. 2: 138–146.

Bartlett, C.A., and S. Ghoshal. 1985. "The New Global Organization: Differentiated Roles and Dispersed Responsibilities." Working paper no. 9–786–013, Harvard Business School.

Birnbaum, P.H., and G.Y.Y. Wong. 1985. "Organizational Structure of Multinational Banks in Hong Hong from a Culture-Free Perspective." *Administrative Science Quarterly* 30, no. 2: 262–277.

Blau, P.M., and R.A. Schoenherr. 1971. *The Structure of Organizations.* New York: Basic Books.

Boulton, W.R., W.M. Lindsay, S.G. Franklin, and L.W. Rue. 1982. "Strategic Planning: Determining the Impact of Environmental Characteristics and Uncertainty." *Academy of Management Journal* 25, no. 3: 500–509.

Brandt, W.K. 1978. "Determinants and Effects of Structural Design in the Multinational Organization." Unpublished paper, Columbia University Graduate School of Business.

Brandt, W.K., and J.M. Hulbert. 1976. *A Empresa Multinacional No Brasil: Um Estudo Empirico.* Rio de Janeiro: Zahar Editores.

Bresser, R.K., and R.C. Bishop. 1983. "Dysfunctional Effects of Formal Planning: Two Theoretical Explanations." *Academy of Management Review* 8, no. 4: 588–599.

Brooke, M.Z., and H.L. Remmers. 1970. *The Strategy of Multinational Enterprise.* New York: Elsevier.

Burns, T., and G.M. Stalker. 1961. *The Management of Innovation.* London: Tavistock.

Burrell, G., and G. Morgan. 1979. *Sociological Paradigms and Organizational Analysis.* Portsmouth, NH: Heinemann Educational Books.

Butler, A.G. 1973. "Project Management: A Study in Organizational Conflict." *Academy of Management Journal* 16, no. 1: 84–101.

Capon, N., C. Christodoulou, J.U. Farley, and J. Hulbert. 1984. "A Comparison of Corporate Planning Practice in American and Australian Manufacturing Companies." *Journal of International Business Studies,* Fall: 41–54.

Chandler, A.D. 1962. *Strategy and Structure: Chapters in the History of Industrial Enterprise.* Cambridge, MA: M.I.T. Press.

Channon, D.F. 1973. *The Strategy and Structure of British Enterprise.* Boston, MA: Division of Research, Graduate School of Business Administration, Harvard University.

Child, J. 1972. "Organizational Structures, Environment and Performance: The Role of Strategic Choice." *Sociology* 6: 1–22.

————. 1973. "Predicting and Understanding Organization Structure." *Administrative Science Quarterly* 18: 168–185.

————. 1975. "Managerial and Organizational Factors Associated with Company Performance, Part 2: A Contingency Analysis." *Journal of Management Studies* 12: 12–27.

Cleland, D.I., and W.R. King. 1968. *Systems Analysis and Project Management*. New York: McGraw-Hill.

Cyert, R.M., and J.G. March. 1963. *A Behavioral Theory of the Firm*. Englewood Cliffs, NJ: Prentice-Hall.

Daft, R.L., and N.B. Macintosh. 1981. "A Tentative Exploration into the Amount and Equivocality of Information Processing in Organizational Work Units." *Administrative Science Quarterly* 26, no. 2: 207–224.

Daft, R.L., and K.E. Weick. 1984. "Toward a Model of Organizations as Interpretation Systems." *Academy of Management Review* 9, no. 3: 284–295.

Daniels, J.D. 1974. "The Education and Mobility of European Executives in U.S. Subsidiaries: A Comparative Study." *Journal of International Business Studies* 5: 9–24.

Daniels, J.D., R.A. Pitts and M.J. Tretter. 1984. "Strategy and Structure of U.S. Multinationals: An Exploratory Study." *Academy of Management Journal* 27, no. 2: 292–307.

———. 1985. "Organizing for Dual Strategies of Product Diversity and International Expansion." *Strategic Management Journal* 6: 223–237.

Davidson, W.H., 1980. *Experience Effects in International Investment and Technology Transfer*. Ann Arbor, MI: UMI Research Press.

Davidson, W.H., and P. Haspeslagh. 1982. "Shaping a Global Product Organization." *Harvard Business Review* 60, no. 4: 125–132.

Davis, S.M., and P.R. Lawrence. 1977. *Matrix*. Reading, MA: Addison-Wesley.

Dill, W.R. 1962 "The Impact of Environment on Organizational Development." In *Concepts and Issues in Administrative Behavior*, edited by S. Mailack and E. Van Ness, pp. 29–48. Englewood Cliffs, NJ: Prentice-Hall.

Donaldson, L. 1984. "Strategy, Structure, Fit and Financial Performance: Validation of a General Model." Paper presented at the Annual Meeting of the Academy of Management, OMT Division, Boston, August 12–15.

———. 1985. *In Defence of Organization Theory*. Cambridge: Cambridge University Press.

Downey, H.K., D. Hellriegel, and J.W. Slocum. 1975. "Environmental Uncertainty: The Construct and Its Application." *Administrative Science Quarterly* 20: 613–629.

Downey, H.K., and J.W. Slocum. 1975. "Uncertainty: Measures, Research, and Sources of Variation." *Academy of Management Journal* 18: 562–577.

Doz, Y.L. 1980. "Strategic Management in Multinational Companies." *Sloan Management Review*, Winter: 27–46.

Doz, Y.L., and C.K. Prahalad. 1980. "How MNC's Cope with Host Government Intervention." *Harvard Business Review*, March-April: 149–157.

———. 1981. "An Approach to Strategic Control in MNCs." *Sloan Management Review*, Summer: 5–13.

Duncan, R.B. 1972. "The Characteristics of Organizational Environments and Perceived Environmental Uncertainty." *Administrative Science Quarterly* 17: 313–327.

———. 1973. "Multiple Decision-Making Structures in Adapting to Environmental Uncertainty: The Impact of Organizational Effectiveness." *Human Relations* 26: 273–291.

Dyas, G.P., and H.T. Thanheiser. 1976. *The Emerging European Enterprise: Strategy and Structure in French and German Industry.* London: Macmillan.

Dymsza, W.A. 1984. "Global Strategic Planning: A Model and Recent Developments." *Journal of International Business Studies,* Fall: 169–183.

Edstrom, A., and J.R. Galbraith. 1979. "Transfer of Managers as a Coordination and Control Strategy in Multinational Organizations." *Administrative Science Quarterly* 22: 248–263.

Egelhoff, W.G. 1982. "Strategy and Structure in Multinational Corporations: An Information-Processing Approach." *Administrative Science Quarterly* 27, no. 3: 435–458.

———. 1984. "Patterns of Control in U.S., UK, and European Multinational Corporations." *Journal of International Business Studies,* Fall: 73–83.

Emery, F.E., and E.L. Trist. 1965. "The Causal Texture of Organizational Environments." *Human Relations* 18: 21–31.

Fayol, H. 1949. *General and Industrial Management.* London: Pitman.

Fouraker, L.E., and J.M. Stopford. 1968. "Organizational Structure and Multinational Strategy." *Administrative Science Quarterly* 13: 47–64.

Franko, L.G. 1973. "Who Manages Multinational Enterprises?" *Columbia Journal of World Business* 8, no. 2: 30–42.

———. 1976. *The European Multinationals: A Renewed Challenge to American and British Big Business.* Stamford, CT: Greylock Publishing.

Galbraith, J.R. 1969. "Organization Design: An Information Processing View." Working paper #425–69, M.I.T., Sloan School of Management.

———. 1970. "Environmental and Technological Determinants of Organization Design." In *Studies in Organization Design,* edited by J. Lorsch and P. Lawrence. Homewood, IL: Irwin.

———. 1971 "Matrix Organization Design." *Business Horizons,* February: 29–40.

———. 1973. *Designing Complex Organizations.* Reading, MA: Addison-Wesley.

———. 1977. *Organization Design.* Reading, MA: Addison-Wesley.

Galbraith, J.R., and D.A. Nathanson. 1978. *Strategy Implementation: The Role of Structure and Process.* St. Paul, MN: West Publishing.

Garnier, G.H. 1982. "Context and Decision Making Autonomy in the Foreign Affiliates of U.S. Multinational Corporations." *Academy of Management Journal* 25: 893–908.

Gates, S.R., and W.G. Egelhoff. 1986. "Centralization in Headquarters-Subsidiary Relationships." *Journal of International Business Studies* 17: 71–92.

Ghoshal, S. 1987. "Global Strategy: An Organizing Framework." *Strategic Management Journal* 8: 425–440.

Giglioni, G.B., and A.G. Bedeian. 1974. "A Conspectus of Management Control Theory: 1900–1972." *Academy of Management Journal* 17: 292–305.

Goehle, D.G. 1980. *Decision Making in Multinational Corporations.* Ann Arbor: UMI Research Press.

Goggins, W.C. 1974. "How the Multidimensional Structure Works at Dow Corning." *Harvard Business Review*, January-February: 54–65.

Gotcher, J.W. 1977. "Strategic Planning in European Multinationals." *Long Range Planning*, October: 7–13.

Gouy, M. 1978. "Strategic Decision Making in Large European firms." *Long Range Planning*, June: 41–48.

Grinyer, P., S. Al-Bazzaz, and M. Yasai-Ardekani. 1980. "Strategy, Structure, the Environment, and Financial Performance in 48 United Kingdom Companies." *Academy of Management Journal* 23: 193–220.

——. 1986. "Towards a Contingency Theory of Corporate Planning: Findings in 48 UK Companies." *Strategic Management Journal* 7: 3–28.

Guth, W.D. 1976. "Toward a Social System Theory of Corporate Strategy." *Journal of Business*, July.

Hage, J. 1965. "An Axiomatic Theory of Organizations." *Administrative Science Quarterly* 10: 289–320.

Hage, J., and M. Aiken. 1967. "Relationship of Centralization to Other Structural Properties." *Administrative Science Quarterly* 12: 72–92.

Hall, R.H. 1972. *Organizations: Structure and Process*. Englewood Cliffs, NJ: Prentice-Hall.

Hannan, M.T., and J. Freeman. 1977. "The Population Ecology of Organizations." *American Journal of Sociology* 82: 929–964.

Harvey, E. 1968. "Technology and the Structure of Organizations." *American Sociological Review* 33: 247–259.

Hawkins, R.G., and I. Walter. 1981. "Planning Multinational Operations." In *Handbook of Organizational Design*, edited by P.C. Nystrom and W.H. Starbuck, pp. 253–267. New York: Oxford University Press.

Hedlund, G. 1981. "Autonomy of Subsidiaries and Formalization of Headquarters-Subsidiary Relationships in Swedish MNCs." In *The Management of Headquarters-Subsidiary Relationships in Multinational Corporations*, edited by L. Otterbeck, pp. 25–78. New York: St. Martin's Press.

Heller, F. 1971. *Management Decision Making*. London: Tavistock.

Herold, D.M. 1972. "Long-Range Planning and Organizational Performance: A Cross-Validation Study." *Academy of Management Journal* 15: 91–102.

Heydebrand, W. 1977. "Organizational Contradiction in Public Bureaucracies: Toward a Marxian Theory of Organizations." In *Organizational Analysis: Critique and Innovation*, edited by J.K. Benson, pp. 85–109. Beverly Hills: Sage Publications.

Hickson, D.J., D.S. Pugh, and D.C. Pheysey. 1969. "Operations Technology and Organizational Structure: An Empirical Reappraisal." *Administrative Science Quarterly* 14: 378–397.

Hinings, C.R., and G.L. Lee. 1971. "Dimensions of Organization Structure and Their Context: A Replication." *Sociology* 5: 83–93.

Hitt, M.A., and R.D. Middlemist. 1979. "A Methodology to Develop the Criteria and Criteria Weightings for Assessing Subunit Effectiveness in Organizations." *Academy of Management Journal* 22: 356–374.

Hofstede, G. 1967. *The Game of Budget Control*. London: Tavistock.

Horovitz, J.H. 1980. *Top Management Control in Europe*. London: Macmillan.

Horovitz, J.H., and R.A. Thietart. 1982. "Strategy, Management Design and Firm Performance." *Strategic Management Journal* 3: 67–76.

House, R.J., and J.R. Rizzo. 1972. "Toward the Measurement of Organizational Practices: Scale Development and Validation." *Journal of Applied Psychology* 56: 388–396.

Hout, T., M.E. Porter, and E. Rudden. 1982. "How Global Companies Win Out." *Harvard Business Review*, September-October: 98–108.

Hulbert, J.M., and W.K. Brandt. 1980. *Managing the Multinational Subsidiary*. New York: Holt Rinehart and Winston.

Jaeger, A.M. 1982. "Contrasting Control Modes in the Multinational Corporation: Theory, Practice and Implications." *International Studies of Management and Organization* 12, no. 1: 59–82.

––––––. 1983. "The Transfer of Organizational Culture Overseas: An Approach to Control in the Multinational Corporation." *Journal of International Business Studies*, Fall: 91–114.

Javidan, M. 1984. "The Impact of Environmental Uncertainty on Long-range Planning Practices of the U.S. Savings and Loan Industry." *Strategic Management Journal* 5: 381–392.

Jennergren, P. 1981. "Decentralization in Organizations." In *Handbook of Organizational Design*, Volume 2, edited by P.C. Nystrom and W.H. Starbuck, pp. 39–59. New York: Oxford University Press.

Karger, D.W., and Z.A. Malik. 1975. "Long-range Planning and Organizational Performance." *Long Range Planning* 8: 60–64.

Katz, D., and R. Kahn. 1966. *The Social Psychology of Organizations*. New York: Wiley.

Keegan, W.J. 1974. "Multinational Scanning: A Study of the Information Sources Utilized by Headquarters Executives in Multinational Companies." *Administrative Science Quarterly* 19: 411–421.

Keeley, M. 1984. "Impartiality and Participant-interest Theories of Organizational Effectiveness." *Administrative Science Quarterly* 29: 1–25.

Khandwalla, P.N. 1974. "Mass Orientation of Operations Technology and Organizational Structure." *Administrative Science Quarterly* 19: 74–97.

Kmetz, J.L. 1984. "An Information-processing Study of a Complex Workflow in Aircraft Electronics Repair." *Administrative Science Quarterly* 29: 255–280.

Kono, T. 1976. "Long Range Planning—Japan—USA—A Comparative Study." *Long Range Planning*, October: 61–71.

Kuhn, T.S. 1970. *The Structure of Scientific Revolutions*, 2d ed. Chicago: University of Chicago Press.

Landsberger, H.A. 1961. "The Horizontal Dimension in Bureaucracy." *Administrative Science Quarterly* 6: 299–332.

Lawrence, P.R., and J.W. Lorsch. 1967. *Organization and Environment*. Homewood, IL: Irwin.

Lindblom, C.E. 1959. "The Science of Muddling Through." *Public Administration Review* 19: 78–88.

Lindsey, W.M., and L.W. Rue. 1980. "Impact of the Organization Environment on the Long-range Planning Process: A Contingency View." *Academy of Management Journal* 23: 385–404.

Lorange, P., and M.S. Scott Morton. 1974. "A Framework for Management Control Systems." *Sloan Management Review*, Fall: 41–56.

Marquis, D.G. 1969. "A Project Team + PERT = Success. Or Does It?" *Innovation* 5: 26–33.

McCaskey, M.B. 1974. "A Contingency Approach to Planning: Planning with Goals and Planning without Goals." *Academy of Management Journal* 17: 281–291.

McKelvey, B. 1982. *Organizational Systematics.* Berkeley and Los Angeles, CA: University of California Press.

Merton, R.K. 1957. *Social Theory and Social Structure.* Glencoe, IL: Free Press.

Miller, D., and P. Friesen. 1980. "Archetypes of Organizational Transition." *Administrative Science Quarterly* 25: 268–299.

Milliken, F.J. 1987. "Three Types of Perceived Uncertainty About the Environment: State, Effect, and Response Uncertainty." *Academy of Management Review* 12: 133–143.

Mintzberg, H. 1978. "Patterns in Strategy Formation." *Management Science* 24: 934–948.

————. 1979. *The Structuring of Organizations.* Englewood Cliffs, NJ: Prentice-Hall.

Mott, P.E. 1972. *The Characteristics of Effective Organizations.* New York: Harper and Row.

Newman, W.H. 1975. *Constructive Control.* Englewood Cliffs, NJ: Prentice-Hall.

O'Reilly, C. 1982. "Variations in Decision Makers' Use of Information Sources: The Impact of Qualtiy and Accessability of Information." *Academy of Management Journal* 25: 756–771.

Ouchi, W.G. 1977. "The Relationship between Organizational Structure and Organizational Control." *Administrative Science Quarterly* 22: 95–113.

Ouchi, W.G., and R.T. Harris. 1974. "Structure, Technology, and Environment." In *Organizational Behavior*, edited by G. Strauss, R.E. Miles, C.C Snow, and A.S. Tannenbaum, pp. 107–140. Madison, WI: Industrial Relations Research Association, University of Wisconsin.

Ouchi, W.G., and M.A. Maguire. 1975. "Organizational Control: Two Functions." *Administrative Science Quarterly* 20: 559–569.

Pavan, R.J. 1972. "The Strategy and Structure of Italian Enterprise." Doctoral dissertation, Harvard Graduate School of Business.

Pennings, J.M. 1975. "The Relevance of the Structural-contingency Model for Organizational Effectiveness." *Administrative Science Quarterly* 20: 393–410.

Perrow, C. 1967. "A Framework for the Analysis of Organizations." *American Sociological Review* 32: 194–208.

Pfeffer, J., and G.R. Salancik. 1978. *The External Control of Organizations: A Resource Dependence Perspective.* New York: Harper and Row.

Picard, J. 1977. "Factors of Variance in Multinational Marketing control." In *Recent Research on the Internationalization of Business,* edited by L.G. Mattson and F. Widersheim-Paul. Uppsala: Almqvist and Wiksell.

Pitts, R.A. 1977. "Strategies and Structures for Diversification." *Academy of Management Journal* 20: 197–208.

Prahalad, C. 1976. "Strategic Choices in Diversified MNCs." *Harvard Business Review* 54: 67–78.

Price, J.L. 1968. *Organizational Effectiveness.* Homewood, IL: Irwin.

Pugh, D.S., D.J. Hickson, C.R. Hinings, and C. Turner. 1968. "Dimensions of Organization Structure." *Administrative Science Quarterly* 13: 65–105.

———. 1969. "The Context of Organization Structures." *Administrative Science Quarterly* 14: 91–114.

Quinn, J.B. 1980. *Strategies for Change: Logical Incrementalism.* Homewood, IL: Irwin.

Randolph, W., and F. Finch. 1977. "The Relationship between Organization Technology and the Direction and Frequency Dimensions of Task Communications." *Human Relations* 30, no. 12: 1131–1145.

Reimann, B.C. 1973. "On the Dimensions of Bureaucratic Structure: An Empirical Reappraisal." *Administrative Science Quarterly* 18: 462–476.

Rousseau, D.M. 1985. "Issues of Level in Organizational Research: Multi-level and Cross-level Perspectives." In *Research in Organizational Behavior, 7,* edited by L.L. Cummings and B.M. Staw, pp. 1–37. Greenwich, CT: JAI Press.

Rumelt, R.P. 1974. *Strategy, Structure, and Economic Performance.* Boston, MA: Division of Research, Graduate School of Business Administration, Harvard University.

Sayles, Leonard R. 1976. "Matrix Management: The Structure with a Future." *Organizational Dynamics,* Autumn: 2–17.

Scharpf, F.W. 1977. "Does Organization Matter? Task Structure and Interaction in the Ministerial Bureaucracy." In *Organization Design: Theoretical Perspectives and Empirical Findings,* edited by E.H. Burack and A.R. Negandhi, pp. 149–167. Kent, OH: Kent State University Press.

Schoonhoven, C.B. 1981. "Problems with Contingency Theory: Testing Assumptions Hidden within the Language of Contingency Theory." *Administrative Science Quarterly* 26: 349–377.

Scott, B.R. 1971. "Stages of Corporate Development" 9–371–294, BP 988, Intercollegiate Case Clearinghouse, Harvard Business School.

Silverman, D. 1968. "Formal Organizations or Industrial Sociology: Towards a Social Action Analysis of Organizations." *Sociology* 2: 221–238.

———. 1970. *The Theory of Organizations.* London: Heinemann.

Simon, H.A. 1957. *Administrative Behavior.* New York: MacMillan.

Snow, C.C., and L. Hrebiniak. 1980. "Strategy, Distinctive Competence, and Organizational Performance." *Administrative Science Quarterly* 25: 317–336.

Steers, R.M. 1975. "Problems in the Measurement of Organizational Effectiveness." *Administrative Science Quarterly* 20: 546–558.

———. 1977. *Organizational Effectiveness: A Behavioral View*. Santa Monica, CA: Goodyear Publishing Co.

Stopford, J.M. and L.T. Wells, Jr. 1972. *Managing the Multinational Enterprise*. New York: Basic Books.

Tannenbaum, A.S. 1968. *Control in Organizations*. New York: McGraw-Hill.

Taylor, F.W. 1911. *Principles of Scientific Management*. New York: Harper and Row.

Terreberry, S. 1968. "The Evolution of Organizational Environments." *Administrative Science Quarterly* 12: 590–613.

Thomason, G.F. 1966. "Managerial Work Roles and Relationships, Part I." *Journal of Management Studies* 3: 270–284.

Thompson, J.D. 1967. *Organizations in Action*. New York: McGraw-Hill.

Thune, S.S., and R.J. House. 1970. "Where Long-range Planning Pays Off." *Business Horizons* 13, no. 4: 81–87.

Tosi, H., R. Aldag, and R. Storey. 1973. "On the Measurement of the Environment: An Assessment of the Lawrence and Lorsch Environmental Uncertainty Subscale." *Administrative Science Quarterly* 18: 27–36.

Toyne, B. 1980. *Host Country Managers of Multinational Firms: An Evaluation of Variables Affecting Their Managerial Thinking Patterns*. New York: Arno Press.

Toyne, B., and R.J. Kuehne. 1983. "The Management of the International Executive Compensation and Benefits Process." *Journal of International Business Studies*, Winter: 37–50.

Turner, S.D. 1977. "Blau's Theory of Differentiation: Is It Explanatory?" In *Organizational Analysis: Critique and Innovation*, edited by J.K. Benson, pp. 19–34. Beverly Hills: Sage Publications.

Tushman, M.L. 1978. "Technical Communication in Research and Development Laboratories: Impact of Project Work Characteristics." *Academy of Management Journal* 21: 624–645.

Tushman, M.L., and D.A. Nadler. 1978. "Information Processing as an Integrating Concept in Organizational Design." *Academy of Management Review* 3: 613–624.

Urwick, L.F. 1947. *The Elements of Administration*. London: Pitman.

Van de Ven, A. 1977. "A Panel Study on the Effects of Task Uncertainty, Interdependence, and Size on Unit Decision Making." In *Organizational Design*, edited by E.H. Burack and A.R. Negandhi, pp. 237–254. Kent, OH: Kent State University Press.

Van de Ven, A.H., A.L. Delbecq, and R. Koenig, Jr. 1976. "Determinants of Coordination Modes within Organizations." *American Sociological Review* 41: 322–338.

Van de Ven, A.H., and R. Drazin. 1985. "The Concept of Fit in Contingency Theory." In *Research in Organizational Behavior*, 7, edited by L.L. Cummings and B.M. Staw, pp. 333–365. Greenwich, CT: JAI Press.

Van de Ven, A.H., and D.L. Ferry. 1980. *Measuring and Assessing Organizations.* New York: Wiley.

Vernon, R. 1971. *Sovereignty at Bay: The Multinational Spread of U.S. Enterprise.* New York: Basic Books.

Weber, M. 1947. *The Theory of Social and Economic Organization.* Trans. by A.M. Henderson and T. Parsons. Glencoe, IL: Free Press.

Weick, K.E. 1976. "Educational Organizations as Loosely-coupled Systems." *Administrative Science Quarterly* 21: 1–19.

———. 1979. *The Social Psychology of Organizing.* Reading, MA: Addison-Wesley.

Wicker, A.W. 1980. Review of *The Social Psychology of Organizing,* 2d ed. by K.E. Weick. *Administrative Science Quarterly* 25: 713–719.

Williams, C.R. 1967. "Regional Management Overseas." *Harvard Business Review* 45: 87–91.

Williamson, O.E. 1975. *Markets and Hierarchies.* New York: Free Press.

———. 1981 "The Modern Corporation: Origins, Evolution, Attributes." *Journal of Economic Literature* 19: 1537–1568.

Wood, D.R., and R.L. LaForge. 1979. "The Impact of Comprehensive Planning on Financial Performance." *Academy of Management Journal* 22: 516–526.

Woodward, J. 1965. *Industrial Organization: Theory and Practice.* London: Oxford University Press.

Youssef, S.M. 1975. "Contextual Factors Influencing Control Strategy of Multinational Corporations." *Academy of Management Journal* 18: 136–143.

Yuchman, E., and S.E. Seashore. 1967. "A System Resource Approach to Organizational Effectiveness." *American Sociological Review* 32: 891–903.

Zammuto, R.F. 1982. *Assessing Organizational Effectiveness.* Albany: State University of New York Press.

AUTHOR INDEX

SUBJECT INDEX

Acquisitions. *See* Foreign acquisitions

Aerospace industry, 92

Age of company abroad, 36-37, 257; and centralization, 140, 142, 146-148, 153, 213; and control systems, 163, 169-170; measurement, 54; and planning, 201, 205-206, 213, 220; and staffing, 181, 188

Age of subsidiary, 36-37, 257; and centralization, 163, 166, 169-170; measurement, 55; and planning, 205-206; and staffing, 181, 188-189

Annual plan, 193, 194, 207, 209, 213; *see also* Planning

Austria, 50

Automobile industry, 142, 181

Brazil, 46, 164, 172

Centralization, 19, 22, 48, 66, 69-70, 129-154, 189, 196, 259; and age of company abroad, 140, 142, 146-148, 153, 213; and age of subsidiary, 140; and company-level organization, 135-136, 142-148, 149, 152, 188, 200-201; and competitive climate, 137, 150-151; and control systems, 170; and day-to-day manufacturing dependency, 136; disadvantages, 131; and environment, 130-133, 137, 150, 153-154, 195; and European MNCs, 140, 141, 228-229, 232, 243; financial, 134, 140, 143, 146-148, 150, 151-152, 153, 180, 228; and foreign manufacturing, size of, 136; and foreign product diversity, 135, 149; and geographical region structure, 138, 230; and hierarchical management, 130-131, 132-133; and industry type, 140, 142; and information processing, 130-133, 149-150, 152, 174, 187, 263; and interdependency of subsidiaries, 132, 136-137, 142-146, 150, 157; and manufacturing, 133-134, 140, 143, 146, 149, 150, 151, 153, 226; and marketing, 133, 135, 138, 140, 142-143, 146-148, 150-151, 153-154, 180, 226; and marketing information dependency, 136, 150; and matrix structure, 230, 232; measures, 133-135; and

ISBN 0-88730-170-3

90000